Grammar Links 3

A Theme-Based Course for Reference and Practice

Workbook

SECOND EDITION

Charl Norloff
University of Colorado,
International English Center

Debra Daise
University of Colorado,
International English Center

M. Kathleen Mahnke
Series Editor
Saint Michael's College

THOMSON
™
WADSWORTH

Australia • Brazil • Canada • Mexico • Singapore • Spain • United Kingdom • United States

Grammar Links 3
Mahnke

Publisher: Patricia A. Coryell
Director of ESL Publishing: Susan Maguire
Senior Development Editor: Kathleen Sands Boehmer
Editorial Assistant: Evangeline Bermas

Project Editor: Robin Hogan
Senior Manufacturing Coordinator: Marie Barnes
Marketing Manager: Annamarie Rice
Marketing Associate: Laura Hemrika

Thomson Higher Education
25 Thomson Place
Boston, MA 02210-1202
USA

For more information about our products, contact us at:
Thomson Learning Academic Resource Center
1-800-423-0563

For permission to use material from this text or product, submit a request online at
http://www.thomsonrights.com

Any additional questions about permissions can be submitted by e-mail to **thomsonrights@thomson.com**

Printed in the United States of America
2 3 4 5 6 7 8 9 10 09 08 07

ISBN-13: 978-0-618-27423-9
ISBN-10: 0-618-27423-5

Contents

ACKNOWLEDGMENTS

We would like to thank the people who helped us in writing the second edition of this workbook. We are especially grateful to Karen Davy, our developmental editor, for her invaluable help and guidance and the care with which she edited the manuscript.

We are indebted to Kathleen Mahnke, the *Grammar Links* series editor, for her unfailing encouragement and support. We thank Jan van Zante, our co-author of the *Grammar Links 3* textbook, for generously sharing her ideas and exercises for the workbook. We are thankful for the support of the other *Grammar Links* authors—Jan, Randee Falk, Elizabeth O'Dowd, Mahmoud Arani, and Linda Butler.

Our gratitude also goes to the people at Houghton Mifflin from whom we have received care and guidance throughout the writing of this book. We thank our editorial team, especially Kathy Sands Boehmer and Evangeline Bermas for their thoughtful handling of our manuscript. We especially thank Susan Maguire, the director of ESL at Houghton Mifflin, for her continued faith in us.

Our thanks, too, to all of our students at the International English Center, who gave us feedback and helped us write better, and to our director, Dr. Bob Jasperson.

Finally, we extend heartfelt love and thanks to those closest to us, Richard, Jonathan, and Joshua Norloff, and Lakhdar Benkobi for their patience, understanding, support, and fast food. Without their willingness to allow us to devote our time and energy to the project once again, we would not have been able to write this book.

Charl Norloff
Debra Daise

Present and Past: Simple and Progressive

Chapter 1

Simple Present and Present Progressive

Simple Present and Present Progressive I

1 **Simple Present—Form and Spelling**

A. Use the words in parentheses to complete the statements and questions in the simple present. Use contractions with *not*.

1. Science __divides__ _____ time into precise units of clock time.
(divide)

2. _____ all their activities, even the natural ones, according
(people / schedule)

    to the clock?

3. We _____ about natural time very often in modern society.
(not / think)

4. _____ a natural, internal clock?
(the human body / follow)

5. Yes, our bodies _____ on an internal clock.
(run)

6. However, most of us _____ our internal clock to schedule our activities.
(not / use)

7. For example, Phil and Carla _____ a typical couple.
(be)

8. What kind of time _____?
(they / follow)

9. _____ to bed when he _____ tired?
(Phil / go) (be)

10. No, he _____ to bed when he _____ his work.
(go) (finish)

11. Carla _____ in bed all morning.
(not / stay)

12. When _____?
(she / get up)

13. She _____ to get up when the alarm clock _____ off.
(hurry) (go)

14. She probably _____ how much she _____ on
    (not / realize)   (depend)

    the clock.

15. How much _____ on the clock?
    (you / depend)

B. Write the third person singular (*he/she/it*) simple present form of each verb.
Pronounce each word as you write it. Write its ending sound: /s/, /z/, or /ĭz/.

1. wash washes /ĭz/   8. talk _____   15. study _____

2. play _____   9. miss _____   16. sleep _____

3. mix _____   10. try _____   17. pay _____

4. start _____   11. carry _____   18. annoy _____

5. watch _____   12. end _____   19. have _____

6. stay _____   13. reach _____   20. drive _____

7. go _____   14. finish _____   21. blow _____

2 **Present Progressive—Form and Spelling**

A. Use the words in parentheses to complete the sentences in the present
progressive. Use contractions with subject pronouns and with *not*.

1. Nowadays, many people are trying   to pay attention to natural time.
                          (try)

2. They _____ as much attention to clock time.
        (not / pay)

3. My roommate and I _____ to schedule our activities in natural time.
                     (try)

4. Now, we _____ that we are late for scheduled activities.
          (not / always / complain)

5. What kinds of things _____?
                        (we / do)

6. I _____ and _____ in natural time.
     (sleep)   (wake up)

7. She _____ right now because she's hungry.
       (eat)

8. _____ for us?
   (natural time / work)

9. We _____ to decide that.
      (still / try)

10. _____ to your internal clock right now?
    (you / listen)

11. What _____?
         (it / say)

12. _____ you to keep studying?
    (it / tell)

B. Write the *-ing* form of each verb.

1. save _saving_
2. leave _____
3. fix _____
4. shop _____
5. see _____
6. begin _____
7. cry _____
8. run _____

9. wave _____
10. stop _____
11. go _____
12. tie _____
13. fly _____
14. pay _____
15. taste _____
16. show _____

17. do _____
18. plan _____
19. come _____
20. let _____
21. hop _____
22. hope _____
23. hike _____
24. die _____

GRAMMAR PRACTICE 2

Simple Present and Present Progressive II

3 Simple Present—Uses

Look back at Exercise 1, Part A on page 2. Why is the simple present used in these sentences? Write the letter of a reason above the verb in each sentence.

a. Habitual or repeated action   b. Scientific fact, thing generally accepted as true

1. Science _divides_ time into precise units of clock time.
   (divide)
   [b written above "divides"]

4 Present Progressive—Uses

Look back at Exercise 2, Part A on page 3. Why is the present progressive used in these sentences? Write the letter of a reason above the verb in each sentence.

a. Action in progress at this moment

b. Action in progress through a period of time including the present

1. Nowadays, many people _are trying_ to pay attention to natural time.
   (try)
   [b written above "are trying"]

5 Adverbs of Frequency and Time Expressions with Simple Present and Present Progressive

Underline the verbs in the sentences. Circle the correct time expression for the meaning of the sentence.

1. I'm reading more (nowadays / always) than I used to.

2. Do you exercise (on the weekends / right now)?

3. They aren't watching a lot of TV (usually / these days).

4. He goes to bed (at 10:00 / tonight).

5. Are you leaving (always / at this time)?

6. She doesn't eat dinner (in the evening / this evening).

6 Simple Present and Present Progressive; Time Expressions

Use the words given to write sentences in the simple present and present progressive. Use contractions with subject pronouns and with *not*.

1. I/go to bed/usually/at 11:00

   I usually *go to bed* at 11:00.

2. he/get up/often/at sunrise

3. this week/we/eat big breakfasts

4. Jon/relax at home/on weekends

5. you/study more/these days?

6. Briana/exercise/not/every day

7. what classes/Sarah/have/on Tuesdays?

8. Lisa/get/enough sleep/at night?

7 Writing

Do your activities follow natural time or clock time? On a separate sheet of paper, use verbs and time expressions like those in Exercise 6 to write seven sentences about when you do things.

Examples: I usually *go to bed when I feel tired.* OR I usually *go to bed at 10:00.*

Nowadays, I'm eating on a regular schedule. OR Nowadays, I'm eating when I feel hungry.

8 **Simple Present Versus Present Progressive**

Use the words in parentheses to complete the statements and questions in the simple present or the present progressive. In some cases, either form may be correct.

Cosmologists are scientists. They ___*study*___ time and the universe.

1 (study)

How _____ their work?

2 (they / do)

A cosmologist _____ the universe as a whole. Cosmologists often

3 (study)

_____ about distances, times, and ideas that are very hard for most people to

4 (think)

imagine. These days, cosmologists _____ to understand the beginning of the

5 (try)

universe and the nature of time. So somewhere right now, a cosmologist _____

6 (ask)

difficult questions: Is it possible to understand the beginning of time? Why

_____ the past, but we _____ the future?

7 (we / remember)   8 (not / remember)

Why _____ forward? Where _____?

9 (time / run)   10 (the universe / go)

GRAMMAR PRACTICE 3

Verbs with Stative Meaning

9 **Identifying Verbs with Active Meaning and Verbs with Stative Meaning**

A. Underline the verbs that have stative meaning. Including the example, there are ten.

My husband <u>has</u> an irregular schedule, so he stays up late to watch TV programs that he doesn't really hear. He rarely exercises and looks tired all the time. He says he's being lazy, but he isn't lazy. He seems unwell in the morning. He knows his schedule is making him unhappy, and he wants to do something about it.

Nowadays, I'm listening to my body's internal clock and paying attention to natural time and my natural work cycle. I'm going to work early and leaving early, too. I go to bed when my body tells me I'm tired, so I don't mind getting up early in the morning. I like my new schedule. I'm feeling great.

Are you following your natural cycle, or are you following clock time?

B. In Part A, there are two verbs that usually have a stative meaning but have an active meaning in the passage. Circle them.

10 Verbs with a Stative and an Active Meaning

Complete the sentences with the verbs in parentheses.
Use the simple present if the verb has a stative meaning.
Use the present progressive whenever the verb can have
an active meaning.

1. a. I __think__ Mars is an interesting planet.
      (think)

   b. I_'m thinking_ about becoming an astronomer.
      (think)

2. a. Astronomers _____ for evidence of ice or water in the photographs of Mars.
      (look)

   b. This photograph _____ like a picture of ice.
      (look)

3. a. Astronomers _____ good telescopes now.
      (have)

   b. We _____ a good time studying about Mars.
      (have)

4. a. Scientists _____ the new meteor samples.
      (weigh)

   b. Rocks _____ less on Mars.
      (weigh)

5. a. Astronomers _____ excited about the possibility that life exists or
      (feel)
      existed on Mars.

   b. The surface of the meteor _____ rough.
      (feel)

6. a. Astronomers _____ scientists and scientists need positive proof.
      (be)

   b. At present, astronomers _____ cautious about declaring the certainty of
      (be)
      life on Mars.

11 Editing

Correct the errors with simple present and present progressive. There is one error
in each sentence.

1. Because the sun ~~is reaching~~ _reaches_ the highest point in the sky about once every 24 hours, it is a
   convenient marker of time.

2. However, the earth doesn't moves around the sun on a consistent basis.

3. It is varying from day to day by as much as 16 minutes.

4. Nowadays, we seldom realizing that clock time and sun time don't match.

5. We are usually making appointments by our watches, not by the position of the sun in the sky.

6. Watches help us agree on what time it is being.

Chapter 2

Simple Past and Past Progressive

Simple Past and Past Progressive I

1 | Simple Past—Form

Complete the chart with the correct irregular past form for each verb.

Base Form	Past Form	Base Form	Past Form
1. become	become	11. leave	
2. blow		12. let	
3. bring		13. make	
4. dig		14. rise	
5. drink		15. read	
6. eat		16. run	
7. feel		17. say	
8. find		18. sleep	
9. fly		19. teach	
10. give		20. wake	

2 Simple Past—Form and Pronunciation

A. Read the conversation between a college student and her advisor. Use the words in parentheses to complete the statements and questions in the simple past. Use contractions with *not*.

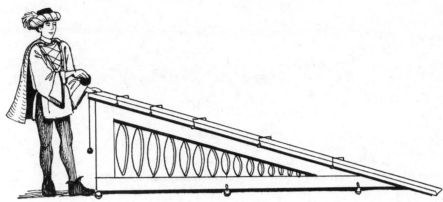

Student: I don't know whether I should study mathematics or music. I like both.

Advisor: Well, in his scientific experiments, Galileo __used__ both music and
                                                      1 (use)

mathematics to find out about speed and time.

Student: How _____ that?
              2 (he / do)

Advisor: Galileo _____ to know if a ball _____ its
                    3 (want)   4 (increase)

speed as it _____ through the air. He couldn't determine changes in
              5 (fall)

speed when he simply _____ a ball, so he had to find a different
                        6 (drop)

way to measure changes in speed.

Student: _____ that?
            7 (what / be)

Advisor: He _____ inclined planes, or flat pieces of wood with one end higher
            8 (set up)

than the other. He _____ some balls down the inclined planes.
                      9 (roll)

Student: Then _____ measure changes in speed?
                10 (Galileo / be able to)

Advisor: No. He _____ a way to measure time first. He _____
                  11 (need)   12 (not / have)

a watch, but he _____ that music has a regular beat, or time
                  13 (know)

between notes.

Student: So, _____ the piano during his experiments?
                    14 (he / play)

Advisor: No. He _____ strings across the inclined planes so that the balls
                       15 (put)

_____ the strings in regular intervals, like the beats in music. The
           16 (hit)

time that it _____ a ball to go from string to string was always the
                  17 (take)

same, but the strings _____ further and further apart. In this way,
                             18 (get)

Galileo _____ that the balls _____ faster and
              19 (show)   20 (go)

faster down the inclined plane.

Student: Wow! Thanks! Math and music *can* work together!

B. Circle the regular (-*ed* form) verbs in Part A. Pronounce each word and listen to
the final sound. Write each word in the correct column in the chart according
to its final sound. (See Appendix 6 in the student book for pronunciation rules
for the -*ed* form of the verb.)

Example: Galileo (used) _____ both music and mathematics.
                                    1 (use)

/t/	/d/	/ɪd/
	used	

3   **Past Progressive—Form**

Use the words in parentheses to complete the statements and questions in the past progressive. Use contractions with *not*.

In 1000 B.C., the Nile River ___was flooding___ every year. _____
                              1 (flood)   2 (the river / hurt)

the farming in the area? Actually, when the Nile invaded the land, it _____
                                                                        3 (bring)

nutrients to the plants. While the farmers _____ help from the
                                              4 (get)

river, they _____ plans to take advantage of its flooding.
              5 (not / make)

Why _____ to anticipate the floods? They couldn't predict its cycles
        6 (they / fail)

because they had no modern calendars.

_____ anything to help the farmers predict the flooding?
      7 (any people / do)

At this time, some people _____ the sky. They _____
                             8 (study)   9 (observe)

the star Sirius very closely. This star appeared in the sky a few weeks before the Nile flooded,

so the astronomers were able to help the farmers and began to develop calendars.

GRAMMAR PRACTICE 2

Simple Past and Past Progressive II

4   **Simple Past and Past Progressive—Meaning**

A. Read each statement. If the sentence is true for the simple past, write **SP**. If the sentence is true for the past progressive, write **PP**.

___SP___ 1. is used with verbs with stative meaning to talk about states in the past

_____ 2. talks about actions in progress at a particular moment or over a period of time in the past

_____ 3. emphasizes that the action was in progress

_____ 4. doesn't specify whether the action was completed

_____ 5. emphasizes completion of the action

_____ 6. gives background information in stories

_____ 7. sets the scene for the action in stories

B. Use the verbs in italics in parentheses to complete the statements. Use the function in the same parentheses to determine the form of the verb: the simple past or the past progressive.

Tycho Brahe __was__ a Danish astronomer. One night at a party when he was
1 (*be, stative meaning*)

attending university, Brahe and another student _____ about a math
2 (*argue, background information*)

equation. The two men _____ to fight, but their friends _____
3 (*start, action*)   4 (*pull, action*)

them apart. Neither Brahe nor the other man _____ about the argument. A week
5 (*forget, stative meaning*)

later, they _____ again, this time with swords. While they _____
6 (*fight, completed action*)   7 (*fight, action in progress*)

the other student _____ off a big part of Brahe's nose. Brahe _____
8 (*cut, completed action*)   9 (*wear, completed action*)

an artificial nose for the rest of his life.

5 Simple Past and Past Progressive

Use the words in parentheses to complete the statements and questions in the simple past or the past progressive. In some cases, either form may be correct.

Isaac Newton __was__ an English physicist. He was born in the year of Galileo's
1 (be)

death, 1642, and he _____ in 1727. As a young man, Newton _____
2 (die)   3 (study)

at Cambridge University when a terrible disease, the plague, _____, and the
4 (break out)

university _____. To avoid the plague, Newton _____ in a village in
5 (close)   6 (stay)

the countryside for nearly two years. While he _____ in the countryside, he
7 (wait)

_____ about mathematics and physics. Once, he _____
8 (think)   9 (sit)

in the garden when an apple _____ from a tree to the ground. The falling apple
10 (fall)

_____ him understand that gravity is the force that holds the planets in their orbits
11 (help)

around the sun. Newton _____ a professor at Cambridge. While he
12 (become)

_____ there, he _____ many other important discoveries about
13 (work)   14 (make)

the nature of motion, light, and time. For Newton, time _____ absolute—it was
15 (be)

constant and unchanging under all conditions.

6 **Writing**

 On a separate sheet of paper, write a story about a science experiment—either a story you know about or one that happened to you. Use the simple past at least seven times and the past progressive at least three times. Write at least seven sentences. What was happening when the experiment began? What happened during the experiment?

Example: *I really liked science when I was growing up. I was always taking things apart to see how they fit together. One day when I was taking apart an old radio, the phone rang.*

GRAMMAR PRACTICE 3

Simple Past and Past Progressive in Time Clauses

7 **Simple Past and Past Progressive in Time Clauses—Meaning**

Read the sentences. Circle the time expressions that begin the time clause. Underline the action or state that started first (earlier in time). If the actions or states happened at the same time, put brackets [ ] around the sentence.

1. (Before) the United States had time zones and standardized time, clock time wasn't very important.

2. Many Americans were farmers and small business owners. [Most people were making their own schedules (while) only factory workers were listening for bells and whistles to tell them at what time to start and stop work.]

3. In the 1880s, when the United States was thinking about instituting standardized time, the railroads were very powerful.

4. Farmers and factory owners needed to get their products to the railway station before the train arrived. Knowing the arrival time of the train became very important.

5. After the farmers and factory owners started paying attention to clock time, other business owners and professionals began using it, too.

6. While clock time was taking over the business world, natural time remained important in people's personal world.

8 Simple Past, Past Progressive, and Time Clauses

Lauren and Paul wrote down their activities one day and compared their lists. Use the activities and time expressions in parentheses to write sentences about their days. Use a time clause in each sentence. Use the simple past or past progressive of the verbs.

	Lauren's Day		Paul's Day
5:00 a.m.	get up, eat breakfast	5:00 a.m.	sleep
7:00 a.m.	go to work	10:00 a.m.	get up
11:00 a.m.	eat lunch	3:00 p.m.	go to work
3:00 p.m.	leave work; do errands	7:30 p.m.	eat dinner
9:00 p.m.	go to bed	11:00 p.m.	finish work; meet friends
2:30 a.m.	sleep	2:30 a.m.	come home

1. (Lauren, get up; Paul, sleep; when) __When Lauren got up, Paul was sleeping.__ OR
   __Paul was sleeping when Lauren got up.__

2. (Lauren, go to work; Paul, get up; after)

   _____

3. (Lauren, work; Paul, get up; while)

   _____

4. (Lauren, eat lunch; Paul, get up; before)

   _____

5. (Lauren, leave work; Paul, go to work; when)

   _____

6. (Lauren, leave work; Paul, eat dinner; before)

   _____

7. (Lauren, go to bed; Paul, work; while)

   _____

8. (Lauren, go to bed; Paul, meet friends; after)

   _____

9. (Lauren, sleep; Paul, come home; when)

   _____

GRAMMAR PRACTICE 4

Used To

9   *Used To—Form*

A. Use the words in parentheses to complete the statements and questions with *used to*. Use contractions with *not*.

Sally: The electricity was off for a while at school today, so I couldn't use the

computer to finish my paper. I had to use a pencil.

Grandpa: I <u>used to write</u> all of my papers with a pencil or pen.
       _{1 (write)}

Schools _____ computers.
     _{2 (not / have)}

Sally: The teacher usually puts on a CD while we clean up, but he couldn't because he

didn't have batteries for the CD player. _____
              _{3 (your teacher / play)}

music for you?

Grandpa: Yes, but she didn't have a CD player. She _____ a
               _{4 (use)}

record player.

Sally: How _____ your math problems? I check mine
     _{5 (you / check)}

with a calculator.

Grandpa: I _____ them by doing them a second time.
     _{6 (check)}

Sally: Who _____ you with your homework?
     _{7 (help)}

Grandpa: My grandpa _____ me.
       _{8 (help)}

Sally: You see, Grandpa? Some things don't change!

B. Go back to Part A. Write *would* above the form of *used to* where it can replace *used to*.

     would
I <u>used to write</u> all of my papers with a pencil or pen.
   _{1 (write)}

Writing

On a separate sheet of paper, write five sentences about differences between you now and your grandparents when they were your age. Use *would* where possible. Use *used to* where *would* is not possible.

11 Editing

Correct the errors with the simple past, past progressive, *used to*, and time expressions. There is one error in each sentence.

1. We ~~were knowing~~ *knew* many years ago that time itself was not constant.

2. Einstein's theory of relativity predicted that motion and gravity used to affect time.

3. However, Einstein never doing an experiment to prove his theory.

4. An experiment on 1971 tested his theory.

5. While one airplane was traveling west carrying an atomic clock, another is traveling

    east with another atomic clock.

6. The atomic clock on the plane traveling east gained time while the one on the plane

    going west losed time.

Unit Wrap-up

Writing

On a separate sheet of paper, write a paragraph comparing your past and present habits and routines. What were you doing in the past? What are you doing now? What do you usually do every day? What did you use to do? Use simple present, present progressive, simple past, and past progressive. Use appropriate time expressions and time clauses.

Example: I was a high school student last year, but now I'm attending a
            community college. I used to get up early every day, but now I'm getting
            up later. I go to class at 11:00 every day. When I was in high school, I
            started class at 8:00 a.m. . . .

TOEFL TIME

Allow yourself 12 minutes to complete the 20 questions in this exercise.
Questions 1 through 10: Circle the letter of the one word or phrase that best completes the sentence.

1. While they _____ Paris last year, thousands of tourists saw Leonardo da Vinci's *Mona Lisa* at the Louvre.
   (A) visit
   (B) are visiting
   (C) were visiting
   (D) would visit

2. At one time the telephone system in the United States was a monopoly; different companies didn't _____ offer telephone service.
   (A) use
   (B) using
   (C) used to
   (D) use to

3. Jurors often deliberate for many hours before they _____ a decision.
   (A) are making
   (B) were making
   (C) make
   (D) made

4. The number of cases of asthma _____ these days, perhaps partly because more people own cats.
   (A) is increasing
   (B) increases
   (C) was increasing
   (D) increased

5. How long before the American Civil War started _____ *Uncle Tom's Cabin*?
   (A) was Harriet Beecher Stowe completing
   (B) did Harriet Beecher Stowe complete
   (C) Harriet Beecher Stowe completed
   (D) Harriet Beecher Stowe was completing

6. Several people, who refused to leave, _____ on Mount St. Helens when it erupted in 1980.
   (A) still live
   (B) still living
   (C) are still living
   (D) were still living

7. Scientists now _____ that it is possible to clone organisms.
   (A) know
   (B) are knowing
   (C) were knowing
   (D) knew

8. George Balanchine _____ the New York City Ballet before 1948.
   (A) wasn't establishing
   (B) didn't establish
   (C) doesn't establish
   (D) used to establish

9. Nowadays, the average American routinely _____ about 20 hours of TV per week.
   (A) watch
   (B) watches
   (C) watched
   (D) watching

10. Before Pasteur developed his theories, people _____ that life could arise spontaneously.
    (A) were believing
    (B) used to believe
    (C) would believe
    (D) believe

Go on to the next page.

Questions 11 through 20: Circle the letter of the underlined part of the sentence that is incorrect.

11. A constitutional amendment <u>established</u> a two-term limit to the presidency <u>while</u>
                              A   B

    Harry S. Truman <u>was</u> <u>being</u> president.
                    C   D

12. Cities <u>are</u> <u>proposing</u> and <u>build</u> new highways as traffic steadily <u>increases</u>.
             A   B   C   D

13. <u>When</u> oxygen <u>combines</u> with hydrogen, it sometimes <u>is creating</u> water.
      A   B   C   D

14. <u>While</u> some senators <u>were</u> <u>looking</u> for a solution to the budget disagreement, others
      A   B   C

    <u>refuse</u> to compromise.
     D

15. <u>Until</u> it <u>sailed</u> on its maiden voyage, people <u>would think</u> that the *Titanic* <u>was</u>
      A   B   C   D

    unsinkable.

16. <u>In what year</u> <u>did</u> Istanbul <u>change</u> its name from Constantinople, the name it <u>use to</u>
         A   B   C   D

    have?

17. Four years <u>after</u> Emily Dickinson <u>was dying</u> <u>in 1886</u>, her family <u>published</u> her poetry.
             A   B   C   D

18. People <u>were</u> already <u>using</u> clocks <u>while</u> Peter Henlein, who <u>was</u> from Nuremberg,
            A   B   C   D

    invented the watch in 1509.

19. A college education <u>costs</u> more <u>today</u> than it <u>costs</u> at any <u>previous</u> time.
                   A   B   C   D

20. <u>Before</u> the 1970s, in many communities, businesses <u>rarely</u> <u>were opening</u> <u>on Sundays</u>.
      A   B   C   D

Present and Past: Perfect and Perfect Progressive

3

Present Perfect and Present Perfect Progressive

Present Perfect and Present Perfect Progressive I

1 Past and Past Participle Forms

Complete the chart with the correct past and past participle form for each irregular verb.

Base Form	Past	Past Participle	Base Form	Past	Past Participle
1. begin	began	begun	11. ride		
2. catch			12. see		
3. draw			13. sell		
4. fall			14. sink		
5. hear			15. strike		
6. keep			16. swim		
7. lead			17. tell		
8. lie			18. think		
9. mistake			19. win		
10. quit			20. write		

2 Present Perfect—Form

At a conference about time management, a moderator and a participant are discussing ideas about the pace of life. Use the words in parentheses to complete the statements and questions in the present perfect. Use contractions with subject pronouns and with *not*.

Moderator: You said technology __has taken__ up our time. It _____

                        1 (take)   2 (not / give)

  us more free time.

Participant: This is true. We _____ many things to save time, but in the

               3 (invent)

  end they _____ that for us.

           4 (not / do)

Moderator: What _____? Why _____

         5 (happen)   6 (technology / not / save)

  us time? Where _____?

         7 (our time / go)

Participant: First, people _____ to work harder and longer to earn

         8 (need)

  enough money to buy the new time-savers. Also, people _____

          9 (spend)

  a lot of time learning how to use them and taking care of them. These "time-savers"

  _____ the fast pace of American life!

  10 (not / change)

3 Present Perfect Progressive—Form

Use the words in parentheses to complete the statements and questions in the present perfect progressive. Complete the short answer. Use contractions with subject pronouns and with *not*.

Moderator: So far, we __'ve been talking__ about the fast pace of life in the

         1 (talk)

  United States. Many Americans _____ this

         2 (not / enjoy)

  pace. Some of them _____ stressed. Why

         3 (feel)

  _____ this way?

         4 (they / feel)

Participant: We _____ to do more in the time that we have.

         5 (try)

Moderator: How _____ this and why?

         6 (we / do)

Participant: We _____ each activity and we
                        7 (speed up)

 _____ two or three things at once because
                8 (do)

we _____ to get more time to spend at home.
                9 (try)

Moderator: But _____ more time as a result?
                    10 (we / get)

Participant: No, _____.
                        11

4 Contractions with Present Progressive, Present Perfect, and Present Perfect Progressive

The moderator has asked the participant to comment on what she has done to slow down the pace of her life. In the sentences, change the contractions with **'s** in bold to *is* or *has*.

Participant: The fast pace of life affects everyone, but my husband, my daughter, and I have

found ways to slow down the pace of our lives. For example, my husband made a

                                         has
decision to reduce his overtime hours. He**'s** been feeling happier because he**'s**
                                     1   2

working fewer hours. My daughter realized that her problem was poor organization.

She**'s** trying to schedule her time better, so she**'s** found that she has more time to
   3   4

relax. I've been paying more attention to my schedule, too. It**'s** not been easy for me,
                                                  5

but I'm learning to say no and it**'s** working! I've actually been able to sit and do
                                        6

nothing!

Moderator: Thank you. It**'s** been interesting to hear that people can slow down the pace of
                           7

their lives.

Present Perfect and Present Perfect Progressive II

5 Present Perfect with *Already, Yet, Still,* and *So Far*

Use the words in parentheses to complete the sentences in the present perfect with *already, yet, still,* or *so far.*

1. Usually, by the time a young man graduates from high school, he <u>has already learned</u>
   (learn / already)
   how to drive, but <u>he hasn't gotten married yet</u>.
   (not / get married / yet)

2. Often, by the time a young woman is 21, she _____,
   (get a job / already)
   but she _____.
   (have a baby / yet)

3. Sometimes, by the time people are 30, they _____
   (buy / already)
   a home, but they _____ a family.
   (not / start / still)

4. Normally, by the time we are 45, we _____ the
   (reach / already)
   top of our earning potential, but we _____.
   (not / achieve all our goals / yet)

5. By the time people reach 65, _____? The answer
   (retire / they / already)
   is yes for some, but many _____ by then.
   (not / retire / still)

6. What _____ in your life?
   (you / do / so far)
   What _____?
   (you / not / do / yet)

6 Time Expressions of Duration

Complete each time expression. Use *for, since,* or *all.*

1. <u>for</u> three months
2. _____ 1999
3. _____ last May
4. _____ a long time
5. _____ day
6. _____ the beginning of the year
7. _____ a few days
8. _____ 9:00
9. _____ about a year
10. _____ months

7 Using Present Perfect Progressive

A. Use the words given to write questions in the present perfect progressive.
Use the dates or words in brackets to write answers to the questions.

1. how long/people/use personal computers   [1977]

   Q: How long have people been using personal computers?

   A: People have been using personal computers since 1977.

2. how long/we/communicate by e-mail   [1972]

   Q: _____

   A: _____

3. how long/people/surf the Internet   [1973]

   Q: _____

   A: _____

4. how long/we/use the World Wide Web   [1989]

   Q: _____

   A: _____

5. how/most people/communicating/lately   [by cell phone]

   Q: _____

   A: _____

B. Look again at the questions in Part A. Write answers about yourself.

Example: I have been using a personal computer since I was five.

1. _____

2. _____

3. _____

4. _____

5. _____

GRAMMAR PRACTICE 3

Present Perfect Versus Present Perfect Progressive

8 **Present Perfect and Present Perfect Progressive**

Match the sentences with the meanings of the present perfect or present perfect progressive.

1. __*a*__ Some Americans have been making changes to slow the pace of their lives.

2. _____ They have been happier because they have had more time for simple pleasures.

3. _____ A friend of mine works in an office, but he has used a computer to "telecommute" to his company from home.

4. _____ I have taken time off from work twice in the last year to pursue other interests.

5. _____ I have been building my own house for the last three years.

a. actions continuing to the present

b. completed actions

c. progress toward a result

d. stating the number of times a completed action is repeated

e. verbs with stative meaning

9 **Present Perfect Versus Present Perfect Progressive**

Look for the time expressions in the sentences. Underline them. Then circle the correct verb to complete the sentences. In some cases, both forms may be correct.

1. I ((have thought)/ (have been thinking)) about changing the pace of my life <u>lately</u>.

2. I (have written / have been writing) a movie script for two years.

3. I (have gone / have been going) to six writers' conventions in the last two years.

4. I (haven't watched / haven't been watching) TV since I started writing the script.

5. My children and husband (haven't seen / haven't been seeing) much of me recently, either.

6. I (have traveled / have been traveling) overseas, and I'd like to do that again.

7. I (have made / have been making) a decision to relax more when I finish this script.

8. (Have you had / Have you been having) time for all the things you want to do recently?

9. Is there anything that you (haven't done / haven't been doing) lately because you (have had / have been having) no time?

10 Writing

A. On a separate sheet of paper, write a paragraph about the pace of your life lately. Use the present perfect and present perfect progressive. What have you been doing? How long have you been doing it? What haven't you done because you don't have time? How have you been feeling about the pace of life?

Example: I've been writing a novel. I've been working on it for two years. I haven't watched TV in the evening since I began to write it.

B. Interview a family member or friend. Ask the questions in Part A. On a separate sheet of paper, write a paragraph about the pace of his/her life.

GRAMMAR PRACTICE 4

Present Perfect Versus Simple Past

11 Present Perfect Versus Simple Past

Underline the present perfect and simple past in the sentences. Write the letter of the correct meaning on the line.

For the present perfect, decide if a past action:
   a. happened at an unspecified time in the past.
   b. continues to the present.

For the simple past, decide if a past action:
   c. cannot occur again.
   d. happened at a specified time.

1. I <u>have seen</u> a human walk on the moon. ____a____

2. Neil Armstrong became the first person to walk on the moon. _____

3. He has lived in Honolulu all his life. _____

4. What's the most exciting experience you have ever had? _____

5. They have been to New York. _____

6. They saw the Statue of Liberty two years ago. _____

7. She has painted pictures since she was a child. _____

8. I saw that movie last week. _____

12 Present Perfect Versus Simple Past

Use the words in parentheses to complete the statements and questions. Use the present perfect where possible. Use the simple past elsewhere. Use contractions with subject pronouns and with *not*.

Shauna: I <u>'ve just finished</u> reading this
              1 (just / finish)

book about sports cars. Do you want to borrow it?

Karl: No, thanks. I _____ it when it was published.
              2 (read)

I _____ interested in sports cars all my life.
          3 (be)

_____ one?
        4 (you / ever / drive)

Shauna: No. I _____ my friend's old Ford Mustang a couple of months
          5 (drive)

ago, but I _____ a real sports car.
        6 (still / not / drive)

Karl: I _____ to own a Ferrari, but
        7 (always / want)

I _____ enough money. I'm saving up to buy one now.
        8 (never / have)

Shauna: Ferraris are really expensive. Do you have a good job?

Karl: I _____ working at a fast-food restaurant a year ago.
        9 (start)

Shauna: _____ a lot of money since then?
      10 (you / save)

Karl: So far, I _____ about enough to buy a spare tire for a Ferrari.
        11 (save)

13 Writing

On a separate sheet of paper, write a paragraph about your past accomplishments and things you haven't accomplished yet. Use the present perfect and simple past. What have you already accomplished in your life? When did you do it? Give details. What haven't you done yet that you would like to do?

Example: I have already graduated from college. I graduated in 2001 with a degree in Business Administration. I have worked for a company, too. But I haven't started my own business yet.

14 Present Perfect, Present Perfect Progressive, and Simple Past

A reporter is talking to a former Boston resident who now lives on a ranch in New Mexico. Use the words in parentheses to complete the statements and questions in the present perfect, present perfect progressive, or simple past. In some cases, you can use either of two tenses. Use contractions with subject pronouns and with *not*.

Q: How long <u>have you lived/have you been living</u> in New Mexico?
                         1 (you / live)

A: We _____ here for two years. We _____
            2 (live)   3 (move)

   here from Boston in 2002.

Q: Why _____ Boston?
           4 (you / leave)

A: Our lives _____ too hectic and stressed there, and we
              5 (be)

   _____ time for the important things.
      6 (not / have)

Q: _____ very different since you moved?
      7 (your lives / be)

A: Yes. Everything is different now. Since we came here, we _____
                                            8 (live)

   very simply, without computers or television. Jack _____
                                          9 (build)

   a new barn, but he _____ it yet. For the last two years, I
                 10 (not / finish)

   _____ the children at home instead of sending them to
      11 (teach)

   school, so they _____ the freedom to develop their interests at their
                12 (have)

   own speed. For example, Cindy _____ a lot of time writing
                         13 (spend)

   short stories. So far, she _____ over 100 stories.
               14 (write)

Q: It sounds like a big change from Boston. _____ happy living in
                                  15 (you / be)

   New Mexico?

A: Yes. We _____ happier here than we _____ in Boston.
          16 (be)   17 (be)

15 Editing

Correct the 8 errors with present perfect, present perfect progressive, and simple past. Some errors can be corrected in more than one way. The first error is corrected for you.

Recently I have been reading a book about people who use their time well. I have

been trying to be more like them since I ~~have found~~ this book.

found

Herb Kelleher, CEO of Southwest Airlines, is a person who uses his time well.

During an interview, someone asked him, "What does a typical day look like for you

now?" He said that he didn't know. He said, "I have never look back. I have always

tried to remain directed forward." He has decided what is important and has setting

his priorities based on those decisions.

Several years ago, he has delegated control of his schedule to his executive vice

president, Colleen Barrett. Herb Kelleher said that before Colleen began handling his

appointments, scheduling his day took up too much time of his time. When he spent

time on scheduling, he hasn't focused on other important matters. Since then, Herb

concentrated on running the company, while she has managed his daily activities.

So far, Herb Kelleher was a good role model for me while I have been trying to

use my time well. I have managed my time better since I have been finishing the

book. There is just one problem. I don't have an executive vice president to schedule

my day!

Chapter 4

Past Perfect and Past Perfect Progressive

Past Perfect and Past Perfect Progressive

1 **Past Perfect—Form**

A. Sadatoshi is an exchange student in the United States. In sentences 1–5, tell what Sadatoshi had done before he came to the United States. In sentences 6–12, tell what Sadatoshi hadn't done before he came to the United States.

1. climb a mountain

   Before he came to the United States, he had climbed a mountain.

2. drive a car

   _____

3. catch a fish

   _____

4. make a lot of friends

   _____

5. ride a horse

   _____

6. fly across an ocean

   Before he came to the United States, he hadn't flown across an ocean.

7. sleep in a tent

   _____

8. go skiing

   _____

9. hear a coyote howl

   _____

10. write e-mail to his parents

   _____

11. read a novel in English

_____

12. have so much fun

_____

B. Circle the past participles in the sentences in Part A. Then look at the blanks below. Under each blank there are the sentence number and another number. The other number is the position of the letter in the past participle that goes in the blank. For example, (*1*) indicates the first letter, (*2*) the second letter, etc. The blanks should spell out the name of a city and state that Sadatoshi visited in the United States.

Example: 1. Before he came to the United States, he had (climbed) a mountain.

M ____ ____ ____ ____ ____ , ____ ____ ____ ____ ____ ____ ____
1. (4) 2. (3) 3. (2) 4. (1) 5. (2)   6. (1) 7. (2) 8. (2) 9. (4) 10. (3) 11. (4) 12. (2)

2 Past Perfect Progressive—Form

Stories called fables often use animals to teach us a lesson about using time. Use the words in parentheses to complete the statements and questions about a grasshopper and some ants. Use the past perfect progressive. Use contractions with *not*.

1. Last fall, a grasshopper didn't have any food.

   What **had the grasshopper been doing?** _____
   (the grasshopper / do)

   during the summer?

2. The grasshopper _____.
   (play)

   It _____ any food for the winter.
   (not / gather)

3. _____ the same thing?
   (the ants / do)

4. No, the ants _____.
   (work)

   They _____ for food all summer.
   (search)

5. Where _____ food?
   (the ants / look for)

6. They _____ everywhere, especially at
   (look)

parties and picnics.

GRAMMAR PRACTICE 2

Past Perfect

3 Past Perfect and Simple Past

Use the words in parentheses to complete the sentences in the fable about the grasshopper and the ants. Use the simple past or the past perfect. In cases where both tenses are possible, use the past perfect. Use contractions with *not*.

1. Last fall, a grasshopper __visited_____ some ants.
   (visit)

2. It _____ them to give it some of the food they
   (ask)

   _____ .
   (store)

3. During the summer, the grasshopper _____ and
   (sing)

   _____ , but the ants _____ .
   (dance)   (work)

4. The grasshopper_____ any food for the winter because it
   (not / have)

   _____ all summer.
   (play)

5. In the summer, food _____ plentiful, but in the fall the grasshopper
   (be)

   _____ find any.
   (not / be able to)

6. The ants _____ what the grasshopper _____
   (think about)   (do)

   while they _____ food.
   (gather)

7. The ants _____ a decision about what the grasshopper
   (make)

   _____ .
   (request)

8. They _____ the grasshopper and _____ it
   (pick up)   (throw)

   out of their home.

9. The grasshopper _____ that it _____ its
   (realize)   (not / use)

   time wisely.

10. It _____ for a second chance, but the ants _____
    (beg)   (not / change)

   their minds.

4 Past Perfect and Simple Past in Sentences with Time Clauses

Use the words given to write sentences in the past perfect or the simple past with the information from the time lines. In cases where both tenses are possible, use the past perfect.

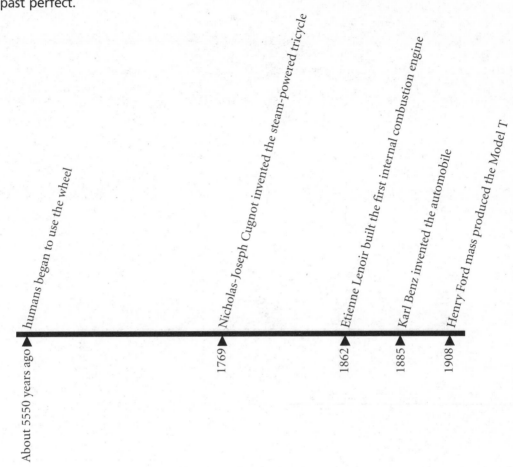

1. Etienne Lenoir/Nicholas-Joseph Cugnot/before

   Before Etienne Lenoir built the first internal combustion engine, Nicholas-Joseph Cugnot had invented the steam-powered tricycle. OR Nicholas-Joseph Cugnot had invented the steam-powered tricycle before Etienne Lenoir built the first internal combustion engine.

2. in 1885/Karl Benz _____

   _____

   _____

3. Etienne Lenoir/already/Karl Benz/when _____

   _____

   _____

4. until 1908/Henry Ford/not _____

   _____

   _____

5. humans/for thousands of years/before/Nicholas-Joseph Cugnot _____

_____

_____

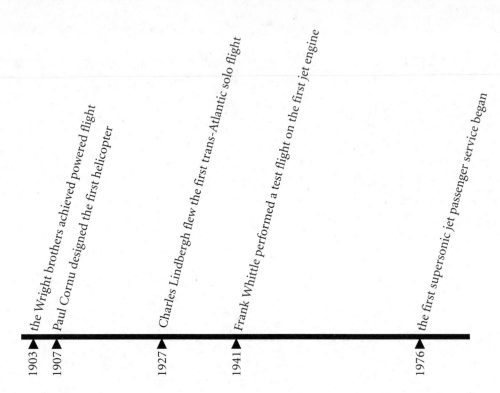

Timeline:
- 1903 — the Wright brothers achieved powered flight
- 1907 — Paul Cornu designed the first helicopter
- 1927 — Charles Lindbergh flew the first trans–Atlantic solo flight
- 1941 — Frank Whittle performed a test flight on the first jet engine
- 1976 — the first supersonic jet passenger service began

6. by 1904/the Wright brothers _____

_____

_____

7. Charles Lindbergh/Paul Cornu/after _____

_____

_____

8. until 1976/the first supersonic jet passenger service/not _____

_____

_____

9. Frank Whittle/the first supersonic jet passenger service/before _____

_____

_____

10. the Wright brothers/already/Paul Cornu/when _____

_____

_____

GRAMMAR PRACTICE 3

Past Perfect Progressive; Past Perfect Progressive Versus Past Perfect

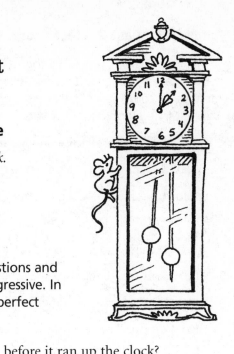

5 Past Perfect Versus Past Perfect Progressive

Hickory Dickory Dock. The mouse ran up the clock.
The clock struck one; the mouse ran down.
Hickory Dickory Dock.

—children's rhyme

Use the words in parentheses to complete the questions and answers in the past perfect or the past perfect progressive. In cases where both tenses are possible, use the past perfect progressive. Use contractions with *not*.

1. Q: What <u>had the mouse been doing</u> before it ran up the clock?
   (the mouse / do)

   A: It _____ food.
   (look for)

2. Q: _____ "one" before the mouse reached the top?
   (the clock / strike)

   A: Yes. The mouse _____ only halfway up when the clock
   (got)

   struck one. It _____ up the clock, but then it turned and
   (climb)

   ran down.

3. Q: Why did the mouse run down after the clock _____ one?
   (strike)

   A: It was scared. The clock _____ many times before, but the
   (strike)

   mouse _____ the clock strike so loudly until then.
   (never / hear)

4. Q: _____ scared before it ran up the clock?
   (it / feel)

   A: No. It _____ about danger or loud noises.
   (not / think)

6 Past Perfect, Past Perfect Progressive, and Simple Past

Another fable about time tells the story of a tortoise* and a hare*. Decide whether past perfect, past perfect progressive, or simple past can be used in the sentences. In some cases, only one is possible. In other cases, both answers are possible. Circle all possible answers.

1. Long, long ago, a tortoise and a hare ((lived)/ had lived) with many other animals.

2. When the animals got together, the hare (bragged / had bragged) about how fast he could run and (teased / had teased) the tortoise about being slow.

3. The tortoise (had told / had been telling) a joke to her friends and was unhappy when the hare came in and interrupted her.

4. The tortoise was angry, so she (challenged / had challenged) the hare to a race.

5. The tortoise (hadn't run / hadn't been running) a race before, but the hare (had won / had been winning) many races.

6. The hare (accepted / had been accepting) the challenge before the tortoise could change her mind.

7. On the day of the race, all the animals (were / had been) excited.

8. The night before, the hare (had danced / had been dancing) with his friends.

9. On the other hand, the tortoise (had gone / had been going) to bed early.

10. The race started, and the tortoise and hare (took / had taken) off.

11. The hare ran fast until he (got / had gotten) tired and thirsty and lay down for a short nap.

12. When the hare woke up, he (realized / had realized) that the tortoise was ahead.

13. Before the hare caught up, the tortoise (crossed / had crossed) the finish line.

14. The tortoise won because she (didn't stop / hadn't stopped) during the whole race.

a tortoise = a turtle that lives on land. *a hare* = an animal like a rabbit, but with longer ears and legs.

7 **Editing**

Correct the 6 errors with perfect and perfect progressive. Some errors can be corrected in more than one way. The first error is corrected for you.

                                                                         have

For a number of years now, career coaches ~~had~~ been giving advice on managing time on the job. One company asked a career coach about one of its policies. The company had requiring its employees to work 60 or 70 hours per week, but most of the people weren't working very efficiently. The company found out that most workers are not very productive after 50 hours per week. After the company cut back on each person's work time, it had started to see better time management.

"We hadn't been taking vacations," said one employee, "but the career coach asked each of us to take just a couple of days off. I had been surprised at how much better I felt at work after a short break away from the office."

Another problem that the career coach noticed was that little things, such as making phone calls, had been distracting the workers. When the workers had began scheduling time to do the little things, they could focus better on the bigger projects. "Answering e-mail was my big time waster," said another employee. "Before the career coach had come, I had been looking at my e-mail constantly. I hadn't been able to concentrate on my work very well. Now I use the time between meetings to read e-mail, and I concentrate better on my projects."

Unit Wrap-up

Writing

On a separate sheet of paper or on the space below, put the important events of your life so far on a timeline. Then write a paragraph about them. Use each tense—past perfect, past perfect progressive, simple past, present perfect, and present perfect progressive—at least once. Use appropriate time expressions.

Example: I was born 20 years ago. By the time I started kindergarten, I had already learned to read. I've been a good reader ever since. I had been enjoying being an only child when my brother was born. . . .

TOEFL TIME

Allow yourself 12 minutes to complete the 20 questions in this exercise.
Questions 1 through 10: Circle the letter of the one word or phrase that best completes the sentence.

1. Scientists _____ the effects of El Niño for many years, but they still don't agree on its impact on our weather.
   (A) have been studying
   (B) had been studying
   (C) are studying
   (D) were studying

2. Because the U.S. _____ trade with Cuba yet, cigars from that island nation are considered contraband by U.S. customs officials.
   (A) reestablished
   (B) has reestablished
   (C) hasn't reestablished
   (D) hadn't reestablished

3. The number of subscribers to cellular service has grown since the technology _____ available in the mid-1990s.
   (A) has become   (B) has been becoming
   (C) had become   (D) became

4. Voters _____ Franklin Delano Roosevelt four times before an amendment to the Constitution limited the number of terms a U.S. president could serve.
   (A) has been electing (B) had elected
   (C) has elected   (D) had been electing

5. Database companies _____ personal information about consumers for years before the government regulations became stricter.
   (A) had compiled
   (B) have been compiling
   (C) was compiling
   (D) are compiling

6. Toni Morrison _____ the 1988 Pulitzer Prize for fiction.
   (A) has won   (B) was winning
   (C) had won   (D) won

7. After the flood of 2003, health workers _____ residents to boil their drinking water until water-purification systems could be repaired.
   (A) have advised
   (B) have been advising
   (C) advised
   (D) had advised

8. Since downsizing during the 1980s, many companies _____ trouble finding loyal new employees.
   (A) had had   (B) have had
   (C) were having   (D) had been having

9. Host cities usually _____ their major highways in preparation for the Olympic Games.
   (A) had been repairing
   (B) have repaired
   (C) are repairing
   (D) were repairing

10. Special crews _____ avalanches for scientific studies until this practice was deemed too dangerous.
    (A) have filmed
    (B) have been filming
    (C) was filming
    (D) had been filming

Go on to the next page.

39

Questions 11 through 20: Circle the letter of the underlined part of the sentence that is incorrect.

11. Humans are refining ways of communicating with each other for thousands of years.
          A   B   C   D

12. Albert Einstein had continued to work on his theory of relativity even after he
                   A   B   C

    had published it.
       D

13. The average score on standardized tests has been dropping since the last 10 years.
                          A   B   C   D

14. Scientists have developed new theories on the collapse of stars, but they have not
                                             A   B

    confirming them yet.
        C   D

15. Before he became famous for opposing the president's policies, Daniel Schorr has
            A   B

    already reported the news for many years.
           C   D

16. The U.S. military has been having the FA-18F Super Hornet fighter jet in service as a
             A   B

    replacement for the FA-18 Hornet for a few years.
                    C   D

17. The National Aeronautics and Space Administration has ever sent a manned mission
                                   A   B

    to the moon, but it hasn't yet put human astronauts on Mars.
                C   D

18. Life became easier for humans while they had learned to use tools.
        A   B   C   D

19. Nicole Kidman had been acting for several years by the time she has won an Oscar
            A   B   C   D

    for best actress.

20. Since 15 people lost their lives on Mt. Everest in 1996, the climbing community had
              A   B

    been discussing whether amateurs should be allowed to climb that mountain.
      C   D

Future; Phrasal Verbs;
Tag Questions

Future Time

Will and *Be Going To* I

 **1** *Will*—Form

Visits to amusement parks are becoming a popular activity on many vacations. The roller coasters, in many shapes and sizes, are the biggest attraction in those parks. Use *will* and the words in parentheses to complete the statements and questions about the roller coasters at a popular amusement park in California. Use contractions with subject pronouns and with *not*.

Josh: I'm so excited to be at Six Flags Magic Mountain. With all the roller coasters

here, this <u>will be</u> a thrilling day.
                     1 (be)

Rachel: How many roller coasters _____?
                              2 (we / ride)

Josh: I'm not sure. The lines _____ long, so we probably

_____ ride them all.
  4 (not / be able to)

Rachel: Which one _____ first?
                   5 (we / go on)

Josh: Look, the sign says the wait time for the Viper _____ one hour
6 (be)

in the morning and two hours in the afternoon. Let's wait in line for the Viper first.

Rachel: I don't know. It looks dangerous. I _____ too scared.
7 (be)

Josh: Don't worry. I _____ you, I promise.
8 (take care of)

Rachel: I _____ the others, but I _____ the
9 (ride)   10 (not / ride)

Viper.

Josh: OK, but _____ at me when I go by?
11 (you / wave)

2 *Be Going To*–Form

Use *be going to* and the words in parentheses to complete the information about one of the popular roller coasters at Six Flags Magic Mountain. Use contractions with subject pronouns and with *not*.

Welcome to the Riddler's Revenge. You __'re going to take_____ the ride
1 (take)

of your life on the world's tallest and fastest stand-up roller coaster. First, the train

_____ you up a 156-foot-tall hill. Be ready! Within
2 (carry)

seconds, the train _____ 146 feet into a vertical loop*.
3 (dive)

You _____ a top speed of 65 mph.
4 (reach)

You _____ six inversions where you're riding
5 (experience)

upside down. You _____ to the platform until you
6 (not / return)

experience a gravity-defying upward spiral. The ride _____
7 (take)

three minutes. The park has several more roller coasters. Which one

_____ next?
8 (you / ride)

vertical loop = straight up and then curved back on itself.

GRAMMAR PRACTICE 2

Will and *Be Going To* II; Future Time Clauses

3 *Will*—Function

Look at the sentences with *will* in Exercise 1. Write the number of the answer that fits each meaning.

1. #3 and #6   ___3___ prediction or expectation

    ___6___ formal announcement

2. #2 and #11   _____ prediction or expectation

    _____ request

3. #7 and #8   _____ prediction or expectation

    _____ offer or promise

4. #4 and #10   _____ prediction or expectation

    _____ refusal

4 *Be Going To*—Function

A. Most of the sentences in Exercise 2 on page 43 use *be going to* to express an expectation about the roller coaster ride. Write two of the sentences that express an expectation.

You're going to take the ride of your life on the world's tallest and fastest stand-up

roller coaster.

_____

_____

_____

_____

B. One sentence in Exercise 2 asks about intentions or plans. Write the sentence.

_____

_____

5 *Will* and *Be Going To*—**Function**

Circle the function of each **boldfaced** verb.

1. A: We've made reservations for our vacation.

    B: When **are** you **going to leave**? [(plan)/ prediction]

2. A: I've packed my winter jacket.

    B: Do you think the weather **will be** cold? [plan / prediction]

3. A: It's an outdoor-adventure vacation.

    B: It's **going to be** exciting. [plan / expectation]

4. A: My arms are getting tired. My suitcase is too heavy.

    B: Give it to me. **I'll carry** it for you. [plan / offer]

5. A: This flight is getting bumpy.

    B: Yeah. Watch out! Your coffee **is going to spill**.

    [intention / prediction about the immediate future]

6. A: Would you like a cheese sandwich or a turkey sandwich?

    B: **I'll have** a turkey sandwich. [prediction / request]

7. A: I've never eaten enchiladas before. Are they good?

    B: You**'ll enjoy** them, I'm sure. [expectation / request]

8. A: Are you a vegetarian?

    B: Yes, I am. I **won't eat** meat. [prediction / refusal]

6 **Expressing the Future in Sentences with Time Clauses**

A. Read about another exciting roller coaster at Six Flags Magic Mountain. Complete the sentences with the correct form of *be going to* or the simple present of the words in parentheses. Use contractions with subject pronouns.

1. When the riders sit down ___sit down___ on Batman the Ride, an
   (sit down)

   inverted* roller coaster, their feet ___are going to dangle___ free.
   (dangle)*

2. The train _____ into a vertical loop as soon as
   (dive)

   it _____ the top of the first hill.
   (reach)

3. Before the riders _____ through the second 68-foot loop,
   (travel)

   they _____ a one-of-a-kind spin.
   (experience)

4. After they _____ through the spin, the riders
   (go)

   _____ through several twisting turns.
   (proceed)

5. Until the ride _____ over, the riders
   (be)

   _____ at speeds up to 50 mph.
   (travel)

6. By the time the train _____ at the end of the ride, some
   (arrive)

   riders _____ very dizzy.
   (be)

* *inverted* = upside down. *dangle* = hang or swing loosely.

B. The following sentences are about another thrilling roller coaster. Combine the pairs of sentences into one sentence using the time word given, the simple present, and *will*. In each pair, the action in the first sentence happens earlier in time.

1. when: You will ride the Viper.

    You will be upside down seven times.

    When you ride the Viper, you will be upside down seven times.   OR   You will be upside down seven times when you ride the Viper.

2. after: You will experience the first drop of 188 feet.

    You will go into the first vertical loop.

    _____

    _____

3. before: The train will enter a high-speed 180-degree turn.

    The train will go through two more vertical loops.

    _____

    _____

4. as soon as: The train will go through the loops.

    The train will fly up a hill.

    _____

    _____

5. when: You will go through the last inversion.

    You will finish the ride.

    _____

    _____

7 Writing

On a separate sheet of paper, write a paragraph that describes the steps that someone is going to go through in experiencing an activity you know. Use *will* and *be going to*. Use time clauses with *when, before, after,* etc.

Example: You're going to take your first snowboarding lesson. Before you practice with both feet on the board, you will learn how to go up and down the hill with one foot on. You won't put both feet on the board until you can stop without falling. When you are ready, we will try to turn. You will fall down, and it isn't going to be easy to get up, but you're going to do fine. . . .

Expressing the Future with Present Progressive, Simple Present, and *Be About To*

8 **Expressing the Future with Present Progressive, Simple Present, and *Be About To***

Match each form with the most appropriate function. Use each form and each function only once.

1. present progressive	a. predict unplanned events in the future
2. simple present	b. talk about the immediate or very near future
3. *be about to*	c. talk about future actions that are scheduled
4. *will* or *be going to*	d. talk about planned future actions

9 **Future Time with Present Progressive and Simple Present**

A. Circle the function of each **boldfaced** verb.

Guide: Tomorrow **we're going** to the Black Hills. (1) [prediction / (planned future action)]

The bus **leaves** at 8:00 in the morning. (2) [prediction / scheduled action]

Dudley: When **are** we **arriving** in Idaho? (3) [unplanned event / planned event]

Guide: **We're** not **going** to Idaho. (4) [prediction / plan] The bus **gets** to Hot Springs,

South Dakota, late in the day. (5) [unplanned event / planned event] It **will**

probably **be** dark before we get there. (6) [prediction / plan] **We're having** dinner

at a buffalo ranch near there. (7) [prediction / planned event]

Dudley: **Are** we **riding** buffaloes after dinner? (8) [prediction / plan]

Guide: No, buffaloes are dangerous animals. Besides, I think **you'll be** pretty tired after

dinner. (9) [prediction / plan]

B. Use the present progressive or the simple present and the words in parentheses to complete the statements and questions. Sometimes both are possible. If neither is possible, use *will*. Use contractions with subject pronouns and with *not*.

Dudley: When we're at the hotel, what time _does room service start?_
                                                    1 (room service / start)

Guide: I think the kitchen _____ at 5:00 a.m. Why?
                                2 (open)

Dudley: Tonight I _____ my earplugs in case my room is next to the
                      3 (pack)

kitchen.

Guide: I see. Remember, everyone, that after breakfast, the tour _____
                                                                                    4 (go)

to Mt. Rushmore and the Crazy Horse Memorial. It _____
                                                                         5 (probably / be)

cool in the morning, so please bring a jacket or a coat.

Dudley: When _____ the Jefferson Memorial?
                          6 (we / visit)

I _____ my camera because I want to get lots of pictures of it.
          7 (bring)

Guide: This tour _____ to the Jefferson Memorial. That's in Washington,
                                8 (not / go)

D.C. Are you sure that you want to go on this tour?

Dudley: Yes, but it _____ a lot different than I expected!
                                 9 (be)

10 Expressing the Future with Present Progressive, Simple Present, and *Be About To*

Circle the forms in parentheses that correctly complete the conversations.

Marissa: Oh, you have the phone in your hand. Who (are you about to / do you) call?
                                                                      1

Clare: I ('m about to call / call) the travel agent to arrange our vacation cruise.
                      2

Marissa: Wow! Where (are you going / do you go) this year?
                                 3

Clare: I don't know yet. I (know / 'll know) more after I call. The travel agent's office
                                          4

(closes / is about to close) in half an hour, so I need to call now.
          5

Later . . .

Marissa: Your trip to the Bahamas sounds wonderful! I know I (am / 'll be) jealous
                                                                               6

when you're there.

Clare: I ('m telling / 'm about to tell) Tom when he gets home from work. I'm so
                          7

excited that we ('re going / go) on this trip! As soon as Tom comes home, we
                              8

('re making / make) a list of all the things we have to pack.
          9

Marissa: You're already making me jealous. I ('m about to pick up / pick up) the phone
                                                                                10

and make my own reservation. In fact, give me that phone. I (go / 'm going) to
                                                                                 11

the Bahamas, too!

11 Writing

On a separate sheet of paper, write a paragraph about a trip that you would like to take. Use *will*, *be going to*, the present progressive, and the simple present to describe your trip. Give the schedule for the time that you will leave and come back and for the activities that you will do.

Example: *The bus leaves for Mt. Rushmore promptly at 9:00 a.m. We're spending two hours there. We're going to watch the video in the Visitors' Center and learn about how the monument was made. . . .*

12 Editing

Correct the 7 errors with future forms. Some errors can be corrected in more than one way. The first error is corrected for you.

USA Weekend, a newspaper magazine, recently chose the 10 most beautiful places

in America. My friends and I are making plans to visit the spot of our choice.

   'm going to visit
I going to visit the number one spot: Sedona, California. With its dramatic red

sandstone rock towers, I'm seeing one of the most beautiful places in the U.S.

My friend is going travel to the number four spot this summer. When she will arrive,

she'll hikes the Kalalau Trail on Kauai, Hawaii's oldest island. She'll see volcanic peaks

and waterfalls surrounded by tropical flowers. Another friend are going to drive the

Great River Road along the upper Mississippi River as it goes through many

nineteenth-century towns. We won't go to the number two spot: the city of

Pittsburgh, or the number five spot: the Golden Gate Bridge in San Francisco.

Which one you will visit?

Chapter 6

Future Progressive, Future Perfect, and Future Perfect Progressive

Future Progressive I

1 **Future Progressive with *Will*—Form**

Use the words in parentheses to complete the statements and questions in the future progressive with *will*. Use contractions with subject pronouns and with *not*.

Before long, robotic submarines* <u>will be exploring</u> the
 $\qquad$ 1 (explore)

oceans. These small subs $\rule{8cm}{0.4pt}$ passengers.
 2 (not / carry)

What $\rule{8cm}{0.4pt}$? These unmanned subs
 3 (they / do)

$\rule{8cm}{0.4pt}$ dangerous missions where no one
 4 (carry out)

has been able to go before. They $\rule{8cm}{0.4pt}$ into
 5 (go)

dark caves. They $\rule{8cm}{0.4pt}$ in the ice-covered
 6 (travel)

Arctic regions. They $\rule{8cm}{0.4pt}$ over hypothermal
 7 (pass)

vents where lava-heated water comes up from the ocean floor. These AUVs (autonomous

underwater vehicles) $\rule{8cm}{0.4pt}$ scientists gather physical,
 8 (help)

biological, chemical, and geographical data.

*submarine = a ship that operates underwater.

51

2 **Future Progressive with *Be Going To*—Form**

Use the words in parentheses to complete the statements and questions in the future progressive with *be going to*. Use contractions with subject pronouns and with *not*.

The Southampton Oceanography Center's Autosub One, an example of an

autonomous underwater vehicle (AUV), <u>is going to be monitoring</u> natural hazards and
                                          1 (monitor)

environmental changes in the ocean. It _____
                                          2 (also / research)

the role that oceans play in climate changes. A fleet of AUVs built by Florida Atlantic

University's Sea Tech _____ even more
                          3 (take on)

dangerous roles by waiting for and recording what is going on when storms hit. AUVs

_____ routine sampling of the seabeds
          4 (carry out)

and ocean surface, too. So AUVs _____ oceanographers
                                      5 (save)

from dangerous work. What _____
                              6 (these scientists / do)

instead? They _____ more time to studying
                  7 (devote)

the data that the AUVs provide.

Future Progressive II; Future Progressive Versus Future with *Will* or *Be Going To*

3 **Future Progressive Versus Future with *Will* or *Be Going To***

A. Circle the forms in parentheses that correctly complete the sentences.

1. In the future, people (will travel / will be traveling) across the ocean in hypersonic* planes.

2. Transoceanic travel (will be / will be being) faster when hypersonic planes begin to fly.

3. The hypersonic plane (will fly / will be flying) at five times the speed of sound.

hypersonic = capable of speed equal to or exceeding five times the speed of sound.

4. With automated baggage handling, when you arrive, your luggage

   (will wait / will be waiting) for you.

5. When the first hypersonic plane lands, the passengers (will cheer / will be cheering).

6. (Are you going to ride / Will you be riding) on a hypersonic plane one day?

7. The first one (will depart / is going to be departing) in 2025.

8. (Will you be / Are you going to be being) on it?

B. In one sentence in Part A where both verb forms are possible, each form gives
the sentence a different meaning. Write the number of the sentence on the line. _____

4 **Future Progressive in Sentences with Time Clauses**

Futurists make predictions about what will be happening in the future. Complete
the sentences on their predictions about the future of personal transportation.
Use the future progressive with *will* and the simple present. Use contractions with
subject pronouns and with *not*.

1. Most people _**will be driving**_____ hybrid* vehicles that combine electric and
   _(drive)

   internal combustion engines when fuel-cell cars (electric cars powered by fuel cells)

   become _**become**_____ available around 2016.
   _(become)

2. By the time people _____ on automated highways two years later, everyone
   _(drive)

   _____ fuel-cell cars.
   _(use)

3. When cars _____ on automated highways, these highways
   _(drive)

   _____ their speed, steering, and braking.
   _(control)

4. When automated highways _____ these intelligent transportation systems,
   _(use)

   drivers _____ so many accidents.
   _(not / cause)

5. People in large metropolitan areas _____ in personal rapid transit
   _(ride)

   (car-like capsules on guide rails) when large cities _____ them in around 2024.
   _(install)

6. Before cities _____ personal rapid transit, people _____
   _(have)   _(live)

   in clustered*, self-contained communities in large urban areas.

7. After cities _____ these clustered communities, people _____
   _(build)   _(not / commute)

   to work, which will reduce the amount of traffic on highways.

hybrid = made up of different types. *clustered* = grouped close together.

GRAMMAR PRACTICE 3

Future Perfect and Future Perfect Progressive I

5 Future Perfect with *Will* and *Be Going To*—Form

A. Use the words in parentheses to complete the statements and questions in the future perfect with *will*. Use contractions with subject pronouns and with *not*.

Ron: Imagine living on Mars! Do you think I can explore there someday?

Carl: Maybe. Before anyone goes there, though, we ___'ll have developed_____
                                        1 (develop)

    a lot of new technology to deal with Mars' problems.

Ron: Oh, yeah? Like what? What problems _____?
                                        2 (we / solve)

Carl: By then, we _____ a way to keep warm at very cold
                             3 (find)

    temperatures. The nighttime low at the surface can be –130°F.

Ron: Oooh, that's cold. I'm sure that I _____ a good heat
                                   4 (put)

    source on board my spaceship.

Carl: Yes, and scientists _____ materials for your spacesuit to
                          5 (discover)

    keep you comfortable at Mars' high temperatures, too.

Ron: Hmm. Does Mars have an atmosphere? Will I be able to breathe the air?

Carl: No. The Martian atmosphere is 95 percent carbon dioxide and has almost no oxygen.

    The atmosphere _____ by the time you get there.
                        6 (not / change)

Ron: _____ on Mars?
            7 (anything / change)

Carl: Maybe not, but you _____ older, and everyone
                      8 (get)

    _____ more about the planet.
          9 (learn)

B. Use the words in parentheses to complete the statements and questions in the future perfect with *be going to*. Use contractions with subject pronouns and with *not*.

Ron: How <u>are we going to have learned</u>
1 (we / learn)

more about Mars by the time I get there?

Carl: Well, in 2003, after NASA scientists successfully

landed two rovers—small vehicles that can move

around—on the surface of Mars, they updated their plans for exploring Mars.

By 2009, they _____
2 (launch)

a space laboratory. Before then, scientists hope they

_____ a "smart lander"
3 (develop)

to help them land the rover in a hard to reach area of Mars.

Ron: Yes, and . . . ?

Carl: So, before there are any plans for a manned mission, the space laboratory

_____ a lot more information
4 (provide)

about the planet. There are also plans to send an orbiter, a spacecraft that will

circle the planet but not land on it. It is going to take close-up photographs of the

surface, so it _____ the surface
5 (map)

of Mars in much greater detail.

Ron: _____ back samples of Martian rocks
6 (they / send)

and soil by 2009?

Carl: No, they _____ that before 2014, but
7 (not / do)

they _____ to look for signs that
8 (continue)

there was life on Mars.

Ron: _____ any life? Am I going to meet Martians?
9 (they / find)

Carl: Who knows what they'll find? That's the excitement of exploration.

6 Future Perfect Progressive with *Will* and *Be Going To*—Form

A. Use the information in the chart and the words in parentheses to complete the statements. Use the future perfect progressive and *will*.

Ron's Terraforming Experiment

Activity	Day																				
	Week 1							Week 2							Week 3						
	1	2	3	4	5	6	7	8	9	10	11	12	13	14	15	16	17	18	19	20	21
plant seeds	X																				
fan 1 running	X	X	X	X	X	X	X	X	X	X	X	X	X	X	X	X	X	X	X	X	X
write in journal	X	X	X	X	X	X	X	X	X	X	X	X	X	X	X	X	X	X	X	X	X
read about terraforming Mars		X	X	X	X	X	X														
read about wind erosion								X	X	X	X	X	X	X							
fan 2 running												X	X	X	X	X	X	X	X	X	X
read about reclaiming deserts															X	X	X	X	X	X	X
end experiment																					X

1. Ron planted three plots with grass seeds on the first day of the experiment. By the end

   of the experiment, the grass __will have been growing_____ for 21 days.

   (grow)

2. Ron started a fan blowing on one plot of grass on the first day of the experiment.

   By the end of the experiment, the fan _____

   (blow)

   for 21 days.

3. Today is the twelfth day of the experiment. Ron is starting a fan on the

   second plot of grass today. By the end of the experiment, the fan

   _____ for 10 days.

   (run)

4. Ron isn't going to start a fan on the third plot. At the end of the experiment, a fan

    _____ on the third plot at all.
    (not / blow)

5. Ron started a journal on the first day to record his observations. By the end of the

    experiment, Ron _____ in his journal
    (write)

    every day for 21 days.

B. Use the information in the chart and the words in parentheses to complete
the statements. Use the future perfect progressive and *be going to*.
Use contractions with subject pronouns.

1. This week, Ron has been reading about wind erosion. By the end of the week, he

    <u>**is going to have been reading**</u> about wind erosion for seven days.
    (read)

2. Next week, Ron is going to read about deserts. By this time next week,

    he _____ about deserts
    (read)

    for five days.

3. By the end of the experiment, what _____
    (Ron / look at)

    every day?

4. He _____ whether the grass can
    (observe)

    grow with wind from the fans blowing on it.

GRAMMAR PRACTICE 4

Future Perfect and Future Perfect Progressive II

7 **Future Perfect and Future Perfect Progressive with *Will* and *Be Going To***

Decide whether future perfect or future perfect progressive can be used in the sentences. Circle the letter of the forms that are possible. In some cases, only one is possible. In other cases, both are possible.

1. By 2020, scientists _____ in space for two years.

   (a.) will have worked   (b.) will have been working

2. By 2020, some private companies _____ several spaceships.

   a. are going to have launched   b. are going to have been launching

3. Before astronauts reach Mars in 2037, we _____ a permanent moon base.

   a. will have established   b. will have been establishing

4. By 2042, spaceships _____ to Mars for five years.

   a. are going to have traveled   b. are going to have been traveling

5. Spaceships _____ at the speed of light until at least 20 years after astronauts land on Mars.

   a. won't have traveled   b. won't have been traveling

6. _____ life on other planets before the end of the twenty-first century?

   a. Will we have discovered   b. Will we have been discovering

8 **Time Clauses, Future Perfect, and Future Perfect Progressive**

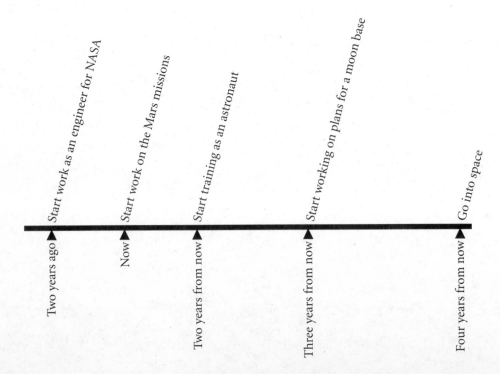

A. Henry is an engineer at NASA. Use information from the time line and the time expression given to combine each pair of sentences into one sentence. Use the simple present and the future perfect with *will*.

1. by the time: He will start training as an astronaut.

   He will work at NASA for four years.

   By the time he starts training as an astronaut, he will have worked at NASA for four

   years. OR He will have worked at NASA for four years by the time he starts training

   as an astronaut.

2. before: He will work on the Mars missions for three years.

   He will begin plans for a moon base.

   _____

   _____

3. when: He will train as an astronaut for two years.

   He will go into space.

   _____

   _____

4. by the time: He won't work at NASA for 10 years.

   He will go into space.

   _____

   _____

   _____

B. Now use the simple present and the future perfect progressive with *will*.

1. when: He will be training as an astronaut for a year.

   He will start working on the moon base.

   He will have been training as an astronaut for a year when he starts working on the

   moon base. OR When he starts working on the moon base, he will have been training

   as an astronaut for a year.

2. before: He will start working on the moon base.

   He will be working on the Mars missions for three years.

   _____

   _____

3. when: He will start working on the moon base.

   He will be working for NASA for five years.

   _____

   _____

4. by the time: He will go into space.

   He will be working for NASA for six years.

   _____

   _____

9 | Writing

Predict the important events of your life and put them on a time line on your own paper. Include activities beginning in the past, present, and future. Then, on a separate sheet of paper, write a paragraph about what you will be doing and what you will have accomplished in 10 years. Use the future progressive, the future perfect, and the future perfect progressive. Use appropriate time expressions.

Example: In 10 years, I will be working as an international business professional. I'll have been working for three years by then. I will have gotten married, but I won't have had any children yet. . . .

10 | Editing

Correct the 6 errors with verbs in the future progressive, future perfect, future perfect progressive, and time clauses. Some errors can be corrected in more than one way. The first error is corrected for you.

will be landing

In the future, robots and other devices that ~~will be land~~ on Mars will probably

have gone to Antarctica before they ever leave Earth. Scientists will be using this cold

continent more and more as they design devices for Mars exploration. They want to

try out the machines there because of the similarities in climate between Mars and

Antarctica. Both of these places have frozen soil, and Antarctic lakes resemble the

Martian lakes of long ago. Before anyone will be setting foot on Mars, scientists are

going to have exploring Lake Hoare in Antarctica for many years. They will have

been looking at the algae that lives at the bottom of the ice-covered lake. They want

to know about it because it is a very simple form of life. In the future, they searching

for similar algae under the surface of Mars in what they think are old lake beds. The

water dried up long ago, but the remains of the algae, if there are any, might still be

there. By 2010, a spacecraft is going to have been returning to Earth with soil

samples. When the spacecraft comes back, scientists may find algae fossils in the soil.

Regardless of what they find, scientists aren't going to give up their search for life too

easily. They will keep looking in other places until they will have reached their goal.

Chapter 7

Phrasal Verbs; Tag Questions

Phrasal Verbs I

1 **Phrasal Verbs Without Objects**

A. Complete the crossword puzzle with the phrasal verbs for the meanings given. Look at the verbs in the box if you need help.

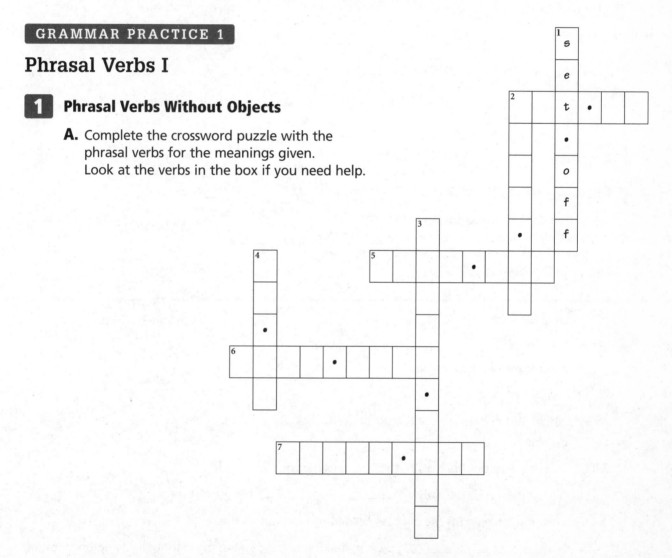

Across
2. begin to happen (for weather)
5. end or result
6. return
7. begin

Down
1. start on a journey
2. appear
3. fail to function
4. continue

| break down | come back | go on | set in | ✓set off | show up | start out | turn out |

B. Use the appropriate form of the phrasal verbs from the crossword puzzle in Part A to complete the paragraph.

Norwegian explorer Borge Ousland _set off_ _____ alone across

_____
1

Antarctica on November 15, 1996. The journey _____ well.

_____
2

In 1995, he had tried to cross the Antarctic continent solo, but only reached the

South Pole. He said, "I _____ to try again. I am determined to succeed,

_____
3

and I _____ to the end this time." Luck was with him. None of his

_____
4

equipment _____, and no bad weather _____

_____   _____
5   6

to stop him. The second crossing _____ well and he

_____
7

_____ as planned at New Zealand Scott Base on January 17, 1997—the

_____
8

first man to cross the Antarctic continent solo and unassisted.

2 Phrasal Verbs; Placement of Pronoun Objects

Underline the phrasal verbs and circle the noun objects in the questions about Borge Ousland's journey. Complete the answers to the questions. Use pronoun objects.

Antarctica

Berkner Island

South Pole

Ross Ice Shelf   Scott Base

Ousland's route

1. Q: How did Borge Ousland bring off (the feat) of crossing Antarctica alone?

   A: He _brought it off_ _____ through careful planning and endurance.

2. Q: Did he use dogs to pull along his sled?

   A: No, he didn't have any help with his sled. He _____ himself on his skis.

3. Q: Did he carry out his plan in the 100 days that he estimated?

   A: No, he didn't. He actually _____ in 64 days.

4. Q: How did he keep up the pace he needed to accomplish this?

   A: He _____ by making better time than he thought using his parasail.

5. Q: When did he first try out the parasail?

   A: The winds were too strong until the third day, so he _____ (not) until then.

6. Q: What held up Borge Ousland?

   A: The lack of wind _____, and he traveled only a few kilometers some days.

7. Q: Was he able to make up the time?

   A: Yes, he was always able to _____ when the wind picked up.

8. Q: What did Borge Ousland say after he arrived at Scott Base and took off his skis?

   A: He _____ and said, "It's done."

Phrasal Verbs II

3 Phrasal Verbs—Meaning

Circle the appropriate particle for each phrasal verb in **bold** to complete the sentences. (If necessary, look in Appendix 8 in the student book for help.)

1. Polar explorers won't let their fears **keep** them (back) up) from reaching their goals.

2. They will **take** (on / over) the challenge of being the first to succeed.

3. Unless the weather is very bad, they won't **call** (off / up) the expedition.

4. They must **check** (in / out) their equipment carefully before they set (back / off) on their journey.

5. The media **plays** (down / up) their successes with many interviews and articles.

6. It's easy to **run** (off / up) thousands of dollars in expenses to **bring** (off / out) an expedition successfully.

7. These explorers will never **turn** (down / off) a chance for a new adventure.

4 Particle Versus Preposition

Rewrite each sentence. Replace the underlined noun in the sentence with a pronoun. Remember: The pronoun must come before the particle of a phrasal verb and after the preposition in a verb followed by a prepositional phrase.

1. He looked up <u>the tree</u>. *He looked up it.*_____

2. Look up <u>the word</u> in your dictionary. *Look it up in your dictionary.*_____

3. She turned up <u>the radio</u>. _____

4. We turned up <u>the path</u> to get to the lake. _____

5. Turn down <u>the road on the left</u>. _____

6. She turned down <u>the job</u>. _____

7. The police ran down <u>the thief</u>. _____

8. I ran down <u>the hill</u>. _____

GRAMMAR PRACTICE 3

Verb–Preposition Combinations; Phrasal Verbs with Prepositions

5 Verb–Preposition Combinations

Complete the conversation between an interviewer and Borge Ousland. Use the appropriate form of the verb–preposition combinations in the boxes. (If necessary, look in Appendix 9 in the student book for help.)

| depend on | happen to | ✓hear of | learn from | plan for | protect from |

Interviewer: Congratulations on being the first man to cross the continent of Antarctica alone and unsupported. Everyone __has heard of__ (1) your amazing feat and wants to know what contributed to your success.

Borge: I knew I would succeed. I can _____ (2) myself. I always _____ (3) an expedition carefully. I _____ (4) my experience reaching the South Pole last year, too. I _____ (5) myself _____ bad weather, but I also know I'm lucky that nothing bad _____ (6) me.

| care about | come from | recover from | suffer from | think about | worry about |

Interviewer: What about injuries and loneliness? Did you _____ (7) those?

Borge: Yes, I did. When you're alone, you always _____ (8) accidents and injuries. I _____ (9) several injuries during my journey, but I _____ (10) them all. It was also hard to _____ (11) Norway without my family, but I know they _____ (12) me and support me.

pay for	read about	talk about	write about

Interviewer: What will you do now?

Borge: I wrote in a journal each day of my journey. I plan to _____
        13

my expedition in a book, and I _____ my expedition to
                                14

interested groups. I _____ my next expedition with the
                      15

money I make on my book and lectures.

Interviewer: Thanks for talking about your incredible adventure. We _____
                                                                     16

it when you publish your book.

6 Phrasal Verbs with Prepositions

A. Match the phrasal verb–preposition combinations with their meanings.
(If necessary, look at Appendix 10 in the student book for help.)

_____*c*_____ 1. come up with   a. return from

_____ 2. get along with   b. meet unexpectedly

_____ 3. get back from   c. discover (an idea)

_____ 4. get down to   d. be careful of

_____ 5. meet up with   e. enjoy the company of

_____ 6. put up with   f. begin (work)

_____ 7. watch out for   g. tolerate

B. Complete the sentences with the correct phrasal verb–preposition
combinations from Part A. Use each verb–preposition combination only once.

Borge Ousland had to:

1. _watch out for_____ crevices.

2. _____ the expedition safely.

3. _____ extreme cold and loneliness.

4. _____ work.

5. _____ a plan for the expedition.

Borge Ousland didn't have to:

6. _____ other people.

7. _____ anyone until he got near Scott Base.

7 Writing

A. Choose three verbs from the box. These verbs are phrasal verbs with one or more meanings. On a separate sheet of paper, write a sentence using each verb you choose in one of its meanings. (If necessary, look in Appendix 8 in the student book for help.)

bring in	call off	come over	keep up	think over	work out

B. Choose three verbs from the box. These verbs are verb–preposition combinations. On a separate sheet of paper, write a sentence using each verb you choose in one of its meanings. (If necessary, look in Appendix 9 in the student book for help.)

come from	forget about	look for	play with	search for	worry about

C. Choose three verbs from the box. These verbs are phrasal verbs with prepositions. On a separate sheet of paper, write a sentence using each verb you choose in one of its meanings. (If necessary, look in Appendix 10 in the student book for help.)

come up with	drop in on	get through with	look forward to
meet up with	run out of	start out for	watch out for

D. Choose three verbs from the box. These verbs are both phrasal verbs with one or more meanings and verbs + preposition. On a separate sheet of paper, write sentences using each verb you choose in two different meanings. (If necessary, look in Appendices 8 and 10 in the student book for help.)

look over	look up	run off	turn down	turn up

GRAMMAR PRACTICE 4

Tag Questions I

8 Tag Questions—Form

Complete the sentences with tag questions and short answers.

1. Q: Learning about explorers past and present is fun, <u>isn't it?</u>

   A: Yes, <u>it is.</u>

2. Q: All of the explorers faced danger and hardship, _____

   A: Yes, _____

3. Q: Nothing stopped them from pursuing their goals, _____

   A: No, _____

4. Q: Borge Ousland was very brave to cross Antarctica alone, _____

   A: Yes, _____

5. Q: Others had gone before him but had never gone alone, _____

   A: No, _____

6. Q: These stories of adventure inspire others to do the same, _____

   A: Yes, _____

7. Q: Explorers have always wanted to travel into the unknown, _____

   A: Yes, _____

8. Q: Someone is always trying to be the first to go somewhere, _____

   A: Yes, _____

9. Q: We'll continue to explore new places in the future, _____

   A: Yes, _____

10. Q: There aren't many places left on earth to explore, _____

    A: No, _____

11. Q: The ocean still offers unknown territory, _____

    A: Yes, _____

12. Q: I am interested in exploration, _____

    A: Yes, _____ (you)

GRAMMAR PRACTICE 5

Tag Questions II

9 Writing

A. Write five tag questions about things that you think you know the answer to. Use different verbs tenses and modals.

Example: **The weather will be nice tomorrow, won't it?**

B. Write five tag questions about things you aren't sure you know the answer to. Use different verbs tenses and modals.

Example: **You haven't been to the Antarctic, have you?**

10 Editing

Correct the 6 errors with phrasal verbs, verb–preposition combinations, phrasal verb + preposition combinations, and tag questions. Some errors can be corrected in more than one way. The first error is corrected for you.

NASA, the National Aeronautic and Space Administration, is preparing a report on the future of space travel. It may be considering sending astronauts back to the moon. This is a good idea, ~~is it~~ *isn't it*? Buzz Aldrin, a former astronaut, says it may not be the best idea. He hopes that they will think the idea up carefully and he has suggested setting up a new space port in an area of space called L 1. If NASA sets up it there, it will offer a place to launch spaceships to the moon, Mars, and anywhere else humans decide to travel in the future. Unlike the moon or the International Space Station, L 1 has low gravitational pull, so a spaceship will require little energy to leave it. It can take up easily. This space port will cost a lot, won't this? How will we pay off it? In fact, it will be relatively cheap. NASA can bring it off for less money than the current International Space Station costs.

Unit Wrap-up

Writing

On a separate sheet of paper, write two travel advertisements or announcements. Your advertisements can be for: (1) a travel agency, (2) a trip or tour, (3) a lecture about exploration, and/or (4) any other travel-related idea you have. Use at least three future forms and two phrasal verbs or verb–preposition combinations in each one. Use a tag question at least once. If you want, you can include drawings. (If necessary, look at the Grammar in Action on page 80 of the student book for examples.)

TOEFL TIME

Allow yourself 12 minutes to complete the 20 questions in this exercise.
Questions 1 through 10: Circle the letter of the one word or phrase that best completes the sentence.

1. Hip-replacement surgery will become more common when the population _____ .
   (A) ages
   (B) will age
   (C) is going to age
   (D) age

2. Before a single term of office is over, a U.S. President _____ a State of the Union Address four times.
   (A) is delivering
   (B) is about to deliver
   (C) will have been delivering
   (D) will have delivered

3. If students can't find a particular source of information, a reference librarian will _____ for them.
   (A) look it up
   (B) look up it
   (C) look up
   (D) look it

4. By 2020, the Internet _____ to meet the needs of a growing number of users.
   (A) will have expanded
   (B) expands
   (C) is expanding
   (D) is about to expand

5. Jobs open up when an economy expands, _____ ?
   (A) aren't they
   (B) are they
   (C) don't they
   (D) won't they

6. The *Farmer's Almanac* tells on what days the new moon _____ in the coming year.
   (A) is about to fall
   (B) falls
   (C) will have been falling
   (D) will have fallen

7. Today's fads _____ completely in a few years or even a few months.
   (A) are disappearing
   (B) will have been disappearing
   (C) are going to have been disappearing
   (D) will have disappeared

8. Because of their economic value, grains are never going to lose importance, _____ ?
   (A) don't they
   (B) do they
   (C) are they
   (D) aren't they

9. When runners _____ a race, they need to block out distractions.
   (A) are about to start
   (B) will start
   (C) will be starting
   (D) will have started

10. No one has solved the problem of global warming, _____ ?
    (A) has he
    (B) have they
    (C) haven't they
    (D) hasn't he

Go on to the next page.

Questions 11 through 20: Circle the letter of the underlined part of the sentence that is incorrect.

11. In the future, engineers will have figure out how to avoid collisions so that accidents
    will not tie up traffic.
    A: will B: have figure out C: to avoid D: tie up traffic

12. Halley's Comet is coming back in 2062 after it will complete another orbit.
    A: is B: coming back C: after D: will complete

13. Many homes will be having more computers when engineers build more "smart houses," isn't that right?
    A: will be having B: when C: build D: isn't that right

14. It is possible that scientists are going to reclassify the planet Pluto as an asteroid after they will have studied it further.
    A: is B: are going to C: will D: have studied

15. Perhaps in the future, detergents will treat any stain and get out it without damaging the fabric.
    A: will B: treat C: get out it D: damaging

16. In future elections, computers will count up results while the voters will be casting their ballots.
    A: will B: count up results C: will be D: casting

17. There is hope that nations will get along each other, isn't there?
    A: will B: get along C: isn't D: there

18. World-class athletes will be succeeding in breaking many records before the next Olympic Games end.
    A: will B: be succeeding in C: breaking D: end

19. Some people believe that taking vitamin C when a cold be about to start will help them get over it.
    A: believe B: be about to C: will D: get over it

20. Because the present generation doesn't preserve natural resources, it will run out them and there will be nothing left for future generations.
    A: doesn't preserve B: will C: run out them D: will be

Noun Phrases

Chapter 8

Nouns, Articles, and Quantifiers

Nouns; Proper Nouns and Common Nouns

1 | **Identifying Proper and Common Nouns**

Read the passage. Capitalize the proper nouns. Underline the common nouns.

Conquest*, travel, and trade have helped spread different kinds of food and

methods of cooking throughout the world. For example, ᴿ̶omans redesigned the

gardens of the countries they conquered, and Christian soldiers returned from

religious wars in the middle east and north africa with new ingredients and recipes.

The travels of marco polo of venice, italy, helped establish trade with china and india,

which gave europeans tea, spices, and the practice of heating the cooking pot with

coal. When columbus and other explorers returned to europe from america, they

brought new food and recipes with them. Then italians traded these things with

turks, who in turn traded with other Eastern europeans, thereby helping to spread

new food throughout most of europe.

*conquest = the act of defeating or taking control of an enemy or territory.

2 Article Use with Proper Nouns

Write *the* where needed with proper nouns. If a proper noun does not use *the*, write *NA* for "no article." (Look in Appendix 11 in the student book for help.)

1. _the_____ Pacific Ocean
2. _NA_____ Indonesia
3. _____ *Mayflower* (a ship)
4. _____ Southwest
5. _____ Lake Michigan
6. _____ Julia Child
7. _____ Amazon River
8. _____ Ural Mountains
9. _____ California
10. _____ *New York Times*
11. _____ Western Hemisphere
12. _____ Boston
13. _____ Philippine Islands
14. _____ Hawaii
15. _____ Indian Ocean
16. _____ South Pole
17. _____ Gulf of Mexico
18. _____ July
19. _____ Africa
20. _____ Statue of Liberty
21. _____ Tuesday
22. _____ Mediterranean Sea
23. _____ Thanksgiving
24. _____ Sahara Desert

3 Articles and Numbers with Proper Nouns

Circle the appropriate article or number, or if an article is not appropriate, circle *NA*.

Scott: Hey, Jenny, are you free on (the / (NA)) Saturday?
1

Jenny: Why do you ask?

Scott: I was wondering if you'd like to come to my cooking class. The instructors, (the / NA)
2

Crèvecoeurs, said that we could bring a guest sometime.

Jenny: I met a man named (a / NA) Paul Crèvecoeur once. Are your instructors from (a / NA)
3   4

Lafayette, Louisiana?

Scott: There's (a / NA) Lafayette in Louisiana? I didn't know that. I only know about (two / NA)
5   6

Lafayettes: one in Indiana and one in Colorado. No, they're from (a / NA) New Orleans,
7

and his name is (a / NA) Robert.
8

GRAMMAR PRACTICE 2

Count Nouns and Noncount Nouns

4 | Identifying Count and Noncount Nouns

The nouns in the list are noncount nouns, singular count nouns, and plural count nouns. Write **N** for noncount nouns, **SC** for singular count nouns, and **PC** for plural count nouns. For singular count nouns, write the plural form, too. (Look in Appendices 14 and 15 in the student book for help.)

SC men	1. man	_____	13. weather
_N_	2. homework	_____	14. potato
_____	3. silver	_____	15. clothing
_____	4. datum	_____	16. fruit
_____	5. news	_____	17. gravity
_____	6. freedom	_____	18. child
_____	7. milk	_____	19. Japanese
_____	8 sheep	_____	20. thesis
_____	9. rice	_____	21. toothpaste
_____	10. clothes	_____	22. wife
_____	11. person	_____	23. police
_____	12. nutrition	_____	24. soccer

5 | Count and Noncount Nouns

Mark the count nouns in bold with a **C** and the noncount nouns in bold with an **N**.

    The Internet has also been instrumental in spreading **ideas** about **cooking**.
                                                  C   N

Many online **bookstores** have a **section** for **cookbooks** that includes **reviews** about

the **books**. Television and radio **programs** often have corresponding **websites** that

give **recipes** and further **information** and **advice** about different **kinds** of **food**.

Some **companies** use the Internet to give **consumers** **help** with their **products**.

For example, one **company** that sells frozen **turkeys** has a very popular **website**

about the Thanksgiving **holiday**.

6 **Count Nouns Versus Noncount Nouns; Plural Count Nouns**

A. Use the correct form of the nouns in parentheses to complete the passage.

Some new _employees_ were listening to their two _____
            1 (employee)   2 (boss)

talk to them about the _____ at a produce market. "Let me give
                        3 (work)

you some _____," said the first one. "There are no _____
            4 (advice)   5 (party)

here! _____ is for our _____, _____,
       6 (fun)   7 (husband)   8 (wife)

and _____—not for us! Our _____ are our
    9 (child)   10 (vegetable)

_____. _____ are our _____!
11 (life)   12 (fly)   13 (enemy)

_____ and their tiny, little _____ are not welcome!
14 (mouse)   15 (tooth)

We won't talk about harmful _____ because we won't have any!
                                16 (bacterium)

The _____ of our _____ is more important than
    17 (health)   18 (customer)

the _____ that we make."
    19 (money)

"Look over there," said the second of the two _____. "The
                                                20 (man)

_____ are in strong, wooden _____. You can pick
21 (tomato)   22 (crate)

them up easily. The _____, on the other hand, is in flimsy, cardboard
                    23 (garlic)

_____. You must be careful when you pick them up. I'm warning you:
24 (box)

if you workers are careless with the garlic, _____ will roll!"
                                              25 (head)

B. The last line in Part A is a double entendre; that is, it has two meanings. One
meaning comes from the idiom *heads will roll*, which means "people will lose
their jobs." What is the other meaning of the last line? (Hint: Consider the fact
that *garlic* is a noncount noun. How do we "count" garlic?)

7 Subject–Verb Agreement

Circle the correct form of the verb.

1. Food science (**has** / have) long included more areas than just recipes.

2. Stimuli for studies (has / have) come from many sources.

3. For example, lead sometimes (enters / enter) food through decorated plates.

4. Hypotheses about safe food (has / have) led to better public health.

5. Physics (plays / play) a role in developing food for the space program.

6. The basis of such research (rests / rest) on adapting many substances for space travel.

7. Certain means of cooking (isn't / aren't) available in space, either.

8. Exciting news about food (is / are) reported every day.

8 Nouns Used as Count and Noncount Nouns

Circle the correct form to complete the sentences.

1. I don't really know much about (**business** / a business).

2. But I'm thinking about becoming a partner in (business / a business).

3. (Pressure / A pressure) that I'll have to face is dealing with employee problems.

4. Well, of course (pressure / a pressure) comes in many forms.

5. Should I do this? I might not have (chance / a chance) like this again.

6. My mother always said that both (chance / a chance) and skill were important in business.

7. Maybe I'll just light (fire / a fire) and make something to eat.

GRAMMAR PRACTICE 3

Articles

9 The Definite Article

Match each boldfaced noun phrase with the most appropriate meaning. Use each meaning only once.

1. __*d*__ **The earth** appears blue from space.

2. _____ Did you feed **the cat**?

3. _____ I bought a cookbook. **The recipes** in it are really good.

4. _____ Please pass **the salt and pepper**.

5. _____ I saw a chef on TV. **The chef** was talking about his new cookbook.

6. _____ **The cookbook** on that shelf is new.

7. _____ **The Vice-President** came for the ceremony.

a. The noun has already been mentioned.

b. The noun is part of or clearly related to something that has already been mentioned.

c. The noun is made clear by other words in the sentence.

d. The noun is unique—there is only one.

e. The noun is part of everyday life for the speaker and listener.

f. The noun is part of the larger social context of the speaker and the listener.

g. The noun is part of the immediate situation—speaker and listener can see or hear it.

10 The Indefinite Article (*A/An*) and the [0] Article

Match each boldfaced noun phrase with the description of the noun. Use each description only once.

1. __*b*__ That man is **a food critic**.

2. _____ He has written **a cookbook**.

3. _____ He likes **some coffee** after dinner.

4. _____ I like **tea**.

5. _____ He eats in **restaurants** often.

6. _____ **Vegetables** provide many vitamins.

a. singular count noun

b. subject complement

c. plural count noun

d. indefinite quantity of the noun

e. category of things

f. noncount noun

11 Definite and Indefinite Articles

Complete the conversation with *a*, *an*, *the*, or [0].

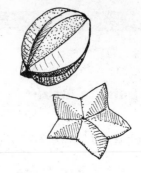

Sara: I want _**a**_ new cookbook.
        1

Dana: But you already have _____ bookshelf full of
                               2

        _____ cookbooks.
        3

Sara: I know, but _____ cookbooks I have aren't like a cookbook I saw in the
                    4

        bookstore yesterday.

Dana: Why? What's so special about it?

Sara: It's _____ astrological cookbook. It lists foods we should eat based on our
            5

        astrological sign and _____ position of _____ sun, moon, and stars.
                              6   7

Later . . .

Dana: So, did you buy _____ astrological cookbook that you wanted?
                        8

Sara: Yes, I did. I've already tried out _____ recipe, too. I had _____ fruit,
                                           9   10

        _____ salad, and _____ bread for _____ lunch.
        11   12   13

Dana: That sounds like _____ normal lunch. I thought _____ recipes in it
                         14   15

        would be more interesting than that.

Sara: I didn't tell you about _____ fruit. It was a carambola.
                                16

Dana: What's that?

Sara: It's also called "star fruit" because when you slice it, it looks like _____ star.
                                                                               17

        _____ cookbook claims it will help me find _____ happiness.
        18   19

Dana: Let me have _____ cookbook. I want to find _____ recipe for my sign
                    20   21

        that will make me happy, too. Here's one: enchiladas with _____ tomatillos.
                                                                  22

        According to _____ recipe, it's going to add spice to my life!
                    23

12 *The, A, Some,* [0]

Circle the correct determiner in the recipes. Where both choices are correct, circle both.

Apple Salad

3 apples, cored and cut into small pieces
1/2 cup raisins
1/2 cup chopped celery
juice of (an, the) orange
        1
8 ounces of yogurt
([0], some) cinnamon
    2

In (a, the) medium bowl, combine (an, the) apples, raisins,
    3   4
and celery. Blend (the, [0]) orange juice into [a, the]
                5   6
yogurt. Pour this mixture over ([0], the) salad and toss
                      7
well. Sprinkle ([0], some) cinnamon on top.
          8

Scrambled Eggs

12 eggs
1/4 cup milk
(the, [0]) salt and fresh ground pepper
    9
butter

Beat (the, some) eggs and milk together. Melt (a, the)
        10   11
butter in (a, the) skillet. Pour (a, the) mixture into
           12   13
(a, the) skillet and stir it until it thickens. Add (some, the)
  14   15
salt and pepper. Continue cooking until ([0], the) eggs
                                16
are soft.

GRAMMAR PRACTICE 4

General Quantifiers

13 General Quantifiers

Write all the noun phrases from the box that can follow each quantifier.

> food   recipe   recipes

1. a great deal of _food_

2. most _food, recipes_

3. quite a few _____

4. not many _____

5. little _____

6. each _____

7. enough _____

8. no _____

9. a large number of _____

10. a great many _____

11. much _____

12. hardly any _____

13. few _____

14. a little _____

15. a large amount of _____

16. plenty of _____

17. some _____

18. not any _____

14 *Much* and *Many*

Write questions with *how many* and *how much* to learn about food ideas for a longer life.

1. ___How much_____ tea is good for me? Drink some every day.

2. _____ fruits and vegetables should I eat in a day? At least five servings.

3. _____ olive oil should I use? Use it sparingly in place of other fats.

4. _____ fish should I eat? Eat two or three servings a week.

5. _____ garlic do I have to eat? As much as you can. Take it in a pill form if you don't like the flavor.

6. _____ servings of soybeans are good for me? Eat several servings a week for their anti-aging effect.

15 General Quantifiers

Circle the correct choice. Where both choices are correct, circle both.

(Many of)/ Much of) today's popular foods have
                    1

been around for (a great many / a great deal of) years.
                              2

Figs are (no / not much) exceptions. They have
                 3

(quite a little / quite a few) stories to their credit.
              4

Figs were probably (one / one of) the first fruits that
                              5

humans dried and stored. The first recorded history of

figs is from about 4000 (year / years) ago, when (several / a large amount of)
                              6   7

countries in Southwest Asia, as well as Egypt, Greece, and Italy, cultivated figs. People

in these areas showered (a great many / a great deal of) honor on the fig. Indeed, at
                                    8

one time, (none / any) of the figs that were grown in Greece could leave the country.
               9

The Greeks kept (all / all of) them for themselves. When the Persian King Xerxes lost
                    10

a battle to the Greeks, he ate (several / some) figs at (each / every) meal to remind
                                      11   12

himself of his defeat.

(Plenty of / Lots of) exporters recognized the value of figs, although
              13

(not all / not much) of them were successful in reestablishing the fruit in other
              14

areas of the world. In 812 A.D. Charlemagne of France tried to plant figs in the

Netherlands, but (none / not any) flourished in the colder climate. In 1759,
                          15

(some / any) Spanish priests planted the first fig trees in California, and today
              16

(many / most) figs in the United States are grown there.
              17

16 Writing

On a separate sheet of paper, write down one of your favorite recipes. Include a list of ingredients and complete instructions for preparing the food. Use articles and quantifiers.

17   **Editing**

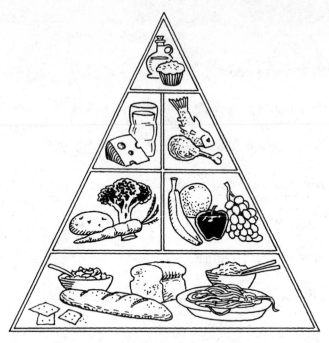

The Food Guide Pyramid

Correct the 10 errors with nouns, articles, and quantifiers. The first one is corrected for you.

                                 an

The Food Guide Pyramid is ~~a~~ outline of what to eat each day. It's a general guide

that lets people choose a diet that's right for them. The Pyramid calls for eating a

variety of foods to stay healthy. The Pyramid also focuses on the fat because most

Americans' diets are too high in fat. Top of the pyramid shows fats, oils, and sweets.

These foods provide little nutrients and are high in calories. They don't provide no

vitamins either, so people should eat less of them. The next level has two groups

of foods that come mostly from animals: milk, cheese, meat, fish, eggs, and nuts.

The guidelines recommend two to three serving a day. The next level is the foods

from plants—fruit and vegetables. Many people don't eat enough of these foods.

People should eat plenty vegetables and fruit because they are good source of

vitamins. At the base of the pyramid are grains—breads, cereal, rice, and pasta.

How much grains should you eat? Get at least four or five servings a day.

Chapter 9

Modifiers, Pronouns, and Possessives

Modifiers

1 **Identifying Modifiers**

A. Find the modifiers that come before the nouns in the sentences. Underline them and circle the nouns they modify.

Every <u>good</u> (cook) knows that even a <u>great</u> (recipe) isn't going to result in a delicious dish without quality ingredients. Professional chefs use only fine, fresh produce. They usually prefer to buy healthy organic fruit and vegetables at small farmer-owned stands at local markets instead of in large grocery stores. For example, they select dark green leafy lettuce and smooth, round tomatoes at the peak of freshness for their summer salads. They pick ripe red strawberries, sweet Persian melons, and exotic tropical fruit for luscious, light desserts.

B. Find adjectives in Part A for . . .

Opinion: _good_ _____ _____

Appearance: _____ _____

Shape: _____

Color: _____ _____

Origin: _____

Find a noun used as a modifier: _____

Find a compound modifier: _____

2   *-ing* and *-ed* Adjectives

Add *-ing* or *-ed* to the word stem in bold to complete the sentences with the correct adjective.

1. Some cookbooks promise **sooth** <u>ing</u> food.

2. **Interest**_____ diners will try a **tempt**_____ new dish.

3. After eating too much chocolate, the **stimulat**_____ child couldn't sleep.

4. There are **heal**_____ recipes in that cookbook.

5. An **excit**_____ new restaurant opened downtown last week.

6. The **refresh**_____ woman had enjoyed the cold, **refresh**_____ iced tea.

7. There's a lot of **confus**_____ information about food and nutrition.

3   Noun Modifiers; Compound Modifiers

A. Change the words in parentheses to noun modifier + noun and complete the titles of the cookbooks. Use capital letters for the important words in the titles.

1. Recipes from a Country <u>Vegetable Garden</u> (vegetables grown in a garden)

2. The _____ Cookbook   (a machine that makes bread)

3. _____ Cooking   (a pot made of clay)

4. The Great _____ Cookbook   (sauce made of chili)

B. Change the words in parentheses to a compound modifier + noun and complete the titles of the cookbooks. Use capital letters for the important words in the title.

1. Great <u>Low-Fat Recipes</u> (recipes that are low in fat)

2. 100 Wonderful _____ (meals that have four courses)

3. Fabulous _____ (recipes that win awards)

4. Quick and Easy _____ (meals that take 20 minutes)

5. The _____ Cookbook   (a meal that has 300 calories)

4 **Order of Modifiers**

Write the modifiers in parentheses in an appropriate order. Include commas when they are indicated.

1. This cookbook offers __authentic, old Southern__ (authentic/old/Southern/,) food.

2. This one promises _____ (easy/quick/really/,) meals.

3. Here is a cookbook with recipes from _____

   (food/great/American) companies.

4. This cookbook has recipes from _____ (art/famous) museums.

5. This one has recipes for _____ (modern/nonstick) cookware.

6. I like this _____ (French/herb) cookbook.

7. Here's a cookbook with _____

   (interesting/regional/very) dishes.

8. There are _____

   (coffee/delicious/international) drinks in this one.

5 **Writing**

On a separate sheet of paper, write five cookbook titles of your own. Use more than one modifier and put the modifiers in an appropriate order. Refer to Exercise 3 for examples.

GRAMMAR PRACTICE 2

Reflexive Pronouns; Reciprocal Pronouns; *Other*

6 **Reflexive and Reciprocal Pronouns**

Circle the correct form to complete the sentences.

Randy: I need help. I have to do a restaurant review. Will you come to the restaurant with

(me / myself)? I don't want to go (myself / by myself).
        1   2

Lee: Yes, unless the restaurant is Bad Bart's Barbecue. The President (himself / by himself)
                                                                        3

couldn't get me to go there. If that's where you're going, you'll have to go

(yourself / by yourself).
          4

Randy: Why? I thought you'd like the restaurant. After all, you barbecue for (you / (yourself))
5

almost every weekend.

Lee: That's the point. We could take turns cooking for (us / (each other)) every Saturday night,
6

and our food would still be more interesting than Bart's food.

Randy: We could sit (ourselves / (by ourselves)) and just talk to (us / (each other)). If Bart came to
7   8

our table, we wouldn't have to talk to (him / himself).
9

Lee: The three of us certainly wouldn't agree with (us / one another)) about food. Maybe we
10

could talk about something else.

Randy: I don't get it. Is it the food ((itself) / by itself) that you don't like, or is it Bart?
11

Lee: Oh, Bart's fine. It's his cooking that I don't like. Don't you know that he's my brother?

Our mother could never get ((us) / ourselves) to agree with (us / (each other)).
12   13

7 Forms of *Other*

Complete the sentences by using *another*, *others*, *the other*, or *the others*.

Sara: The food in this restaurant is wonderful! I love places like this! Do you know some

_____others_____ that we can try?
1

Bernie: Sure. There's _____another_____ one just down the street. Why?
2

Sara: I was just suggesting that since our first date is going well, we might have

_____another_____ next Saturday. What do you think?
3

Bernie: I'm happy with that. For next Saturday, I have three ideas. One is that we go to a little

French place that I know. _____Another_____ is that we pack a lunch and go on a
4

hike. _____The other_____ is that we cook something at your place.
5

Sara: I like those ideas. Do you have any _____others_____?
6

Bernie: Yes, but I'm not telling you about them. I'm keeping _____the others_____ a secret.
7

Sara: Hmm. It sounds as if this won't be the only Saturday evening that we spend together.

Am I right? Are there going to be ___others___?
8

Bernie: I hope so. I hope there will be many more.

GRAMMAR PRACTICE 3

Indefinite Pronouns

8 **Indefinite Pronouns**

Use combinations of the words in the box to complete the sentences. More than one answer may be possible. In sentences with verbs in parentheses, circle the correct verb.

some	one
any	body
no	thing
every	

Henry: Tell me __something__. What are your plans for tonight? Are you doing
1

_____ special?
2

James: I'm not doing _____ so far. What do you have in mind?
3

Henry: There's a new restaurant downtown. _____ at the office (was / were)
4

talking about it, but she hadn't been there yet.

James: Is it the new Indian restaurant? _____ I know (has / have) been there,
5

either, but it's the main topic of conversation at the office. _____
6

(wants / want) to go there.

Henry: I hadn't heard _____ about an Indian restaurant. I know absolutely
7

_____ about it. I was talking about a new Algerian restaurant. I haven't
8

heard _____ say _____ negative about it.
9   10

James: It sounds interesting. It's _____ I'd like to try. Let's go!
11

GRAMMAR PRACTICE 4

Possessives

9 **Possessives—Form and Uses**

A. Underline the possessives and the words that they modify.

1. About 9000 years ago, the <u>people</u> <u>of Mexico</u> started cultivating chilies.

2. In the 1500s, European traders' ships carried the chilies to other places.

3. The length of a century was the time needed for chilies to spread throughout the world.

4. A Hungarian cook has her recipes for chili peppers, and a Chinese cook has his, too.

5. Mexico's chili peppers are especially famous for their flavor and heat.

6. The chili pepper's seeds and ribs make it hot.

7. If your skin is as sensitive as mine is, wear gloves when handling hot chilies.

B. Complete the chart with examples from Part A. Write an example for each form and for each function. You may use an example more than once.

Form	Function
1. possessive determiner **their**	1. ownership
2. singular possessive noun	2. amount
3. plural possessive noun	3. something that is part of another thing
4. possessive pronoun	4. origin
5. possessive phrase	

10 **Forming Possessive Determiners, Possessive Pronouns, and Possessive Nouns**

Complete the sentences with the correct possessive form of the pronoun or noun in parentheses.

Can you imagine living without rice? __Archaeologists'__ discoveries about

        1 (Archaeologists)

rice include grains that are about 7000 years old. These grains were found in an

ancient village in _____ Yangtze River valley.

        2 (China)

European cooks expanded _____ skills when rice came to
_____ 3 (they)

Europe, and Native Americans in South America sharpened _____,
_____ 4 (they)

too, when the Europeans introduced it. Africans have long cultivated this crop, and in

the United States, _____ rice fields date back to the 1600s.
_____ 5 (South Carolina)

More than half of _____ population eats rice every day. Many
_____ 6 (the world)

_____ nutrition depends on _____ availability.
7 (people)   8 (it)

Some _____ diets may contain over a pound of rice every day. One
_____ 9 (Asians)

of _____ friends eats rice at every meal. _____
10 (I)   11 (She)

eating habits are much different from _____ _____
12 (I)   13 (family)

eating habits. _____ diet includes more wheat and corn, whereas
14 (We)

_____ doesn't include wheat at all.
15 (she)

11 Possessive Nouns Versus Possessive Phrases

Complete the sentences by forming possessive nouns and possessive phrases with
the words in parentheses. In each, use the preferred possessive form. Add *the*
when necessary.

__Mama's kitchen__ was always the _____.
1 (Mama / kitchen)   2 (house's activities / center)

On chilly mornings, the _____ drew us there.
3 (stove / warmth)

The kitchen was the first place the neighbors came to tell the

_____.
4 (neighborhood and wider community / gossip)

On holidays, the whole family would gather at _____.
5 (my parents / house)

The _____ permeated the house, and
6 (cooking holiday food / smells)

again we found ourselves in the kitchen as _____
7 (my uncles / funny stories)

kept us entertained.

12 Editing

Correct the 9 errors with modifiers, pronouns, and possessives. Some errors can be corrected in more than one way. The first error is corrected for you.

much-loved
Cacao seeds are valued for producing a ~~much-loving~~ product: chocolate.

Researchers disagree with one other about the origins exact of chocolate, but they

tend to agree that the first domestication of cacao trees was at least 3000 years ago

in the low-lying forests of what is now Mexico. Almost everyone are surprising to

find out that the Mayans, who lived in that part of Mexico, had several ways of

preparing chocolate, including flavoring it with chilies peppers, and almost always

drank it. The Mayans probably spread their chocolate-drinking habits to others in

Central America, eventually reaching the Aztecs in the highlands of Mexico.

The Aztecs valued the caffeine-rich seeds so much that they used them as

currency. Because of this, only royalty and the upper class consumed the rich

chocolate drinks. Montezuma by himself, one of the Aztec last rulers, probably gave

chocolate to Hernán Cortés, a Spanish explorer. The Spanish introduced chocolate

into Europe, where the bitter drink was first mixed with sugar. Nowadays, people

from all over the world enjoy this highly appreciating treat from the Americas.

Unit Wrap-up

Writing

On a separate sheet of paper, write a paragraph about a holiday meal you are familiar with. Describe the holiday and the food that people eat on the holiday you choose. Use nouns, determiners, and modifiers in your paragraph.

Example: On Thanksgiving, the fourth Thursday of November, Americans usually gather with their family to give thanks for all they have and to eat a big meal together. The main course of the meal is a large stuffed turkey that has been roasted in a slow oven for a long time. Tart ruby red cranberry sauce is a must with the turkey as are creamy hot mashed potatoes and rich brown gravy.

TOEFL TIME

Allow yourself 12 minutes to complete the 20 questions in this exercise.
Questions 1 through 10: Circle the letter of the one word or phrase that best completes the sentence.

1. For the indigenous people of Australia, the land and everything on it are deeply woven into all aspects of _____.
   (A) the life
   (B) a life
   (C) life
   (D) lives

2. Orchids come in two basic types: One type grows at the base of the tree, and _____ grows on the tree itself.
   (A) others
   (B) other
   (C) another
   (D) the other

3. Americans get _____ of their news from television rather than from newspapers.
   (A) much
   (B) many
   (C) several
   (D) few

4. Many composers have extensive formal training, but Rimsky-Korsakov taught _____ the fine points of music.
   (A) himself
   (B) he
   (C) his
   (D) him

5. Although Buddhism was founded in India, there are _____ Buddhists living there now.
   (A) a few
   (B) few
   (C) a little
   (D) little

6. The woolly mammoth, which has been extinct since the Ice Age, had _____ tusks.
   (A) long-16-foot
   (B) long-16-feet
   (C) 16-foot-long
   (D) 16-feet-long

7. Although some of the vitamin C that a person ingests is retained, _____ is lost and must be replenished.
   (A) several
   (B) any
   (C) a great many
   (D) a great deal

8. _____ seed will sometimes germinate after 200 years.
   (A) An unpreserved flowering lotus
   (B) A flowering lotus unpreserved
   (C) A lotus unpreserved flowering
   (D) An unpreserved lotus flowering

9. A government employee with a high-level security clearance isn't permitted to discuss his or her work with _____.
   (A) one another
   (B) anyone
   (C) any other
   (D) each other

10. _____ who killed Abraham Lincoln, John Wilkes Booth, was a very popular actor of his time.
    (A) The man   (C) Some man
    (B) A man   (D) Man

Go on to the next page.

Questions 11 through 20: Circle the letter of the underlined part of the sentence that is incorrect.

11. <u>Some of archaeologists</u> believe that <u>people</u> from the Americas have been cultivating
         A   B

    <u>hot peppers</u> for <u>6500 years</u>.
       C   D

12. <u>Research</u> has shown that <u>efficient care</u> in <u>a hospital</u> usually results in <u>shorter stay</u>.
     A   B   C   D

13. <u>Wood</u> from <u>the white oak</u> is not only burned in fireplaces but also used to make
     A   B

    <u>the furniture</u> and <u>whiskey barrels</u>.
       C   D

14. <u>Some of</u> the <u>interested</u> <u>hanging</u> bridges that <u>the Incas</u> built lasted for over 500 years.
     A   B   C   D

15. <u>Cadiz</u>, in <u>the south</u> of Spain, is the oldest continuously <u>inhabited</u> city in <u>Western world</u>.
     A   B   C   D

16. <u>Some of</u> <u>Van Gogh's</u> most famous paintings are of <u>fields</u> of <u>sunflower</u>.
     A   B   C   D

17. Richard G. Drew, a <u>Minnesota-born</u> engineer, was <u>person</u> who invented <u>adhesive tape</u>
              A   B   C   D

    in 1925.

18. In <u>hers</u> <u>1929</u> book, *A Room of One's Own*, <u>Virginia Woolf</u> described the benefits of
       A   B   C

    having <u>a fixed, steady income</u>.
              D

19. <u>Cats and dogs</u> tend to favor one front paw or <u>the other</u>; that is, they prefer to use
     A   B

    either <u>the</u> their left or right <u>paw</u>.
          C   D

20. <u>Shakespeare's</u> characters Romeo and Juliet loved each <u>another</u> even though <u>their</u>
     A   B   C

    <u>families</u> were enemies.
      D

Adjective Clauses

10

Adjective Clauses

Adjective Clauses

1 Identifying Adjective Clauses

In the sentences, underline each adjective clause and circle the noun it modifies.
Put a second line under the relative pronoun in the clause.

1. Intelligence and creativity are two (areas) that psychologists study.

2. One Harvard professor who has studied intelligence and creativity for over 30 years is Howard Gardner.

3. Gardner developed his theories on intelligence by doing research on artistic talents that children have.

4. He proposed that intelligence is something which is made up of different aspects.

5. Gardner called the aspects that make up intelligence "multiple intelligences."

6. Gardner reported on the relationship that he found between types of intelligence and creativity.

7. Gardner first studied two men who demonstrated different kinds of intelligence, Sigmund Freud and Pablo Picasso.

8. Both men were considered creative because of the innovations which they made in their fields.

9. The traits of the people he studied helped Gardner develop ideas about creativity.

2 Position of Adjective Clauses

Complete the sentences with the adjective clauses in parentheses. Write the adjective clauses after the nouns that they modify.

               which everyone has
1. Personality traits are something. (which everyone has)
                   ^

2. A psychologist is a person. (who helps us learn about our personalities)

3. A personality test is something. (which helps people understand their unique traits)

4. Almost everyone can know herself or himself better. (who takes a personality test)

5. People can make better career decisions. (that know their positive traits)

6. Something is your career. (that you should think about carefully)

GRAMMAR PRACTICE 2

Adjective Clauses with Subject Relative Pronouns

3 Subject Relative Pronouns

Complete the sentences with adjective clauses with *be*. Use each adjective only once. Use any appropriate subject relative pronoun (*who*, *which*, *that*).

adventurous	✓creative	dangerous	stressful	talkative

1. A person _who / that is creative_ often becomes an artist or a writer.

2. A person _____ might be among the first to colonize Mars.

3. People _____ might become teachers or salespeople.

4. A job _____ is good for a thrill-seeking person.

5. Careers _____ aren't good for nervous people.

4 Adjective Clauses with Subject Relative Pronouns; Combining Sentences

Combine the pairs of sentences. Use the second sentence to form an adjective clause modifying the appropriate noun in the first sentence. Use any appropriate subject relative pronoun (*who*, *which*, *that*).

1. Psychologists develop tests. The psychologists are interested in personality.

   Psychologists who/that are interested in personality develop tests.

2. They are personality tests. They indicate a person's traits.

   _____

3. People will probably succeed. People have the right personality traits for a certain job.

   _____

4. These are traits. These traits are important for a particular job.

   _____

5. Someone probably won't be happy at a job. He or she doesn't have these traits.

   _____

GRAMMAR PRACTICE 3

Adjective Clauses with Object Relative Pronouns

5 Adjective Clauses with Object Relative Pronouns

Complete the sentences by using the adjectives in the box to form adjective clauses with *we consider*. Use each adjective only once. Use a different object relative pronoun (*who*, *whom*, *which*, *that*, [0]) in each clause.

> conscientious ✓dynamic enterprising exciting important

1. A person _who/whom/that/[0] we consider dynamic_____ would make a good CEO.

2. A person _____ should do well in business.

3. People _____ will be good workers.

4. A profession _____ is professional sports.

5. Jobs _____ will keep our attention and interest.

6 Adjective Clauses with Object Relative Pronouns; Combining Sentences

Combine the sentences. Use the second sentence to make an adjective clause. Use any appropriate object relative pronoun: *who*, *whom*, *which*, *that*, or [0].

1. That man has an exciting job. Everyone knows him.

   _That man who/whom/that/ [0] everyone knows has an exciting job._____

   _____

2. His job is a difficult job. Not many people would want his job.

   _____

   _____

3. The hours are long. He spends the hours at work.

   _____

   _____

4. People want something from him. He meets them.

   _____

   _____

5. That man is the president. We saw him on television.

   _____

   _____

7 **Subject and Object Relative Pronouns**

Complete the passage with all the choices (*who, whom, which, that,* [0]) that are possible.

The Keirsey Temperament Sorter is a personality test ___that / which___
                                                              1

categorizes people into four basic temperaments: artisan, guardian, idealist, and

rational. People _____ take the test answer a series of questions
                        2

_____ are designed to determine their temperament. Traits
         3

_____ are associated with each temperament are also associated
         4

with careers. For example, artisans are people _____ we find in fields
                                                          5

_____ allow them to use their creativity, like art and entertainment.
         6

A famous artisan was Elvis Presley. Guardians are people _____ are
                                                                    7

good at planning and carrying out processes, so they make good supervisors.

A president of the United States _____ was a guardian was
                                          8

George Washington. Idealists are people _____ want deep and
                                                  9

meaningful relationships. Plato, a famous Greek philosopher, was an idealist.

Rationals are abstract thinkers _____ are good at planning.
                                         10

Bill Gates, the founder of Microsoft, is a rational.

The Keirsey Temperament Sorter is a test _____ you can take on
                                                   11

the Internet to help direct you to a career _____ is right for you.
                                                      12

8 **Writing**

On a separate sheet of paper, describe each of the following people and things in two or three sentences. Use adjective clauses with subject and object relative pronouns.

Example: My mother is someone who is always kind and gentle. She has a smile which makes everyone feel good.

Your best friend   Your favorite activity

The person you admire most   The job you would most like to have

9 Editing

Correct the 6 errors with adjective clauses. Some errors can be corrected in more than one way. The first error is corrected for you.

The Greek philosopher Plato wrote about four kinds of characters ~~who~~ that/which humans have. Because Plato was interested in the societal role that these types of characters played, he focused on the actions that each type displayed them. He wrote about artisans, guardians, idealists, and rationals.

Aristotle, Plato's student, also defined four types of people, but he defined them on the basis of happiness. Someone who he or she found happiness in sensual pleasure was different from someone whom wanted to acquire assets. Others found happiness in acting in a moral fashion, while Aristotle's fourth type of person enjoyed logic.

While Plato was alive, Hippocrates, a Greek physician, proposed that people have distinct temperaments from birth. He identified four personality types that was based on bodily fluids: eagerly optimistic, doleful, passionate, and calm. A Roman physician in the second century A.D., Galen, furthered Hippocrates' ideas.

The four personality temperaments who Hippocrates and Galen described complemented Plato's four descriptions of social actions. Hundreds of years later, others interested in personality types also found four types. Perhaps our personalities haven't changed much in the last 2000 years.

More About Adjective Clauses

Adjective Clauses with Relative Pronouns That Are Objects of Prepositions

1 **Adjective Clauses with Relative Pronouns That Are Objects of Prepositions**

Underline the adjective clause in each sentence. Then change each adjective clause to show all possible patterns.

1. A job <u>that you are interested in</u> should fit your personality.

   which you are interested in / you are interested in/ in which you are interested

2. For a short time, you can probably do a job that your personality isn't well suited for.

3. In the long run, however, you will be better off if you do a job that you are happy at.

4. A person that you can talk with honestly may help you decide on a good career.

2 **Adjective Clauses with Relative Clauses That Are Objects of Prepositions; Combining Sentences**

Combine the sentences. Use the second sentence to make an adjective clause. Use any appropriate object relative pronoun, *who, whom, which, that,* or [0].

1. A person is Nora Swann. I can talk to her.

   A person who(m) I can talk to/ that I can talk to/ to whom I can talk is Nora Swann.

2. She is an employment counselor at the company. I have a job at the company.

   _____

   _____

3. I'm not particularly suited for the job. I'm working in the job.

   _____

   _____

4. Nora encourages me to look for a position. I can get excited about the position.

   _____

   _____

5. I may find a new job. I can move into the job.

   _____

   _____

GRAMMAR PRACTICE 2

Adjective Clauses with Possessive Relative Pronouns

3 **Combining Sentences; Clauses with *Whose***

Combine the pairs of sentences. Use the second sentence as an adjective clause with *whose.*

1. A test asks questions about a person's thoughts and feelings.
   Its purpose is to match personality with careers.

   A test whose purpose is to match personality with careers asks questions about a

   person's thoughts and feelings.

2. An immediate response on these tests is preferred to a later response.
   A later response's accuracy may decrease with too much thought.

   _____

   _____

3. People may answer as they wish they were, not as they really are.
   Their responses are slow.

   _____

   _____

4. Answers based on wishes will not help a person.
   His or her personality is actually quite different.

   _____

   _____

5. A person has a strong preference in one aspect of work.
   His or her answers tend toward a specific trait.

   _____

   _____

6. For example, a person probably prefers to work with other people.
   His or her responses indicate an outgoing personality.

   _____

   _____

4 **Relative Pronouns as Objects of Prepositions; Possessive Relative Pronouns**

Complete the sentences with all the choices (*whom, who, which, that, whose,* [0])
that are possible.

1. I've been thinking about taking a personality test, but I'm afraid it will be a test
   __that/which/[0]_____ I won't do well on.

2. My ex-girlfriend told me I had the personality of a rock. When we broke up, I wanted to
   return the personality, but I didn't know the rock _____ I had
   borrowed it from.

3. My ex-girlfriend also told me that you can tell a guy _____
   personality is like mine, but you can't tell him much.

4. I know what kind of personality I have. I am someone for _____
   "living in the moment" is important. I think that that moment was sometime in 1999.

5. My mother tried to get me to keep my eyes open and my mouth shut. This is an awkward
   way in _____ to work when you're a radio announcer.

6. I am a person _____ thoughts never change. I thought that they
   had changed once, but I was wrong.

7. There are some things _____ I just won't speak about. I'd tell

   you what they were, but then I'd have to speak about them.

8. I've always thought of myself as someone _____ others

   don't talk about much. Why should they? I talk about myself enough for all of us.

5 More Practice with Relative Pronouns

Complete the passage, using all the choices (*whom, who, which, that, whose,* [0])
that are possible.

    Personality tests often use terms **which/that** _____ have one

1

meaning in "everyday" language and a different, specific meaning for the test.

The ideas _____ the terms represent are more important

       2

than the terms themselves. For example, one personality test contrasts *factual* with

sensitive, two terms _____ we usually don't think of as

       3

opposites. This contrast is between people _____ like to

         4

deal with facts and logic and people to _____ feelings

       5

and intuition are more important. Someone _____

        6

answers indicate a strong tendency to be "factual" may prefer work

situations for _____ there are clear objectives.

    7

A job _____ allows for more personal expression

    8

appeals to someone _____ tends to be more "sensitive."

      9

Remember that these are terms _____ the test designers

       10

have used in specific ways.

Adjective Clauses with *Where* and *When*

6 Adjective Clauses with *Where*

Use the information in the box to write sentences about John and George with *the place* + adjective clauses. Use *where* in sentences about John. Use different alternatives to *where* to write two sentences about George.

John	George
study/in a quiet corner of the library	study/in the student union
eat/at a small table alone	eat/at a large round table with friends
relax /at home with a good book	go/to a lively night spot
feel comfortable/in a small group of close friends	feel comfortable/in a large noisy crowd

1. The place where John studies is a quiet corner of the library.

   The place in which George studies is the student union. OR The place which George studies in is the student union. OR The place that George studies in is the student union. OR The place that George studies in is the student union.

2. _____

   _____

   _____

   _____

3. _____

_____

_____

_____

4. _____

_____

_____

_____

B. An introvert is shy, and an extrovert is outgoing. Look at the sentences in
Part A about John and George. Who is the introvert? _____
the extrovert? _____

7 **Adjective Clauses with *When***

A. Use the appropriate adjective clause with *when* to complete the sentences.

an artist feels creative ✓a couple feels happy an employee feels nervous	students feel many emotions you felt bored we feel confused or frustrated

1. A day __when__ __a couple feels happy__ is their wedding day.

2. A period in life _____ _____
   is before we decide on a career.

3. A time _____ _____
   is the first few days of a new job.

4. A month in life _____ _____
   is the last month of high school.

5. A time in life _____ _____
   is the most productive period for that person.

6. Was there a time in your life _____ _____
   with what you were doing and wanted a change?

B. Rewrite the sentences in Part A in two different ways: with an appropriate
preposition + *which*, with *that*, or with [0].

1. A day on which a couple feels happy is the day they get married OR A day which a
    couple feels happy on is the day they get married. OR A day that a couple feels happy
    is the day they get married. OR A day a couple feels happy is the day they get married.

2. _____

    _____

    _____

3. _____

    _____

    _____

4. _____

    _____

    _____

5. _____

    _____

    _____

6. _____

    _____

    _____

8 Writing

 On a separate sheet of paper, write two or three sentences about each of the
following times and places.

A time when my life changed   A moment when I felt creative

A place where I had a great adventure   A place where I feel comfortable

Example: A time when my life changed was when I started classes at the university.
            I was meeting people from all over the country, so it was a time when everything
            seemed exciting. . . .

9 Editing

Correct the 6 errors with adjective clauses. Some errors can be corrected in more than one way. The first error is corrected for you.

Traditionally, a creative person is someone ~~whose~~ *who is* able to find a new solution to a problem. Many "creativity tests" were created during a time when this position was taken in. However, this definition has been expanded by psychologists who their work enlarges older views of creativity. A place where there is some disagreement is in the idea of general creativity. The definition that Howard Gardner came up with says that people are creative in a specific domain. A gifted musician may show innovation in music but not in another area in that she has less talent. An expansion of the traditional theory says that there are many periods of time when people are creative. There can also be many different ways in which creativity is demonstrated in. Two areas where are not part of traditional creativity tests, fashioning new products and asking new questions, are part of Gardner's definition of creativity. Gardner's definition also differs in that a judgment about creativity must be made by a group of people, not by a single individual.

Unit Wrap-up

Writing

 On a separate sheet of paper, describe the kind of job that you would like, based on your personality. Use the phrases in the box or your own phrases. Use adjective clauses with subject and object relative pronouns, at least one adjective clause with a relative pronoun that is the object of a preposition, one adjective clause with *whose*, one adjective clause with *where*, and one adjective clause with *when*.

work alone	work in groups	work with things
work with ideas	use numbers	use words
use tools or machines	make your own schedule	have a fixed schedule

Example: My ideal job is one where I can make my own schedule and my own rules. I don't want to work in a company that has a lot of people . . . .

TOEFL TIME

Allow yourself 12 minutes to complete the 20 questions in this exercise.
Questions 1 through 10: Circle the letter of the one word or phrase that best completes the sentence.

1. Scientists all over the world are trying to save species _____ are endangered.
   (A) what
   (B) in which
   (C) that
   (D) who

2. Placido Domingo is a well-known opera singer _____ from Spain.
   (A) which is
   (B) who is
   (C) is
   (D) that he is

3. Garage sales are a way many Americans recycle possessions _____.
   (A) that they don't want to keep
   (B) they don't want to keep them
   (C) which they don't want to keep them
   (D) what they don't want to keep

4. James Michener was an American author _____ books were bestsellers for years.
   (A) of whose
   (B) whose
   (C) who's
   (D) his

5. Although he has been dead for many years, Elvis Presley is a person _____ many people continue to be interested.
   (A) in that
   (B) in whom
   (C) whom
   (D) in him

6. Anthropologists research the habits of people who _____ in the past.
   (A) was living
   (B) has lived
   (C) lived
   (D) living

7. The Pentagon is a five-sided building _____.
   (A) where the U.S. Army headquarters are located in
   (B) where the U.S. Army headquarters are located
   (C) where are the U.S. Army headquarters located
   (D) which the U.S. Army headquarters are located

8. Geography is a subject about _____ many Americans know very little.
   (A) that
   (B) it
   (C) whom
   (D) which

9. In the northern hemisphere, December is the month _____.
   (A) when winter begins in
   (B) winter begins in it
   (C) in which winter begins
   (D) then winter begins

10. The film character James Bond likes martinis _____ shaken, not stirred.
    (A) which is
    (B) who are
    (C) which they are
    (D) which are

Go on to the next page.

Questions 11 through 20: Circle the letter of the underlined part of the sentence that is incorrect.

11. Physicist Murray Gell-Mann first proposed the existence of the subatomic particle <u>who</u>
A

 scientists <u>called the quark</u> and <u>which they</u> believe <u>is</u> the fundamental unit of matter.
B   C   D

12. A scientist <u>who</u> was trying to improve agriculture in the South, George Washington Carver,
A

 showed <u>the peanut</u> could replace soil minerals <u>that</u> cotton had depleted <u>them</u>.
B   C   D

13. Mineralized water that <u>drips</u> in caves <u>forms</u> both structures <u>which build up</u> from the floor
A   B   C

 and structures <u>which hangs down</u> from the ceiling.
D

14. During the presidential election <u>when</u> George W. Bush <u>ran against</u> Al Gore, news
A   B

 organizations <u>covered</u> the campaigns were often criticized <u>on how</u> they reported on them.
C   D

15. One American state <u>where</u> has a capital city <u>which</u> is neither the biggest nor the most
A   B

 important <u>city</u> <u>in the state</u> is New York.
C D

16. There are some American authors <u>whose</u> <u>their</u> books have been translated into <u>many</u>
A   B   C

 languages, <u>including</u> Spanish and Japanese.
D

17. The Pennsylvania Dutch <u>are</u> the descendants of a group of German immigrants <u>who</u>
A   B

 settled in an area of the country where <u>they</u> began farming <u>in</u>.
C   D

18. Bill Gates <u>is</u> someone <u>who's</u> fortune <u>came</u> in a relatively short <u>time from</u> the computer
A   B   C   D
industry.

19. After 1929, <u>when</u> the stock market crashed, the government <u>began</u> the program
A   B

 <u>that people knew it</u> as the New Deal; this was a time <u>in which</u> millions of Americans were out
C   D
of work.

20. In 1876, at a <u>place</u> near <u>the Little Big Horn River is</u>, Indian warriors <u>whose</u> leader was Crazy
A   B   C

 Horse killed General Custer and most of the <u>soldiers he commanded</u>.
D

Gerunds and Infinitives

Chapter 12

Gerunds and Infinitives

Gerunds

1 **Gerunds as Subjects, Objects of Verbs, and Objects of Prepositions**

A. Correct the passage by changing verbs to gerunds where appropriate. Including the example, there are 9 changes.

    Appearing

~~Appear~~ on television helped the career of musician Ricky Martin. At the

1999 Grammy Awards, sing "The Cup of Life" earned Martin a standing ovation.

He certainly must have been happy about receive this recognition of his music,

and he also must have enjoyed accept the award for Best Latin Pop Performance.

After his appearance on the Grammys, Martin's fame kept increase. His song

"Livin' La Vida Loca" soared to the top of the pop charts, and people looked

forward to buy his album. From grow up in San Juan, Puerto Rico, to live the

crazy life, Martin has always been fond of sing.

B. Find examples in Part A of gerunds performing these functions.

Subject of a sentence: <u>Appearing</u>   _____

Object of a verb: _____   _____

Object of a preposition: _____   _____

Be + adjective + preposition: _____   _____

2   **Gerunds; *By* + Gerund; *Go* + Gerund**

A. Correct the passage by changing verbs to gerunds where appropriate. Including the example, there are 10 changes.

> *becoming*
> By ~~become~~ famous, Ricky Martin increased both his problems and his
>
> pleasures. If he goes dance or on a date, he has a problem blend into the crowd.
>
> Fans can't help approach him for an autograph. Maintain his private life is hard.
>
> On the other hand, he has a good time perform. When he goes out on stage, he
>
> stands there expose his thoughts and feelings to his fans. Perhaps he can't go
>
> shop by himself without draw attention, but by remind himself of the line
>
> between his personal life and his private life, he may be able to live quite well
>
> with his fame.

B. Find examples in Part A of gerunds performing these functions.

By + gerund: <u>   becoming   </u>   <u>   </u>

Go + gerund: <u>   </u>   <u>   </u>

Subject: <u>   </u>

Object of a preposition: <u>   </u>

Gerunds used with   <u>   </u>   <u>   </u>

    other expressions: <u>   </u>   <u>   </u>

3   **Writing**

Imagine that you are a pop musician. On a separate sheet of paper, use gerunds and other appropriate words to finish the sentences that tell about your life as a musician.

1. Since I've become famous, I really appreciate . . .
2. Nowadays, I spend time . . .
3. Before I was famous, I used to go . . .
4. On the other hand, I enjoy . . .
5. I think I'll keep my sanity by . . .
6. I'm always busy . . .
7. I avoid . . .
8. I had to quit . . .
9. I miss . . .
10. It's no use . . .

Example: **Since I've become famous, I really appreciate having some time alone.**

GRAMMAR PRACTICE 2

Infinitives I

4   *It* + Infinitive; Infinitive as Subject

A. Rewrite the sentences using *it* + infinitive.

1. To choose a program on TV isn't easy these days.

   <u>It isn't easy to choose a program on TV these days.</u>

2. To learn about all the programs takes time.

   _____

3. To decide what to watch is difficult.

   _____

4. Not to waste time on programs that don't interest you is a good idea.

   _____

B. Rewrite the sentences using the infinitive as the subject.

1. It's fun to channel surf.

   <u>To channel surf is fun.</u>

2. It's necessary to have a remote control.

   _____

3. It's interesting to see how quickly you can become interested in each program.

   _____

4. It's a good idea not to channel surf when someone else is watching a program.

   _____

5 Verb + Infinitive Patterns

I Love Lucy, starring Lucille Ball, was one of the first situation comedies on American television. Complete the sentences with an infinitive or an appropriate pronoun and infinitive.

In most episodes of *I Love Lucy*, Lucy

managed ___*to get*___ herself
         1 (get)

into trouble. He husband, Ricky, often

needed _____ her. In a
        2 (rescue)

famous episode entitled "Job Switching,"

Lucy and her good friend Ethel Mertz decided _____ jobs in a candy factory
                                              3 (take)

while their husbands attempted _____ the house.
                               4 (take care of)

Lucy and Ethel had no experience in factory work, but they talked to the man who was

the manager of the candy factory and persuaded _____ them try the job.
                                                5 (let)

Lucy and Ethel claimed _____ how to do the work. Their supervisor, a
                       6 (know)

woman, told _____ the chocolate candies into paper wrappers as they came
            7 (put)

down a conveyor belt. The supervisor warned _____ too slowly or they
                                             8 (not / work)

would fall behind. She expected _____ the job satisfactorily. Lucy and Ethel
                                9 (do)

attempted _____ the job well, but very quickly they were struggling
          10 (do)

_____. They failed _____ all the chocolates, so they
11 (keep up)   12 (wrap)

began stuffing chocolates into their hats and mouths. Falling further behind, Lucy and Ethel

refused _____ and ate even more chocolates and stuffed the rest in their
        13 (give up)

pockets. The supervisor discovered what they were doing. They begged _____
                                                                     14 (keep)

their jobs, but the candy company chose _____ them anyway.
                                        15 (fire)

GRAMMAR PRACTICE 3

Infinitives II

6 Adjectives Followed by Infinitives

Daytime talk shows are a popular type of program in the United States, but they are also controversial and not everyone thinks they are good television. Here are some reactions to what happens on these shows. Complete the sentences with an appropriate form of *be* + the adjective and verb in parentheses.

1. I <u>was astonished to see</u> people fighting on yesterday's show.
    (astonished / see)

2. We _____ that we watched the guests tell
    (ashamed / admit)
    embarrassing things about their personal lives on the show.

3. People _____ that some guests on a talk
    (stunned / learn)
    show were actors who were paid to fight with each other.

4. Viewers* _____ that a popular talk show
    (delighted / hear)
    host was not going to air people's fights on her show anymore.

5. In the future, _____ what people say on
    (you / surprised / hear)
    these talk shows?

viewer = a person who watches TV

7 Infinitive of Purpose

Murder mysteries are another favorite type of TV program. In one popular show, the murder has often happened before the first scene. Complete the sentences with the phrases in the box. Use infinitives of purpose with *to* or *in order to*.

arrest the murderer figure out if they are lying ✓find clues	fool us find out who committed the crime conceal his or her guilt

1. As the show begins, the detective examines the crime scene <u>(in order) to find clues.</u>

2. _____, the detective asks
    people questions. The detective already knows the truth.

3. The murderer lies _____.

4. _____, the writer always
    includes another suspect who seems to have committed the crime.

5. The detective hunts for the proof he needs _____

_____ .

6. We watch the show _____ .

8 Infinitives with *Too* and *Enough*

A. Jon and Matt are cousins. Write sentences about each boy with an appropriate adjective + *too* or *enough* + infinitive.

Jon, 12

Matt, 24

1. drive a car

   Jon is too young to drive a car.   Matt is old enough to drive a car.

2. watch an R-rated movie at a theater alone

   _____

   _____

3. buy a child's ticket to a movie

   _____

   _____

B. Write sentences about Jon and Matt with the words given and *enough* + infinitive.

1. Jon/time/play video games

   Jon has enough time to play video games.

2. Matt/money/go to a concert

   _____

3. Matt/not/time/play video games all day

   _____

4. Jon/not/money/buy a lot of CDs

   _____

9   **Infinitives as Noun Modifiers**

Many young people in music bands dream of success. Imagine you are in a band.
Complete the sentences with an appropriate infinitive phrase.

1. I think we have the chance _to become the next famous rock band._

2. I know I have the ability _____

3. We have the desire _____

4. With good luck, we have the possibility _____

5. We'll find a way _____

10   **Writing**

On a separate sheet of paper, complete the sentences using infinitives or an
appropriate pronoun and infinitive and your own ideas.

1. It's fun . . .   5. Students have enough time . . .
2. I can't wait . . .   6. I'm glad . . .
3. I'm too young . . .   7. My friend trusts . . .
4. We listen to music . . .   8. It isn't a good idea . . .

Example: It's fun to watch cartoons on TV.

11   **Editing**

Correct the 6 errors with gerunds and infinitives. The first one is corrected for you.

      launching

  One result of launch Music Television (MTV) in 1981 was that both the

television and the music industries took off in new directions. Before this time, it was

unusual seeing music videos, but televising them 24 hours a day became a winning

formula for attracting young viewers. News and documentaries about music and

performers were included on the broadcasts to supplement the videos. Young "VJ's,"

or Video Jockeys, hosted the programs and recommended to listen to artists that they

liked to hear. By promoting rock concerts and by holding interviews with artists,

MTV attracted and exposed viewers to a wide variety of performers. Since the early

1980s, MTV has become enough popular for launching another channel, MTV2, and

it is always looking for ways keeping bringing in new viewers.

Chapter 13

More About Gerunds and Infinitives

Verbs + Gerunds and Infinitives

1 **Verbs That Take Only Gerunds or Only Infinitives**

Complete the sentences with *going*, *to go*, or *them to go*.

1. I enjoy _going_____.

2. We can't afford _____.

3. She forced _____.

4. You can learn a lot by _____.

5. Please think about _____.

6. They intend _____.

7. We're glad _____.

8. We trust _____.

9. Is he looking forward to _____?

10. I suggest _____.

11. It's no use _____.

12. He reminded _____.

13. She recalls _____.

14. He had the opportunity _____.

15. They will wait _____.

16. We have hired _____.

2 **More Practice with Verbs That Take Only Gerunds or Only Infinitives**

Use the words in parentheses to complete the sentences with an infinitive or a gerund.

The prize that most movie actors hope ___to win____ is an

1 (win)

Academy Award. Since 1929, people in the motion-picture industry

have hoped _____ the gold-plated statue, or Oscar,

2 (earn)

given with this award. Winners appreciate _____ this

3 (get)

recognition. No one can deny _____ honored when

4 (feel)

they receive a nomination. Imagine _____ your name announced as the best
                                       5 (hear)

actor of the year. In the excitement, you may forget what you have planned _____.
                                                                              6 (say)

You will need _____ many people before you finish _____.
                 7 (thank)   8 (speak)

3 Gerunds and Infinitives

Special effects are an important element of movies. Use the words in parentheses
to complete the sentences with a gerund or an infinitive. Where both are possible,
include both.

1. In a minute-long movie called *The Conjurer*, magician Georges Melies appeared

    <u>to disappear</u>_____.
              (disappear)

2. Then, he seemed _____ himself into his female assistant.
                         (turn)

3. Today, whole cities appear _____ with great realism in movies like
                                   (vanish)

    Independence Day.

4. Who could have anticipated _____ what it would be like to travel
                                   (experience)

    inside the human body?

5. Imax Theaters showed the movie *Everest*. Moviegoers liked _____ on
                                                                   (stand)

    top of the world without leaving their seats.

6. The creators of special effects hope _____ even better illusions in
                                             (create)

    future films.

7. How ever special effects are created, every moviegoer loves _____ them.
                                                                     (see)

8. The special effects in movies will continue _____ even more
                                                     (get)

    spectacular in the future.

4 Verbs That Take Gerunds and Noun Phrases + Infinitives

Use the words in parentheses to complete the sentences with a gerund or
an infinitive.

I don't always advise <u>looking for</u>_____ deep meanings in pop movies, but the
                          1 (look for)

continuing popularity of the *Star Wars* saga has required _____ for the
                                                               2 (search)

origin of its appeal. Please permit me _____ this with you.
                                            3 (explore)

The *Star Wars* films encourage us _____ the characters in terms
4 (see)

of good and evil. As the heroes fight external forces and internal passions, they urge us

_____ the darkness in our lives. The films allow us _____
5 (examine)   6 (be)

heroes, too, and they encourage _____ in the power of good.
7 (believe)

5   **Verbs That Take Gerunds and Infinitives but with a Difference in Meaning**

Circle the gerund or infinitive that better completes each sentence.

1. I'd like to see *Star Wars* again; we should remember _____ at the video store.

    stopping   (to stop)

2. Some fans remember _____ to the first showing of the movie *Star Wars* in 1977.

    going   to go

3. If they forgot _____ early for tickets, they didn't get into the theater.

    going   to go

4. Darth Vader was so imposing that I've never forgotten _____ him for the first time.

    seeing   to see

5. When Luke Skywalker was learning to use a light saber, he tried _____ it in his left hand and
    then in his right hand to see which felt better.

    holding   to hold

6. R2D2 got hurt. C3PO tried _____ him, but he didn't have the parts he needed.

    repairing   to repair

7. Classic heroes such as Luke Skywalker never stop _____ the forces of evil.

    opposing   to oppose

8. From time to time, the heroes stopped _____ their good fortune and celebrate.

    enjoying   to enjoy

6   **Writing**

On a separate sheet of paper, write a paragraph about a character in a movie or
story that you like. Use at least three of these verbs followed by a gerund or
infinitive: *remember*, *forget*, *stop*, and *try*. Also, use at least two verbs that are
followed only by gerunds, at least two that are followed only by infinitives, and
one that can be followed by both.

Example: *My favorite character in the movie To Kill a Mockingbird was Atticus
             Finch. In the movie, Finch always tried to do the right thing even when
             others were afraid, and he hoped to teach his children to be like him. . . .*

GRAMMAR PRACTICE 2

Performers of the Actions of Gerunds and Infinitives

7 Performers of Gerunds and Infinitives

Use the words in parentheses to complete the sentences with a gerund or an
infinitive. When a noun phrase or pronoun is given, include an appropriate form
of the performer of the action.

With the movie *Toy Story*, Disney and Pixar Studios succeeded in __creating__ the

1 (create)

first all computer-animated full-length movie. The animators planned __for the toys to look__

2 (the toys / look)

realistic. They intended _____ many of the

3 (the audience / recognize)

toys from their childhood. Movie viewers enjoyed _____ the toys

4 (watch)

behave like humans. They tolerated _____ less than life-

5 (the humans / look)

like because the story was really about the toys.

The story was a tale of rivalry between the two main characters. Disney persuaded

_____ in the struggle between Cowboy Woody and Buzz

6 (we / believe)

Lightyear. _____ the favorite toy annoyed Woody. Viewers

7 (Buzz / become)

understood _____ jealous of Buzz Lightyear, the new toy.

8 (Woody / feel)

Disney Studios chose _____

9 (popular actor Tom Hanks / do)

the voice of Woody. They hoped _____ the character appealing.

10 (he / make)

They were eager _____ Buzz Lightyear's voice for the same

11 (Tim Allen / do)

reason. The studio trusted _____ the toys to life.

12 (these two actors / bring)

GRAMMAR PRACTICE 3

Verbs Followed by Base Forms

8   Forms Following Causative Verbs, Verbs of Perception, and Other Verbs

Use the words in parentheses to complete the sentences. In some cases, more than one form is correct. Give all correct forms.

1. a.   In 1899, audiences watched George Melies _disappear, disappearing_ in
         (disappear)
         The Conjurer and were amazed.

    b.   He made himself _____ by stopping the camera,
         (disappear)
         changing the scene, and restarting the camera.

2. a.   In *Honey I Blew Up the Baby*, we saw the baby _____
         (grow)
         larger right before our eyes.

    b.   Filmmakers make people and things _____ larger or
         (appear)
         smaller by changing the perspective.

3. a.   In the 1977 *Star Wars* movie, moviegoers observed spaceships

         _____ in outer space.
         (battle)

    b.   In this film, George Lucas, the director, had his special effects crew

         _____ complex battle scenes using a computer.
         (create)

    c.   Computerized motion control let him _____
         (create)
         specialized effects.

4. a.   Viewers also heard the lasers _____ as Han Solo fought
         (fire)
         the Empire.

    b.   Directors can have the computer _____ different elements
         (add)
         into their scenes, including realistic sounds.

    c.   All of these elements help us _____ that what we are
         (believe)
         seeing and hearing is real.

9   Writing

On a separate sheet of paper, give your own examples of special effects from movies you have seen. Use performers of infinitives and gerunds, sensory verbs, and causative verbs.

Example: In *Raising Arizona*, a speeding car appeared to stop within inches of a
            baby on a highway. I saw the baby move, so I knew it wasn't a doll, but I
            couldn't believe any mother would let her child sit there with a car coming
            so fast....

10 Editing

Correct the 6 errors with gerunds and infinitives. The first one is corrected for you.

Eric Clapton earned his fame through ~~play~~ ^{playing} his guitar, but he may have kept his solo career alive because of his singing. As a teenager, Clapton took up playing the guitar, and he later started performing in public. Practicing the guitar improved his music but left little time for schoolwork, so he stopped to go to school to pursue a career in music. After he joined the Yardbirds, he became known for being one of the best blues guitarists playing at that time. As his reputation grew, Clapton seemed to be moving from one band to another. Within 10 years of he having dropped out of school, Clapton was considered to be a leading rock guitarist. However, he didn't appreciate having become so well-known, and at one time he seemed to be trying to hide in an unknown band. Clapton's popularity faded for a while, but he continued to record albums. The soundtrack of the 1992 film *Rush* included for Clapton singing "Tears in Heaven," a tribute to his son, who had recently died. Clapton's performance of "Tears in Heaven" and other songs on a special television program made it possible for his to reach a new audience. This success let him to release another album, and he kept on writing and performing songs for other movies.

Unit Wrap-up

Writing

On a separate sheet of paper, write eight statements that are true about your preferences and activities. In each statement, use a different verb or expression from the list + a gerund or an infinitive.

Example: I enjoy listening to pop music.

1. enjoy
2. dislike
3. refuse
4. be afraid

5. be interested in
6. be used to
7. have a good time
8. like + go + a recreational activity

TOEFL TIME

Allow yourself 12 minutes to complete the 20 questions in this exercise.
Questions 1 through 10: Circle the letter of the one word or phrase that best completes the sentence.

1. _____ to Ireland in the late 1990s was surprising, especially given their exodus in the 1980s.
   (A) It was thousands of Irish emigrants returning
   (B) For thousands of Irish emigrants to return
   (C) Thousands of Irish emigrants returned
   (D) Thousands of Irish emigrants return

2. Proponents of gun-control legislation were disappointed _____ that it hadn't passed.
   (A) them to learn
   (B) learning
   (C) to learn
   (D) learn

3. The surgeon general recommends that everyone who smokes try _____.
   (A) to stop smoking
   (B) stopping to smoke
   (C) stop smoking
   (D) stop to smoke

4. Fans of Emily Dickinson appreciated _____ her work, which she had chosen to keep secret while she was alive.
   (A) to publish
   (B) publish
   (C) her family to publish
   (D) her family's publishing

5. Some ethicists dispute the Hemlock Society's position that for the terminally ill, life is not worth _____.
   (A) living   (C) live
   (B) to live   (D) to be living

6. Injuries and deaths on the highway can be prevented _____ that children are properly buckled into an appropriate seat.
   (A) making sure
   (B) to make sure
   (C) by making sure
   (D) for making sure

7. Recognizing that _____ to a new home can be time consuming, some companies are assisting their employees in relocating.
   (A) by moving   (C) to move
   (B) for moving   (D) move

8. Individual Retirement Accounts, IRAs, let _____ money for retirement.
   (A) employees accumulating
   (B) employees to accumulate
   (C) for employees to accumulate
   (D) employees accumulate

9. One trend in the United States is for parents to advise _____ home when the children are facing financial difficulties.
   (A) to return
   (B) their children returning
   (C) their children to return
   (D) returning their children

10. Some car experts recommend _____ a used car rather than a new one because, in the long run, it is less expensive.
   (A) buying
   (B) to buy
   (C) buy
   (D) for buying

Go on to the next page.

Questions 11 through 20: Circle the letter of the underlined part of the sentence that is incorrect.

11. Arctic mosquitoes, which can make a caribou herd <u>to stampede</u>, tend <u>to grow</u> <u>to be</u> a
                                          A   B   C

    quarter of an inch long and are known for <u>swarming</u> around unlucky mammals.
                                                D

12. Doctors sometimes remove the tonsils of children who fail <u>to sleep</u> well <u>to unblock</u> their
                                                       A   B

    airways, thereby helping them <u>to stay</u> asleep instead of <u>to wake up</u> throughout the night.
                                        C   D

13. <u>By stroking</u> her baby's chin and throat, a mother may assist the child <u>in learning</u>
       A   B

    <u>to nurse</u>, an action which is crucial for newborns <u>mastering</u>.
       C   D

14. In a 1996 survey, which 950 people were willing <u>to participate</u> in, <u>doing</u> household
                                              A   B

    chores <u>were</u> among the top three things that couples reported <u>fighting</u> about.
           C   D

15. It's difficult <u>to watch</u> television without <u>see</u> reports of harmful bacteria, but food safety
                 A   B

    experts have recommendations <u>to keep</u> us from <u>ingesting</u> unsafe food.
                                C   D

16. <u>For preparing</u> a stranded gray whale <u>to reenter</u> the ocean, rehabilitation specialists are
       A   B

    prohibited from <u>spending</u> time with the animal once they <u>have finished working</u>.
                   C   D

17. Financial experts don't advise <u>investing</u> all of one's money in a single company as, <u>by doing</u>
                                A   B

    that, one risks <u>losing</u> everything at once; instead, they suggest <u>to diversify</u> one's assets.
                   C   D

18. "Pingers" prevent dolphins from <u>becoming</u> entangled in fishing nets by
                                  A

    <u>scaring or alerting</u> them, and they allow fishermen <u>working</u> without <u>hurting</u>
             B   C   D

    marine mammals.

19. Researchers are telling doctors <u>to urge</u> <u>to eat</u> dark green, leafy vegetables <u>to get</u> more
                                     A   B   C

    vitamin K, which seems <u>to strengthen</u> bones.
                              D

20. Once patients get used <u>to using</u> digital hearing aids, these aids may give them the
                            A

    opportunity <u>to hear</u> more sounds that have been <u>too high</u> or <u>not enough loud</u>.
             B   C   D

Modals

Modals

Overview of Modals

1 Overview of Modals

Read the passage. Circle the one-word modals. Underline the phrasal modals. Put a check above the modal-like expressions.

Tony's Tips for Meeting People

(Can) you walk into a room full of people and start talking imediately? You ought to try it sometime. All of us are supposed to be able to meet new people, but some of us find that a little hard. Try my tips and start making new friends today.

• You must show confidence! If you think you are worth knowing, other people will agree! You could try saying to yourself, "I am an interesting person!" Believe it.

• You should look people in the eye! People aren't going to speak to you if you look at their shoes!

• Of course, you ought to smile! You may be able to get someone else to speak with just a nice smile. Try it and see!

• You have got to say something! "Hi!" is a good start! You are allowed to keep your remarks simple. You don't have to be funny; just be sincere!

• You must not talk only about yourself! In fact, you had better let the other person talk more than you do. You might learn interesting things if you just listen.

So, what do you think? Are you going to be able to do these simple things? Of course you are! Start today! You should see results soon!

GRAMMAR PRACTICE 2

Modals of Ability

2   Present, Past, and Future Ability

Complete the sentences with appropriate forms of *be able to*. Where *can* or *could* is possible, write it as well. Use negatives where indicated. Use contractions with *not*.

What attracts people to others? Research ___is able to/can___ tell us something about
                                                                1
attractiveness. A research team asked people to judge which faces were most attractive.

They _____ experiment with real, live faces, but they
                    2 (not)

_____ alter photographs to make them more feminine or
             3

masculine. Using computers, a researcher _____ make the chin
                                                                    4

smaller (a feminine trait) or the eyebrows bigger (a masculine trait). Even though the photos were

very similar, the people in the study _____ select the same faces
                                                          5

consistently. A Scottish researcher _____ get the same results as
                                                    6

researchers in Japan and South Africa did. Thus, the researchers _____
                                                                                  7

draw conclusions across three different ethnic groups: feminine features—for example, fuller lips

and smaller noses—were preferred for both men and women.

An interesting side note to this story is that many people are using the Internet to meet each

other. On the computer, one person _____ see another without
                                                        8 (not)

special equipment. Couples _____ focus on things besides
                                          9

physical attributes. An attractive person _____ feel that he
                                                              10

or she isn't being judged on looks alone. In the future, some of the current Internet couples

_____ meet in the real world, but some of them
             11

_____ get together. Will physical attractiveness still be important
         12 (not)

for the couples that _____ meet in person? People who have
                                  13

already met this way think that we _____
                                                      14 (not)

completely forget our ideas about beauty, but we also don't have to make them our first priority.

GRAMMAR PRACTICE 3

Belief Modals Used to Talk About the Present

3   **Belief Modals and Other Ways of Expressing Degrees of Certainty**

A. Rewrite the sentences using the belief modals in the box that express a similar meaning.

may	might not	must	✓ought to

1. She is probably married by now.

    She ought to be married by now.

2. They are possibly engaged.

    _____

3. He is certainly single.

    _____

4. Maybe they aren't happy together.

    _____

B. Rewrite the sentences using *It's* + the adjectives in the box that express a similar meaning.

✓certain	impossible	not likely	possible

1. He must be her husband.

    It's certain that he's her husband.

2. He shouldn't be at work today.

    _____

3. She may be at home.

    _____

4. They couldn't be on their honeymoon.

    _____

4   Belief Modals About the Present

Gerald is giving a report on attraction. Look at his notes and complete the sentences with *must*, *have to*, *have got to*, *should*, *ought to*, *may*, *might*, and *could*. In each blank, write one of the forms that you think expresses the intended meaning. Use contractions with *not*.

possible	most likely possibility	almost certainly true
• subconsciously looking for a kind man • men with feminine features: gentler • looking very feminine not good	• women concerned with protection • choosing well leads to finding a good mate • no regrets about decision	• reason for attraction • feminine features not the only factor: other influences. . . . too

Why do people seem to be attracted to feminine faces? No one knows for sure, but because

the evidence is so strong, there ___must/has to/has got to___ be a reason.
                                          1

One idea that _____ explain this situation is that,
                        2

subconsciously*, a woman _____ be looking for a man
                                 3

that will be kind to her. A man with softer, more feminine-looking features

_____ seem gentler than a man with harder, more masculine-looking
            4

features. On the other hand, looking too feminine _____ not be
                                                              5

good, either, as a woman _____ be concerned with finding
                                  6

someone who looks like he can protect her. Men with all kinds of features are selected as mates*,

so feminine facial* features alone _____ not be the only factor
                                           7

in women's decisions. There _____ be other
                                   8

influences. If a woman chooses well, she _____ end up with
                                                  9

a man who will be good for her, and she _____ not regret
                                                 10

her decision.

subconsciously = having thoughts or feelings without being aware of them;
mate = a husband or wife; *facial* = related to the face

5 Writing

A. On a separate sheet of paper, tell whether you think each statement about marriages and families in the United States is almost certainly true, possibly true, or almost certainly untrue. Write affirmative and negative statements using the following modals: *must, could, might, may, can.* Tell your reason for thinking a statement is true or false.

1. More weddings occur in New York than in any other state.

   Example: **That might be true because there are a lot of people in New York.** OR
   That couldn't be true because California must have more weddings.

2. Couples are engaged for an average of two years before getting married.
3. January is the most popular month for weddings.
4. Nine out of 10 Americans are married at some point in their lives.
5. Americans are marrying at a younger age than ever before.
6. The bride is older than the groom in one out of four marriages.
7. The average number of children in an American family is four.

B. Look at the end of the unit to find out which statements are true.

GRAMMAR PRACTICE 4

Belief Modals Used to Talk About the Future

6 Belief Modals About the Future

Circle the correct form. If both forms are correct, circle both.

Some trend watchers expect that increasing numbers of people (will) / (are going to)
    1
be using the Internet to find potential mates. The use of online dating services (should / ought to)
                                                                                       2
grow as users become more comfortable with the technology. Even though it is now possible to

see someone on another computer through the use of a camera, this option (may / has got to)
                                                                                3
not become more popular because many people seem to enjoy being able to ignore physical

characteristics. What other changes (will we / do we have to) see in dating practices?
                                            4
We (might / could) find services that cater to international couples who have met over the
       5
Internet, or we (may / might) find more localized services that bring together only people
                         6
in the same geographical area. We (should / ought to) not expect to see people give up on
                                        7
more traditional ways of meeting each other, but we (may / could) see an increase in
                                                            8
electronic "matchmakers." A computer (might / must) set you up with others that you
                                           9
(may / must) not meet otherwise. Whatever the future holds, it (will / has to) be interesting!
  10   11

GRAMMAR PRACTICE 5

Social Modals I: Modals for Permission, Requests, and Offers

7 **Permission, Requests, and Offers**

Use an appropriate modal from the boxes to complete the conversations.
More than one modal may work. Use each modal only once.

1.
> ✓can   could   shall   will

Keiko: What are you reading?

Emily: It's a book about marriage and wedding customs around the world.

Keiko: It looks interesting. __Can__ I borrow it when you're finished?

a

Emily: I'm sorry, but I checked it out of the library and it's due tomorrow. I

_____ ask them to hold it for you.

b

Keiko: That's fine. _____ we go to the library together? Then I can check it out

c

as soon as you return it.

Emily: Sure. _____ you be ready at 9:00?

d

2.
> can   may   would

Librarian: _____ I help you?

a

Keiko: My friend is returning this book, and I want it. _____ I check it

b

out now?

Librarian: Yes, that's not a problem. I see you have some other books. _____

c

you like to check them out as well?

Keiko: Yes, please.

8 **Writing: Permission, Requests, and Offers**

On a separate sheet of paper, write a conversation for each of the situations.
Make polite requests and offers, or ask permission. Use appropriate responses for
the information given.

1. Steve wants to know the number of Matematch Dating Service. The operator
   knows the number.

   Example: Operator: Directory Assistance, may I help you?

Steve: Yes. Could you give me the number of Matematch Dating Service?

Operator: One moment, please. The number is 800 get-mate (438-6283).

2. You're at your brother's home. You ask your 10-year-old nephew to show you how
   to play a new computer game. He is happy to teach you the game.

3. You're at a store. You ask the salesperson to gift-wrap the wedding present you've just bought. The salesperson agrees but asks you to come back later.

4. You don't have any money. You ask a friend to lend you some. He refuses because he doesn't have any money, either.

5. You ask a classmate to go hiking with you this weekend. The classmate agrees.

6. Create a dialogue for a situation of your own.

GRAMMAR PRACTICE 6

Social Modals II: Modals for Suggestions, Advice, Expectations, Warnings, and Necessity

9 Social Modals

A. Match each social modal with the best meaning.

1. could   a. lack of necessity

2. should   b. warning

3. not have to   c. suggestion

4. have got to   d. advice/opinion

5. had better not   e. prohibition

6. be supposed to   f. expectation

7. must not   g. necessity/obligation

B. Complete the sentences with the modals in Part A.

1. You _could_____ ask her to go to a movie with you.
   (suggestion)

2. You _____ ask her out at least two days in advance.
   (advice / opinion)

3. You _____ pay for the movie.
   (expectation)

4. You _____ come late.
   (warning)

5. You _____ ask her out again if you don't want to.
   (lack of necessity)

6. You _____ walk her to the door of her house.
   (necessity)

10 **Suggestions, Advice, Expectations, and Necessity**

A teacher is discussing how young people find marriage partners. Use any appropriate modal to complete the sentences with the meaning given in parentheses. Use contractions with *not*.

Teacher: I've been reading this book about marriage customs and weddings around the world. The author states that young people in almost every culture in the world are expected to find a marriage partner. They _____are supposed to / are to_____ get married. According
1 (expectation)
to this book, in many cultures families still _____ take an
2 (necessity)
active role in arranging for the marriage of their children. How do young people find a marriage partner in your country?

Abdullah: In Saudi Arabia, to find a bride, the man _____ get help
3 (expectation)
from the female members of his family. Most families still agree that young people
_____ meet before marriage arrangements have begun.
4 (prohibition)
However, contrary to what some people believe, the woman
_____ accept the man's proposal. She can refuse.
5 (lack of necessity)

Hye Won: In Korea, a family _____ consult a matchmaker to
6 (suggestion)
find a suitable partner for their son or daughter. But young people
_____ do that. Nowadays, many find a mate on their own.
7 (lack of necessity)

Toshi: In Japan, most people still believe a couple _____ have equal social
8 (advice / opinion)
standing. Computer-based marriage information agencies are available now, and
young people _____ use one if they haven't found a suitable
9 (advice / opinion)
partner on their own.

Wornpahol: In Thailand, although we are free to date now, a Thai son or daughter
_____ pay a debt of gratitude to his or her parents,
10 (necessity)
which often delays the marriage.

Jaime: In Mexico, couples used to be chaperoned on dates, but they may now meet on

unchaperoned dates. The couple _____ have the approval of the
                                    11 (advice / opinion)

woman's parents first, though.

Teacher: Although there are differences in the customs of your cultures, there are also similarities.

This has been so interesting, but we _____ stop now. I see that our
                                          12 (warning)

time is up. Thank you all for sharing your ideas.

11 Writing

On a separate sheet of paper, write a paragraph about marriage customs and
finding a mate. Use modals for expectation, advice, suggestion, and necessity.
Tell what is necessary, what isn't necessary, and what is prohibited.

Example: In the United States, you should find a husband or wife on your own.
            You could use a dating service, or you might go to places where young single
            people socialize. You must get the person to agree to marry you. You don't
            have to get the approval of your family, but it's better if you do. . . .

12 Editing

Correct the 7 errors with modals. The first one is corrected for you.

                                                                          find

Anthropologists have seldom been able to ~~finding~~ a society in which men and women

don't marry, even though when and how they marry might vary. In some cultures, couples

are supposed to marry as soon as they reach adulthood. In others, couples may be delay

marriage until they want children. But most cultures believe that couples should to marry.

Types of marriage also vary. The most prevalent practice is monogamy, a marriage

between one husband and one wife. There are also polygamous societies. In these, a man

may have more than one wife, but he must not. A wife, however, mayn't have more than one

husband. Polyandry, in which a wife can have more than one husband, is extremely rare,

occurring in only 1 percent of the world population.

Will you marry? Will you can choose your own mate? Many societies are changing, and

attitudes about marriage should changing along with them. It is unlikely, however, that

marriage, in some form, is going to disappear anytime soon.

Chapter 15

More About Modals

Perfect Modals

1 Perfect Modals—Form

Julie has made a choice to remain single and is satisfied with her lifestyle, but her mother doesn't agree. Use the words in parentheses to complete the conversation with perfect modals. Use contractions with *not* where possible.

Mom: You __should have gotten_____ married by now.
            1 (should / get)

Julie: I'm happy with my life. My career is going well, and I have a very active social life.

I _____ good decisions about other things, but I made a
         2 (may / not / make)

good decision about not getting married.

Mom: That's silly. With a little more effort, I'm sure you _____
                                                                            3 (could / be)

happily married by now. You have dated some very nice men. What about Jeff?

You _____ Jeff. You _____
          4 (might / marry)   5 (should / not / tell)

him that you planned to remain single. Maybe he's still interested.

Julie: He _____ married by now. Besides, I
              6 (must / get)

_____ happy with him because he wanted a stay-at-home
        7 (could / not / be)

wife and children.

Mom: (*Sigh.*) I _____ grandchildren by now.
                        8 (could / have)

Julie: What made you think of Jeff, anyway?

Mom: I saw his mother at the supermarket last week, and I . . .

Julie: Oh, Mother! I just had a message from Jeff's mother on my voicemail.

You _____ something about me to her!

9 (must / say)

Mom: Well, I did tell her you were still single.

Julie: You _____ her that I like my life as it is.

10 (ought to / tell)

Mom: I _____ you to be so independent.

11 (should / not / raise)

You _____ a career instead of marriage.

12 (might / not / choose)

Julie: You raised me fine. I'm a well-adjusted single person with an exciting career!

GRAMMAR PRACTICE 2

Belief Modals Used to Talk About the Past

2 Belief Modals About the Past

No one has seen Caroline, her fiancé Eric, or her former boyfriend Gene since yesterday afternoon. Caroline is supposed to marry Eric soon. Read the statements and complete the sentences with *must have*, *have to have*, *have got to have*, *should have*, *ought to have*, *may have*, *might have*, *could have*, and, in negative sentences only, *can have*. In each blank, write the modals that work best in the context. Use *not* where necessary. Use contractions with *not* where possible.

1. Caroline

   a. Caroline is missing, and she didn't sleep in her bed.

      Caroline __might have/may have/could have__ stayed with her best friend, Sally, last night.

(not very certain)

   b. When Caroline's mother called Sally, Sally hadn't seen Caroline in two days.

      Caroline _____ stayed with Sally.

(strongly certain / not)

   c. Caroline is planning to marry Eric next month.

      Caroline _____ looked happy,

(most likely)

      but she has seemed sad lately.

   d. Caroline was engaged to Gene a year ago.

      Caroline _____ been serious

(strongly certain)

      about him then.

2. Gene

   a. Gene is missing and his friends haven't seen him since yesterday afternoon.

     Gene _____ gone on a business trip.
                     (not very certain)

   b. Gene never travels on business. His friends aren't sure about where he went.

     Gene _____ gone on a business trip.
                   (strongly certain / not)

   c. Gene and Caroline had a fight and she broke off their engagement a year ago.

     Gene _____ felt sad because he
                 (strongly certain)

     stayed home a lot and never dated anyone else.

   d. Gene has seemed happier lately.

     Gene _____ found a new
                 (not very certain)

     girlfriend.

3. Eric

   a. Eric wasn't at home when Caroline's mother called.

     Eric _____ gone away with
                (not very certain)

     Caroline.

   b. Eric's boss told Caroline's mother that he sent him on a business trip.

     Eric _____ gone anywhere with
                (strongly certain / not)

     Caroline.

3 **Writing**

On a separate sheet of paper, write what you believe happened to Caroline, Gene, and Eric. Write sentences about what might have happened to them, what couldn't have happened to them, and what must have happened to them.

Example: **Eric might not have gone on the business trip for his boss. He and Caroline could have gone away together.** OR **Gene and Caroline might have fallen in love again.**

GRAMMAR PRACTICE 3

Social Modals Used to Talk About the Past

4 **Social Modals About the Past**

Read the letter to Addy Viser, an advice columnist, as well as Addy's response. Complete each sentence with an appropriate social modal in the past. Use *not* where necessary. Use contractions where possible.

Dear Addy Viser,

My husband loves to cook, but he really had too much equipment for our small kitchen. We _had to_
  1 (necessity)
do something. So yesterday I got rid of some things that he

_____
  2 (advice / opinion)
thrown out long ago. When my husband came home after work, he said I

_____
  3 (a bad idea, but it happened)
touched his things without consulting him. He also said that I

_____
  4 (warning)
thrown out his favorite stew pot. When he found out that I had, he was really angry and said that I

_____
  5 (prohibition)
use any of his equipment again.

Addy, I know that I

_____
  6 (suggestion)

asked him to get rid of things himself, but I have tried that and nothing ever happens. He

_____
  7 (expectation)
cleaned out the kitchen last month.

What do you think?

Adele

Dear Adele,

Your head was obviously in the right place, but you

_____ been
  8 (suggestion)
a little more diplomatic.

You _____
  9 (lack of necessity)
get rid of your husband's things when he was at work. You

_____
  10 (good idea, but it didn't happen)
waited until he got home. Next time, talk more and act slowly.

Addy Viser

5 Belief and Social Modals About the Past

Luis and Taka are walking downtown. Complete their conversation. Circle the correct choice. If both are correct, circle both.

Luis: Do you know where there's a phone near here? I (should) / (ought to) have called my
1

girlfriend about five minutes ago.

Taka: Yeah, after all, it (must / has to) have been all of 30 minutes since you last talked to her.
2

Luis: Give me a break, will you? She (might / could) have changed her mind about going out
3

tomorrow.

Taka: No way! She (couldn't / must not) have changed her mind that fast. Besides, she
4

(didn't have to have / mustn't have had) much to do if she agreed to go out with you.
5

Luis: Very funny. Her grandfather was visiting, and he (must / had to) leave soon, so she
6

(couldn't talk / must not have talked) very long when I called before.
7

Taka: So what makes you think she (might / could) have decided not to go out?
8

Luis: Oh, I don't know. I probably (shouldn't / must not) have said anything.
9

Taka: Yeah, you know she (didn't have to accept / couldn't have accepted) your invitation.
10

She (must / has to) have been excited about it.
11

Luis: Well, maybe. So where's that phone? I (must have called / was supposed to call) her 10
12

minutes ago. Is there a phone on the next corner?

Taka: Even better! Isn't that your girlfriend on the next corner?

6 Writing

What do the people say to each other or to themselves in these situations? On a separate sheet of paper, write sentences using *could have*, *might have*, *should have*, and *ought to have*. Use negatives where appropriate.

1. Rex didn't call Marta until a week after he promised to. Marta was unhappy with him.

   She complained to him: <u>You could have called me a week ago.</u>

2. I wanted to go to a movie with Emily on Saturday night, but she had made other plans. I waited until Saturday to call her. I'm sorry about this. I said to myself:

3. Jane kept all of the love letters that her boyfriend had sent her. She discovered that her roommate had found and read them. Jane was angry. She told her roommate:

4. Hilda's boyfriend gave her an electric can opener for Valentine's Day. She wanted a romantic gift. Hilda was unhappy. She told her boyfriend:

5. Bart, a talented college football player, was asked to play for a professional team, but his girlfriend didn't want him to do it, so Bart became a football coach instead. All Bart's friends thought that he had lost an opportunity. They said to each other:

6. I went out with a group of people last night. I talked about myself the whole evening. I was sorry about this. I said to myself:

7 Editing

Correct the 7 errors with modals. The first one is corrected for you.

couldn't

My boyfriend has disappeared. I ~~can't~~ find him all day, and he hasn't answered

his phone. Last night he was really tired. While we were eating dinner, he tried, but

he couldn't have stayed awake. He kept falling asleep, so he went home early. He told

me that he had some work he must have to do this weekend. It was really important

to him to finish it today. It's possible that he went to his office to work. He could

have or he couldn't have; I really don't know. He ought to have called me, but his

phone mayn't have been turned on. Sometimes he turns it off when he wants to

concentrate. He had better not have gone fishing with his friends. He knew he must

to go shopping with me earlier, but I went by myself since I didn't know where he

was. Maybe I should have call the police earlier. Now I'm really beginning to worry.

Unit Wrap-up

Writing

 On a separate sheet of paper, write a letter to Addy Viser's advice column. Describe a problem and ask for advice. In your letter, use at least one belief modal in the past, at least two social modals in the past, and at least one phrasal modal.

Example: Dear Addy Viser,
Last week, my husband and I invited our friends to come to our new house. We were supposed to go out to dinner and to a movie with them. They should have arrived at about 6:00. At 7:30, they still hadn't come. . . .

TOEFL TIME

Allow yourself 12 minutes to complete the 20 questions in this exercise.
Questions 1 through 10: Circle the letter of the one word or phrase that best completes the sentence.

1. Although the U.S. Congress passed a law in 1974 that the Navaho _____ from the Big Mountain area in Arizona, many have refused to leave their land.
   (A) had to move
   (B) couldn't move
   (C) must have moved
   (D) might have moved

2. In the mid 1960s, scientists considered the possibility that astronauts _____ die when they returned from the weightlessness of space.
   (A) can   (C) might
   (B) must   (D) should

3. Twenty years from now, Iceland could _____ liquid hydrogen—rather than fossil fuels—to power land and water vehicles.
   (A) to use   (C) used
   (B) use   (D) using

4. People believe scientists _____ to find a cure for the common cold by now.
   (A) could
   (B) must be able
   (C) should have been able
   (D) had to be able

5. A careful reevaluation of the terminal illness suffered by Edgar Allen Poe has led doctors to believe that this American author _____ from rabies, an infectious disease that affects the central nervous system.
   (A) may have died
   (B) might be dying
   (C) could die
   (D) should have died

6. Partly because a Florida anti-smoking campaign _____ the ideas and energies of teenagers, it was called the most effective such campaign of the late 1990s.
   (A) can use   (C) had better use
   (B) ought to use   (D) was able to use

7. Without an establishment such as the World Trade Organization to settle disputes, nations may _____ into protectionism.
   (A) retreat   (C) retreating
   (B) retreated   (D) to retreat

8. Although they _____ the armed forces when the draft ended in the 1970s, many young people enlisted for the benefits, which included education and health care.
   (A) mustn't join
   (B) mustn't have joined
   (C) didn't have to join
   (D) couldn't join

9. Recognizing that disabled children _____ have good access to playground facilities, one nonprofit organization builds areas where children in wheelchairs can participate more easily.
   (A) mustn't   (C) ought to
   (B) can't   (D) better

10. Because of federal laws, Alaskan fishermen who are licensed to catch cod and pollack _____ other species of fish that they catch by accident.
    (A) can't have kept
    (B) can't keep
    (C) might not have kept
    (D) might not keep

Go on to the next page.

Questions 11 through 20: Circle the letter of the underlined part of the sentence that is incorrect.

11. In the Gemini project, NASA <u>was able</u> <u>to conduct</u> a number of tests, so without
     A   B
    Gemini, the 1968 Apollo mission to the moon <u>might never</u> <u>happen</u>.
                                                C   D

12. The Komodo dragon, which <u>can</u> <u>grow</u> to over 10 feet in length, produces a protein
                              A   B
    molecule that scientists soon <u>may</u> <u>be able</u> use to synthesize a new antibiotic.
                                  C   D

13. Actress Mira Sorvino <u>must</u> <u>have returned</u> to China after she graduated from Harvard,
                          A   B
    but she <u>couldn't</u> <u>make</u> the trip and so went into acting instead.
            C   D

14. As a child, horror author R. L. Stine <u>was not allowed</u> <u>to buy</u> horror comic books, but
                                          A   B
    he <u>could</u> to <u>read</u> them at the local barber shop.
       C   D

15. A female black widow spider <u>will</u> eats her mate; she <u>may</u> <u>be able to</u> <u>consume</u> up to
                                A   B   C   D
    25 males a day.

16. Motivational speakers often advise that people <u>mustn't</u> <u>give up on</u> dreams; instead,
                                                   A   B
    they <u>should</u> <u>have tried</u> to use every opportunity they can.
         C   D

17. Although global warming <u>may</u> <u>coming</u> soon, some researchers believe that a past
                            A   B
    era of warming <u>might</u> <u>have been</u> beneficial to humans.
                   C   D

18. Police <u>could</u> take a long time to respond to a call, especially where they may <u>must</u>
           A   B
    cover a considerable distance or where the roads <u>might not</u> <u>be</u> in good condition.
                                                     C   D

19. By using a laser, doctors <u>should</u> <u>be able to</u> deal with some chronic ear infections that
                              A   B
    in previous treatments <u>might not have</u> <u>respond</u> to antibiotics.
                           C   D

20. Finding a new drug <u>may</u> <u>costing</u> an average of $600 million, so pharmaceutical companies
                       A   B
    feel that they <u>must</u> <u>protect</u> their most valuable assets: patents.
                   C   D

142   Copyright © Houghton Mifflin Company. All rights reserved.

Passives

Introduction to the Passive

The Passive I

1 **Passive Sentences in the Simple Present**

Use the words in parentheses to complete passive sentences in the simple present.

1. A ball __is used__ in many sports.
   (use)

2. Balls _____ in
   (use)

   both team and individual sports.

3. In basketball, the ball _____ down the court and
   (dribble)

   _____ through a hoop.
   (throw)

4. In baseball, balls _____ by the pitcher and
   (pitch)

   _____ with a bat by the players from the other team.
   (hit)

5. In soccer, the ball _____ down the field and into the net to score.
   (kick)

6. In bowling, pins _____ with the ball.
   (knock down)

7. In football, the ball _____ by the quarterback and
   (throw)

   _____ by a receiver who runs with it for a touchdown.
   (caught)

8. In golf, the ball _____ down a grassy area called a fairway and
   (drive)

   _____ into a hole to score.
   (putt)

2 **Passive Sentences in the Simple Past**

Complete the sentences about ice hockey. Use the words in parentheses to complete passive sentences in the simple past. Use contractions with negatives.

1. Ice hockey as we know it _was first played_ in eastern Canada.
   (first / play)

2. The rules _____ until they appeared in the *Montreal Gazette* in 1877.
   (not / publish)

3. In 1888, the Amateur Hockey Association of Canada _____ with
   (form)

   six Canadian teams.

4. The first women's hockey game _____ in Ontario, Canada.
   (play)

5. In 1893, Lord Stanley of Preston donated a trophy which _____ the
   (later / call)

   Stanley Cup.

6. In the early 1900s, the goal net and blue lines to divide the ice into three zones

   _____.
   (add)

7. Ice hockey debuted at the Winter Olympics in 1924, and the gold medal

   _____ by Canada.
   (win)

8. A gold medal _____ by the U.S. in women's ice hockey until 1998
   (not / win)

   when they defeated Canada.

3 **Forming Passive Sentences**

Write questions about the rules of ice hockey. Use the words given to write passive questions in the simple present and simple past. Write answers with the information given in brackets.

1. how many/players/a team/compose of   [six]
   Q: _How many players is a team composed of?_
   A: _A team is composed of six players._

2. when/the number of players/reduce/to six from seven   [1912]
   Q: _____
   A: _____

3. who/appoint/for each game   [a team captain]
   Q: _____
   A: _____

4. what/permit/only to the team captain   [discussions with the referee]

   Q: _____

   A: _____

5. how many goalkeepers/allow/for each team   [only one]

   Q: _____

   A: _____

6. when/goalkeepers/permit/to fall to the ice to make "saves"   [1911]

   Q: _____

   A: _____

7. what happens/when/a player/injure   [another player/substitute]

   Q: _____

   A: _____

4 Transitive and Intransitive Verbs

Rewrite the active sentences as passive sentences when possible or write *No change*. Include the subject of the active sentence in a prepositional phrase with *by*. Use contractions with negatives.

1. Nagano, Japan, hosted the 1998 Winter Olympics.

   The 1998 Winter Olympics were hosted by Nagano, Japan.

2. Many exciting events happened there.

   No change.

3. Both news reporters and sports announcers from a major U.S. television network covered the event.

   _____

4. They wore the Nike logo on their jackets during their broadcasts.

   _____

5. Why did they wear the Nike logo?

   _____

6. Did these news reporters and sports announcers endorse* Nike?

   _____

7. Many viewers appeared to believe this.

   _____

8. The major television network agreed with them about the news reporters.

   _____

*endorse = show support or approval of.

9. Now, news reporters don't wear corporate logos.

    _____

10. But the network allows sports announcers to wear corporate logos.

    _____

11. Are sports announcers different from news reporters?

    _____

12. This seems a contradiction to some viewers.

    _____

GRAMMAR PRACTICE 2

The Passive II

5 Meaning of Passive Sentences

Read the passage. Underline the passives. Then, in the sentences that follow, put a check next to the sentence in each pair that gives the information that is in the passage.

Most football teams in the United States have their team logos on both sides of their team helmets, but the logo of the Pittsburgh Steelers is painted on only one side. In 1962, the logo was created for the Steelers by the United States Steel Corporation (US Steel). At that time, the public's reaction to the logo wasn't known, so it was put on only one side of the helmets in case the Steelers decided to change it. The team is often asked about their helmets. To keep people talking about the logo and the team, the logo is still painted on only one side of Steeler helmets.

1. _____ The Pittsburgh Steelers paint the logo on their own helmets.

    ✓_____ Someone paints the logo on the Pittsburgh Steelers' helmets.

2. _____ The Steelers designed the logo.

    _____ US Steel designed the logo.

3. _____ The team knew that the public liked the logo.

    _____ The team didn't know if the public liked the logo.

4. _____ The players ask questions about the helmets.

    _____ People ask the players questions about the helmets.

5. _____ Players still wear the logo.

    _____ Players used to wear the logo, but they don't anymore.

6   Receivers in Active and Passive Sentences

Underline the receiver of the action of the verbs in boldface. Circle the performer of the action, if it is given.

The most remarkable growth of a sport in the twentieth century **wasn't achieved** by basketball or baseball. Soccer **achieved** this increase. This fast-growing sport **was** originally **played** by amateurs in British-influenced countries, but now it **is dominated** by professionals worldwide. Much of the growth occurred in the second half of the century, and three reasons **are** usually **given** for the spread of soccer.

First, the World Cup **is televised** throughout the world. During the Cup, work schedules **are rearranged** and millions of people **watch** the games.

Second, the growth of the game **was influenced** by the high-level play of the club teams. The best players from all over the world **are recruited** to keep the clubs competitive with one another, and the careers of these players **are followed** by the fans in their home countries.

Third, the fans also **play** soccer. Youth clubs **are organized** throughout the world, and children **start** their practice sessions at ages four, five, and six. In the last 50 years, soccer has truly become the world's game.

7   Omitting the *By* Phrase

Circle the verbs in the passive sentences. (Some sentences have more than one verb.) Cross out *by* phrases if the agent isn't important or necessary.

1. He was honored by sportswriters before his third birthday.

2. He was called by someone "the greatest athlete ever."

3. He was named Secretariat by his owner, and he was voted Horse of the Year by people in both of his competitive years.

4. The Triple Crown is awarded by racing officials to any horse winning the Kentucky Derby, the Preakness, and the Belmont Stakes all in the same year.

5. The 1973 Triple Crown was won by Secretariat in grand style.

6. Horse racing's Triple Crown wasn't won by a horse in any of the previous 25 years.

7. The Kentucky Derby was run by Secretariat in world-record time.

8. Secretariat won the Belmont Stakes by 31 lengths, a distance so great that the images of Secretariat and the next-closest horse weren't captured at the same time by TV cameras.

8 The *By* Phrase

Write passive sentences with the information given. Include the agent in a *by* phrase only if the agent is important or necessary information. Use appropriate tenses.

Swimming

	Agent	Action	Receiver	Other Information
1.	people	enjoy	the sport of swimming	today
2.	the Japanese	set up	swimming competitions	in the first century B.C.
3.	the ancient Greeks and Romans	use	this sport	to train warriors

1. ___The sport of swimming is enjoyed today.___
2. ___Swimming competitions were set up by the Japanese in the first century B.C.___
3. _____

Table Tennis

	Agent	Action	Receiver	Other Information
4.	the English	play first	table tennis	on dining room tables
5.	people	also called Ping-Pong	table tennis	in the early 1900s
6.	the U.S. Table Tennis Association	govern	tournaments in the U.S.	today

4. _____
5. _____
6. _____

Mountain Climbing

	Agent	Action	Receiver	Other Information
7.	athletes	start	the sport of mountain climbing	in eighteenth-century Europe
8.	Edmund Hillary and Tenzing Norgay	conquer	Mt. Everest	in 1953
9.	climbers	still not climb	many of the highest mountains in South America	today

7. _____

8. _____

9. _____

Ice Skating

	Agent	Action	Receiver	Other Information
10.	people	first use	ice skates	as transportation
11.	the people from the Netherlands	hold	speed races	in the Netherlands in the fifteenth century
12.	the Dutch	develop	"clap skates"	in 1997 so that skaters could go faster

10. _____

11. _____

12. _____

9 Writing

On a separate sheet of paper, write a news report on a topic of your choice. Use at least five passive sentences in your report. Try to use more than one tense and at least one negative.

Example: The star quarterback of the Middletown Wolves was injured yesterday in the last play of the game. He was tackled just as he threw the ball to the wide receiver. He was taken to the hospital where x-rays were taken of his right knee. It isn't known if the injury will keep him out of next week's game. . . .

10 **Editing**

Correct the 7 errors with passives. The first one is corrected for you.

dominate
Every year, four tournaments are dominated the men's professional golf season.

They are called the Majors and define the best players in the sport. The tournaments—

the Masters, the U.S. Open, the British Open, and the PGA—are considered to be

challenging and pressure-filled. No player called great unless he has won a Major.

In 1953, three of the four tournaments were won by the same man, Ben Hogan.

That year, Hogan was become the only golfer to have won these three tournaments in

the same year. Hogan didn't enter the PGA, partly because it was held too soon after

the British Open and partly because Hogan hadn't fully recovered from a near-fatal

accident in 1949. Perhaps, too, Hogan didn't enter the PGA because it was never giving

the same respect as the other tournaments.

A record 18 Major tournaments were won a single individual: Jack Nicklaus.

Nicklaus made it clear that these four tournaments were the ones he was training to

win. Because Nicklaus was the best golfer of his era, he copied by other professional

golfers, and the Majors truly became the tournaments to win.

After the PGA tournament finishes in August, other tournaments on the

professional tour are still play. Competition isn't stopped after the last of the

Majors is over, but some golfers may already be looking ahead to the next year.

More About Passives

Passives in Progressive and Perfect Tenses

1 **Passive Sentences in Present Progressive**

Frank, the sports announcer, doesn't seem to be able to get anything correct today. Write two sentences in the passive, one in the negative using the object of the active sentence and one with the words given to correct Frank's mistakes. Include the subject of the active sentence in a *by* phrase. Use contractions with negatives.

1. Frank: Elvis Presley is singing the National Anthem.

   The National Anthem isn't being sung by Elvis. It's being sung by an Elvis impostor.
   (an Elvis impostor)

2. Frank: The governor is throwing out the opening pitch.

   _____
   (the mayor)

3. Frank: Jay White is pitching the first inning.

   _____
   (Mark Erikson)

4. Frank: Bill Watson is hitting the ball into right field.

   _____
   (left field)

5. Frank: The outfielder, Sam Jacobs, is catching it.

   _____
   (a fan in the stands)

6. Frank: The fans are running the bases.

   _____
   (Bill Watson)

2   Active and Passive Sentences in Past Progressive

A. Use the words in parentheses to complete the sentences with the past
progressive. Use the passive where it is appropriate.

It was Mother's Day, May 14, 1939. The baseball game __was being played_____

_____ 1 (play)

in Chicago. It _____ by the parents of pitcher
                        2 (watch)

Bob Feller, who played for Cleveland, Ohio. They _____
                                                          3 (attend)

the game to watch their son throw baseballs to the batters. That day, the balls that

_____ were hard, and the balls that
             4 (throw)

_____ were like rocks. Feller threw a ball, and
             5 (hit)

Marv Owen hit it. As the ball _____ through the air, it
                                          6 (fly)

_____ with force and speed. By chance, that baseball
             7 (move)

hit Feller's mother, broke her glasses, and cut her above her eye. While his mother

_____ medical attention, Feller went to see if she was all
             8 (give)

right. Feller returned to the game and struck out Owen. On a day when mothers across the

country _____, Feller's mother
                   9 (honor)

_____ for her injuries.
             10 (treat)

B. Imagine that you are the announcer at the game described in Part A. On a
separate sheet of paper, rewrite the story, using the present tense, including
both active and passive forms of the present progressive.

3   Passive Sentences in Perfect Tenses

Use the words in parentheses to complete passive sentences in the present perfect
or past perfect.

Before the game began,

1. all the seats __had been cleaned_____,
                                (clean)

2. lines _____ on the field,
                   (paint)

3. plays _____,
                   (practice)

4. audio equipment _____,
                             (test)

5. referees _____,
                      (hire)

6. tickets _____, and
   (sell)

7. snack food _____.
   (prepare)

Now the game is over, and

8. one team has won and the other team <u>has been defeated</u> _____,
   (defeat)

9. fans _____,
   (entertain)

10. food _____,
    (eat)

11. drinks _____,
    (spill)

12. songs _____,
    (sing)

13. stories _____, and
    (tell)

14. news _____.
    (make)

GRAMMAR PRACTICE 2

Passives with Modals

4 **Passives with Modals**

Use the words in parentheses to complete the passives with modals.
Use contractions with negatives.

Olympic sites <u>should be chosen</u> _____ to host the Olympics in a
1 (should / choose)

fair way. Sites _____ priority simply because they
2 (must / not / give)

have held the Olympics before. However, sites _____ because
3 (can / pick)

they have facilities in place. Committee members _____
4 (ought to / appoint)

from different countries. Which sites _____ for the
5 (will / consider)

next Olympics? Many factors _____. The sites
6 (have to / consider)

_____ the opportunity to explain why they are the
7 (are going to / give)

best choice. A site that _____ the Olympics
8 (may / offer)

_____ to spend the money necessary to have the
9 (must / prepare)

required facilities.

5 Passive Sentences with Verbs in Different Tenses

Use the words in parentheses to complete the passive sentences.
Use appropriate verb tenses. Use contractions with negatives.

The International Olympic Committee (IOC)

<u>was founded</u> _____ in 1894, and
                    1 (found)

two years later the first modern Olympic games

_____ in Athens, Greece. These early
        2 (hold)

games later evolved into the Summer Olympics. The Winter Olympics

_____ until 1924. From then until 1994, the Summer and
        3 (not / begin)

Winter Olympics took place in the same year every four years. From 1994 until the present,

they _____ in alternate even-numbered years. The Olympics
            4 (hold)

_____ in 1916, 1940, and 1944 because of the World Wars.
        5 (not / hold)

In 1896, 42 events _____ in 9 sports, and 285 athletes
                        6 (schedule)

participated. In 1992 in Barcelona, Spain, 28 sports _____
                                                            7 (include)

in the games and over 10,600 athletes participated. Since 1896, the dreams of more

and more athletes _____, many athletic records
                        8 (realize)

_____, and many medals—gold, silver, and bronze—
        9 (break)

_____.
        10 (win)

The site for the Olympics _____ six years in advance.
                                11 (usually / choose)

Many nations vie for the chance to host these special events. Even though Berlin

_____ as the site for the Olympics long before 1916, the games
        12 (choose)

there _____ because of the First World War. Many of the sites for
            13 (cancel)

the Olympics have been surrounded by controversy. At the time, some people said of the 1936

Olympics in Berlin, "They _____." But athletes believe that
                                14 (should / not / hold)

politics _____ out of the games. Nowadays, there is less

15 (can / keep)

controversy of a political nature, and Olympic games _____

16 (attend)

by teams from more countries. Which site _____ next?

17 (will / choose)

When it is time to pick a new site, the nations in the running will wait eagerly to hear the

announcement of the winner.

   The Olympics open with an elaborate ceremony. All the athletes file into the stadium.

They _____ by the Greek athletes. The host nation's athletes are

18 (lead)

the last to enter. Then the Olympic hymn _____, and the

19 (play)

Olympic flag _____. The runner enters carrying the Olympic

20 (raise)

torch that _____ by the rays of the sun in Olympia, Greece, and

21 (light)

_____ from there by a series of runners. Imagine the thrill of

22 (carry)

watching as the Olympic flame _____ by the last runner.

23 (light)

GRAMMAR PRACTICE 3

Get Passives

6 *Get* **Passives**

Despite high expectations for the team by their
new owner, the local baseball team has been
having a bad season and needs to change its luck.
A sports announcer is interviewing the team owner.
Complete the sentences with the words in
parentheses. Use a *get* passive in an
appropriate tense.

Announcer: Why are you having this bonfire rally?

Owner: We hope to change our luck by getting rid of the things that are bringing us bad

           luck. A bonfire rally seemed a good way to do that.

Announcer: What kinds of things <u>have already gotten thrown</u> into your bonfire?

1 (already / throw)

Owner: Well . . . , several bats _____ and caps
                                                        2 (burn)

_____ in by several players.
                3 (toss)

Announcer: What about the manager? Did he add anything to the fire?

Owner: A pair of old shorts _____ in by the
                                                         4 (pitch)

manager, who participated in spite of thinking it was pretty weird. Look, right now

shoes and gloves _____ in by the pitcher
                                          5 (put)

and catcher. All kinds of sports souvenirs _____
                                                                  6 (add)

by our fans, too.

Announcer: What happens if your luck doesn't change?

Owner: We'll have another bonfire. Things _____
                                                                7 (burn)

until our luck changes.

Announcer: But, what if the bonfire rallies don't help?

Owner: Well, I certainly hope they do, but if they don't, then I guess I'll have to consider

other things. Players _____. Managers
                                        8 (trade)

_____. The team _____.
              9 (fire)   10 (may / sell)

7 Writing

On a separate sheet of paper, write a sentence with the *get* passive or stative
passive for each verb in the list. Use different tenses. Use *very* with the stative
passives.

Examples: **They haven't gotten finished with the work yet.**
              He got very excited at the news.

1. finish   6. worry
2. excite   7. prepare
3. scare   8. pay
4. confuse   9. pack
5. lose   10. do

Passive Causatives

8 Passive Causatives

The United States Women's Soccer Team enjoys some privileges today, but that hasn't always been true. Look at the statements in the *Early Days* column. Then use the words given in the *Later Days* column to write sentences with passive causatives. Use *the players* as the subject of each sentence. Do not include a *by* phrase if the agent is not important.

Early Days	Later Days
1. The players were served food they couldn't eat.	1. Team chefs prepare their food.
2. The players carried their own bags.	2. Someone carries their bags.
3. The players bought their own practice gear.	3. Someone buys their practice gear for them.
4. The players stayed in cheap hotels.	4. Someone books their rooms in nice hotels.
5. Few people knew the players.	5. Someone sent a postcard of the team to a late-night TV program for publicity.
6. The players didn't have many endorsements.	6. Agents handle their many contracts for them.

1. *The players have/get their food prepared by team chefs.*
2. _____
3. _____
4. _____
5. _____
6. _____

9 Editing

Correct the 7 errors with passives, including *get* passives and passive causatives. The first one is corrected for you.

                             selected

Athletes and teams that get ~~select~~ to be on the *Sports Illustrated* magazine cover

may be both happy and sad. They may feel that they are being honored by the

magazine. However, they may believe in the jinx, or bad luck, that comes with being on

the cover.

Sports Illustrated (*SI*) got started in 1954. At the end of 1955, the editors decided to name a "Sportsman of the Year" and put his picture on the cover of the magazine. Unfortunately, the man who has been chosen, William Woodward, Jr., accidentally got shoot by his wife and had been died before he had his picture taken for the cover. One story says that Mr. Woodward's ghost is responsible for the bad luck that has been followed the people on the cover.

Over the years since *SI* first got published, about 37 percent of the athletes and teams that have been featured on the cover have had bad luck. Some have lost games that they were expected to win. Others have been suffered family tragedies or personal injuries that have ended their careers in sports. These people may have been affected by the *SI* jinx just by believing it. They may have thought that they would have bad luck after they were on the *SI* cover. But if that was true, why they got their photos taken?

The belief in the *SI* jinx may continue, but it won't stop athletes from posing for the cover. Just ask professional basketball player Michael Jordan, who was successful despite being on the cover more than 50 times.

Unit Wrap-up
Writing

 On a separate sheet of paper, write a paragraph about a product, service, or natural resource you are familiar with. Write at least five passive sentences in different tenses, including modals. Include the agent in a *by* phrase where necessary. Use *get* passives and passive causatives.

Example: Thousands of pairs of sports shoes are produced each year by companies such as Nike and Reebok. Many different styles have been designed for various activities and sports. These shoes get purchased by both professional and amateur athletes. Many professional athletes have special shoes designed for them by these big companies. In turn, the shoes are endorsed by the famous athletes with the result that more shoes can be sold by these companies. . . .

TOEFL TIME

Allow yourself 12 minutes to complete the 20 questions in this exercise.
Questions 1 through 10: Circle the letter of the one word or phrase that best completes the sentence.

1. The entire plot of *Dr. Jekyll and Mr. Hyde* _____ in a dream by the author, Robert Louis Stevenson, before he wrote the novel.
   (A) had seen
   (B) had been seeing
   (C) had been seen
   (D) had it seen

2. In order to cut costs, the United States government often _____ by outside contractors rather than by civil servants.
   (A) gets work done
   (B) has done work
   (C) gets worked
   (D) has been worked

3. In 1609, corn _____ for the first time by Virginia colonists.
   (A) planted
   (B) has planted
   (C) was planted
   (D) has been planted

4. The Globe Theater, where Shakespeare's plays _____, was opened in Southwark, London in 1599.
   (A) were performing
   (B) were performed
   (C) performed
   (D) had performed

5. A three-month area-specific online dating service _____ cost a lot of money.
   (A) was
   (B) could be
   (C) got
   (D) could

6. In 1939, Hollywood film companies _____ produced every day.
   (A) were an average of two movies
   (B) got an average of two movies
   (C) an average of two movies
   (D) an average of two movies got

7. Leonardo da Vinci _____ the scissors.
   (A) was invented
   (B) was invented by
   (C) invented
   (D) has been invented by

8. Before 1804, the candidate who _____ second place in a presidential race automatically became vice-president.
   (A) had been earned
   (B) had earned
   (C) had it earned
   (D) got earned

9. The amount of land lost to forest fires in the United States _____ from 32 million acres in 1944 to an average of 3.7 million acres today.
   (A) had it reduced
   (B) has reduced
   (C) has been reduced
   (D) was reducing

10. People all over the world were shocked when Princess Diana died while she _____ driven through Paris.
   (A) was being   (C) had been
   (B) been   (D) has been

Go on to the next page.

Questions 11 through 20: Circle the letter of the underlined part of the sentence that is incorrect.

11. One theory about why the dinosaurs <u>were disappeared</u> is that the earth <u>was</u> <u>hit</u>
                                                       A   B C

    <u>by a comet</u> around 65 million years ago.
      D

12. Navy SEALs <u>are</u> <u>expected</u> to be in top physical shape, and they <u>get</u> trained
               A   B   C

    <u>their instructors</u> to work together as a team under adverse conditions.
      D

13. The tragic sinking of the *Titanic* <u>was</u> <u>happened</u> at a time when the ship <u>was</u> <u>believed</u>
                                     A   B

    to be impossible to sink.

14. Tomatoes <u>were</u> <u>introducing</u> in England in 1596, where they <u>were</u> <u>grown</u> as
           A   B

    ornamental plants.

15. About 24 billion tons of topsoil <u>are</u> <u>lost</u> every year to wind and water erosion,
                                   A   B

    <u>indicating</u> that one-third of the world's arable land <u>will</u> depleted in 20 years.
      C   D

16. Trees that <u>have</u> <u>lined</u> rural roads for over a century are <u>be</u> cut down because they
              A   B   C

    <u>have been</u> called a danger to motorists.
      D

17. If hydrogen that is <u>used</u> for power can itself <u>be created</u> through renewable energy
                  A   B

    sources, urban air quality <u>should</u> be <u>improve</u>.
                           C   D

18. The Black Death <u>was</u> killed 20 million people in fourteenth-century Europe, but it <u>is</u>
                 A   B

    now <u>being</u> <u>rivaled</u> by AIDS as the most destructive infectious disease.
        C   D

19. More than 90 books <u>have</u> <u>been</u> come from a small room which <u>is</u> inhabited
                   A   B   C

    <u>by Engish writer</u> Dick King-Smith.
      D

20. Advances in genetic engineering <u>are</u> <u>being</u> <u>made</u> at such a fast pace that the ethical
                              A   B   C

    dilemmas surrounding the technology <u>are appeared</u> unanswerable.
                                     D

Conditionals

18

Factual Conditionals; Future Conditionals

Overview of Conditionals

1 **Conditional Statements and Questions**

A. In each sentence, write *C* above the condition and *R* above the result.

        C   R

1. If snow contains more ash than usual, it melts faster.

2. Snow reflects less heat back into space if it melts fast.

3. If less heat is reflected back into space, more heat is kept around Earth.

4. The temperature of the planet rises if more heat is kept around Earth.

5. If the temperature of the planet rises, many different climate changes occur.

B. Write a *yes/no* question for each statement in Part A.

1. If snow contains more ash than usual, does it melt faster?

2. _____

3. _____

4. _____

5. _____

GRAMMAR PRACTICE 2

Factual Conditionals

2 **Factual Conditionals with Present Tense Verbs and Modals**

Complete the factual conditionals so that each sentence has an *if* clause and a result clause. Put *if* in the appropriate place in the sentence. Use *then* where possible. Punctuate carefully.

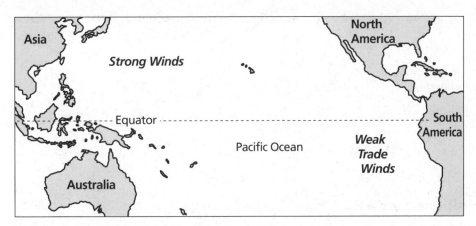

1. Trade winds are blowing in normal patterns.

   <u>If trade winds are blowing in normal patterns, then</u> they maintain a balance between warm
   (cause)

   western Pacific water and cool eastern Pacific water.

2. Warm water in the western Pacific flows east.

   <u>Warm water in the western Pacific flows east if</u>
   (result)

   easterly trade winds decrease, causing a condition we call El Niño.

3. The trade winds relax.

   _____
   (cause)

   the sea surface temperature rises.

4. Cooler, nutrient-rich water is pushed deeper.

   _____
   (result)

   there is an El Niño condition, and sea life suffers from lack of food.

5. El Niño conditions exist.

   _____
   (cause)

   they produce extreme weather such as heavy rainfall and flooding.

6. For example, there is flooding in Peru.

    _____
                       (result)

    rainfall follows the warm water eastward.

7. Scientists can get a wide range of accurate information on the Pacific.

    _____
                       (result)

    they use information gathered by buoys anchored along the equatorial Pacific, statistical data,

    and climate modeling.

8. Scientists understand El Niño better.

    _____ they
                       (cause)

    may be able to predict the effects so people can prepare for the extreme weather conditions.

3   **Factual Conditionals with Past Tense Verbs**

Complete the factual conditionals so that each sentence has an *if* clause and a
result clause. Put *if* in the appropriate place in the sentence. Use *then* where
possible. Punctuate carefully.

1. They expected heavy rain and flooding.

    Because the Incas of Peru knew about the effects of El Niño, _they expected heavy rain_
                                                                          (result)

    and flooding if it was an El Niño year.

2. They built new cities.

    _____
                       (cause)

    they put them on the tops of hills.

3. They built on the coast.

    _____ they didn't build near rivers.
                       (cause)

4. The Incas suffered.

    _____ there was a strong El Niño.
                       (result)

5. Therefore, the Incas made sacrifices to their gods.

    _____
                       (result)

    it was an El Niño year.

4 **Using Factual Conditionals with Modals and Imperatives**

Complete the factual conditionals with modals and imperatives. Give advice and suggestions with *must*, *should*, *ought to*, *might*, and *could*. Then give a command using an imperative.

1. If you want weather information, <u>you could watch the Weather Channel.</u>

   If you want weather information, <u>watch the Weather Channel.</u>

2. If you go to the mountains in the winter, _____

   If you go to the mountains in the winter, _____

3. If it is cold and snowy, _____

   If it is cold and snowy, _____

4. If the weather is warm and sunny, _____

   If the weather is warm and sunny, _____

GRAMMAR PRACTICE 3

Future Conditionals

5 **Future Conditionals—Form and Function**

Use the words given to write future conditionals. Write the words in the order that they are given. (El Niño is the cause in each sentence.)

1. another El Niño/come/weather/change all over the world

   <u>If another El Niño comes, weather will change all over the world.</u>

2. it/be/an El Niño year/Peru and parts of the United States and Europe/suffer from damaging floods

   _____

3. Many countries/have/flash floods/El Niño/bring too much rain

   _____

4. Indonesia, Australia, and India/experience/drought/El Niño/happen

   _____

5. El Niño/occur/the next year/be/a La Niña year

   _____

6. countries/have/drought during El Niño/they/have/too much rain during La Niña

   _____

6 Writing

 On a separate sheet of paper, write a paragraph about the causes and results of a severe weather condition you are familiar with. Use factual conditionals with present and past tense verbs, modals, and the future conditional.

Example: If it's a late summer day, storm clouds are probably gathering over Denver. If you hear thunder, then lightning will follow. . . .

7 Editing

Correct the 7 errors with factual and future conditionals. The first one is corrected for you.

                                  region,

    If people live in a snow ~~region~~ they will probably see snow every year. Snow is often fun and beautiful, but it can be dangerous if it is heavy and accompanied by strong winds. This combination of snow and wind is called a blizzard. If the blizzard be so bad that no one can see very far, "white-out" conditions may exist. In white-out conditions, everything looks white and it's easy to get confused. People may know an area well, but they go out in white outs, if they can still get lost.

    There are many stories about people in blizzards. These people had a better chance of surviving if they had shelter. If they were outside. They probably got very cold very quickly. If they got too cold, they freeze. They could even have been close to shelter but not known it.

    If you will be in a blizzard, stay home. You should survive a blizzard if you are warm and have food and water. We can't control snow or wind, but if we will prepare for snowstorms, we can lessen their damage.

Chapter 19

Present and Past Unreal Conditionals; *Hope* and *Wish*

GRAMMAR PRACTICE 1

Present Unreal Conditionals

1 Present Unreal Conditionals—Form

Complete the present unreal conditional sentences using the words in parentheses. Use *would* in the result clause. Use contractions with negatives.

1. If we __counted__ the number of lightning strikes
   (count)

   on Earth every second, the number __would be__
   (be)

   about 100.

2. If lightning _____ dangerous, hundreds of people _____
   (not / be)   (not / get)

   hurt or killed by it every year.

3. A meteorologist _____ "lightning and floods" if we _____
   (answer)   (ask)

   about the most life-threatening weather hazards in the U.S.

4. If the amount of lightning-caused property damage in a year in the U.S. _____
   (be)

   calculated, the result _____ in the millions of dollars.
   (be)

5. If people _____ to talk about other problems caused by lightning,
   (want)

   they _____ fires and injuries to animals.
   (not / forget)

2 Present Unreal Conditionals—Meaning

Read each sentence and mark the sentences that follow it *T* (true) or *F* (false).

1. If lightning weren't dangerous, we wouldn't have to be careful in a thunderstorm.

   __F__ a. Lightning didn't use to be dangerous.

   __T__ b. Lightning is dangerous.

2. If air were a good conductor of electricity, the forces that produce lightning wouldn't have to be as powerful as they are.

   _____ a. Air is a good conductor of electricity.

   _____ b. Powerful forces produce lightning.

3. We could swim safely in a thunderstorm if lightning didn't travel well through water.

   _____ a. It's not safe to swim during a thunderstorm.

   _____ b. Lightning travels well through water.

4. If a woman were on a bicycle in a thunderstorm, she wouldn't be safe from lightning.

   _____ a. This sentence talks about something that happened in the past.

   _____ b. It's safe to ride a bike in a thunderstorm.

3 Factual Versus Unreal Conditionals

Complete the factual conditionals and unreal conditionals with the correct form of the verbs in parentheses. Use *would* in the result clause of the unreal conditionals. Use contractions with negatives.

1. Lightning sometimes strikes people. If someone __gets__ hit by lightning and survives, he
   (get)

   or she __is__ likely to suffer serious long-term effects from it.
   (be)

2. Lightning kills more people every year than any other weather-related event. If lightning

   _____ anyone, we _____ other disasters.
   (not / hurt)   (still / have)

3. Eighty to 90 percent of lightning-strike victims survive. If no one _____
   (live)

   after getting hit by lightning, we _____ this weather phenomenon more.
   (respect)

4. People are better electricity conductors than air and trees are. Lightning _____
   (not / hit)

   people so often if they _____ bad conductors.
   (be)

5. Staying outside in a thunderstorm isn't a good idea. If people _____ inside a
   (go)

   building, they _____ safer.
   (be)

4 Writing

 A thunderstorm just started. On a separate sheet of paper, write advice for the following situations. Use *If I were you, . . .*

> All of my windows are open.   I am in a small boat on a lake.
> My computer is on.   I am playing golf.

Example: **If I were you, I'd close my windows.**

GRAMMAR PRACTICE 2

Past Unreal Conditionals

5 Past Unreal Conditionals

Use the words in parentheses to complete the past unreal conditionals. Use *would*, *might*, or *could* in the result clause to express the meaning indicated in brackets. In cases where two forms are possible, write both forms. Use contractions with negatives.

1. In 1790, Kilauea, a volcano in Hawaii, erupted, killing 80 people marching across it. If those people __hadn't been walking__ on the volcano, they __might not have been__ killed. [possibility]
                      (not / walk)   (not / be)

2. In 1912, Novarupta, a volcano in Alaska, was the site of the largest eruption of the twentieth century. It _____ incredible damage if it _____
                            (cause)   (erupt)
   in a populous area. [certainty]

3. The eruption of Mount St. Helens in the state of Washington in 1980 shot ash 12 miles into the air. This eruption _____ scientists by complete surprise if there
                              (take)
   _____ earlier earthquakes and minor eruptions. [possibility]
        (not / be)

4. Before 1980, Mount St. Helens had not erupted for 123 years. If anyone _____
                                                                              (see)
   it erupt, he or she _____ others about it. [ability]
                            (tell)

5. The eruption of Mount St. Helens killed 57 people. If it _____ on a
                                                                  (happen)
   Monday instead of a Sunday, several hundred loggers at work on the mountain
   _____ in the explosion. [certainty]
        (die)

6 Past Unreal Conditionals—Meaning

Read each sentence and mark the sentences that follow it *T* (true) or *F* (false).

1. The eruption that formed the volcano Paricutin started in 1943. Today's scientists wouldn't have learned so much about volcanoes if Paricutin hadn't erupted recently.

    ____F____ a. Scientists didn't learn anything from Paricutin's eruption.

    ____T____ b. Paricutin didn't form thousands of years ago.

2. Paricutin was born in Mexico. If Paricutin hadn't developed on land, scientists wouldn't have been able to see the new volcano form.

    _____ a. Scientists observed Paricutin as it grew.

    _____ b. Paricutin developed in the ocean.

3. If the volcano hadn't formed in the middle of a cornfield, it might have caused more damage.

    _____ a.   Paricutin didn't cause as much damage as possible.

    _____ b. The volcano formed in an agricultural area.

4. If the owner of the cornfield, Dominic Pulido, hadn't watched the volcano form, he would have missed an historic event.

    _____ a. The owner of the cornfield missed seeing the volcano form.

    _____ b. The forming of the volcano was an historic event.

5. The Pulidos heard something like underground thunder before the volcano erupted. Smoke and ash came from the ground, trees shook, and Pulido could smell sulfur. Pulido might have realized what was happening if he had been a volcanologist.

    _____ a. Pulido was a scientist that studies volcanoes.

    _____ b. Pulido knew what was happening when he smelled the sulfur.

7 Past Unreal Conditionals

Read the passage about a very destructive volcano. Then use the information given to write past unreal conditionals. Use the clauses in the order that they are given. Use contractions with negatives.

In 1883, the Indonesian volcano Krakatau exploded dramatically. For several days before the explosion, there were eruptions, raining ash and blocks of lava onto the surrounding area. The volcano chamber that this ash and lava were coming from was under the sea. On August 28, the chamber collapsed*. Millions of tons of ocean water and two-thirds of the volcano fell into the molten lava in the chamber. The resulting explosion was the loudest noise on earth in recorded history. It was heard over 3000 km away in Australia; 5000 km away, a British army officer thought it was distant gunfire. Wind created in the explosion circled the earth seven times before it finally died out.

*collapse = fall down or inward suddenly.

1. There were eruptions before the explosion. As a result, there wasn't enough material in the chamber to support it.

   If there hadn't been eruptions before the explosion, there would have been enough material in the chamber to support it.

2. Because the chamber wasn't above sea level, ocean water rushed into it.

   _____

   _____

3. The volcano didn't remain standing because it collapsed in the explosion.

   _____

   _____

4. The explosion was so loud that people in Australia could hear it.

   _____

   _____

5. The wind from the explosion didn't circle the earth more times because the force of the explosion decreased.

   _____

   _____

8 Writing

On a separate sheet of paper, write affirmative and negative statements about your life and activities.

1. Write three factual statements about your life and activities now. Then write a present unreal conditional sentence about each statement.

   Example: I'm taking organic chemistry. I could go out more often if I weren't taking organic chemistry.

2. Write three factual statements about your life and activities in the past. Then write a past unreal conditional sentence about each statement.

   Example: I didn't have a job last year. If I had had a job, I might not have had time to study.

GRAMMAR PRACTICE 3

Sentences with *Hope* or *Wish*

9   *Hope* and *Wish* About the Present and Future

Complete the conversation by using the correct forms of the words in parentheses
to express hopes or wishes about the present and future. Where more than one
form is possible, use any appropriate form. Use contractions with negatives.

Host: Thanks for talking with me today.

I hope we <u>can/will find out</u>
                1 (find out)
more about wildfires and

firefighting policies. Are all

wildfires caused by natural forces?

Scientist: I wish that only nature

_____ fires, but,
            2 (start)
unfortunately, human beings still

cause wildfires as well, often

through carelessness with cigarettes or campfires.

Host: Lightning from thunderstorms sometimes causes fires, too, right? When you see a

thunderstorm, do you hope that the lightning from it _____
                                                           3 (not / start)

a fire?

Scientist: I wish things _____ that easy. Fires have beneficial effects, so when
                          4 (be)

I see a thunderstorm, I hope that it _____ with us. For
                                              5 (cooperate)

example, lightning from a thunderstorm may start a fire tomorrow. We hope that the

fire_____ the dry, old vegetation that has accumulated.
          6 (burn)

Host: Can't people clean out the dead vegetation?

Scientist: We wish they _____, but we're talking about millions of acres in national
                          7 (can)

parks and forests.

Host: What about fire-fighting policies in the future?

Scientist: We will always fight fires to protect lives. We hope we _____
8 (also / save)

property. We wish we _____ protect everyone's property, but we know we
9 (can)

can't. We hope that people _____ with us to keep everyone safe.
10 (work)

10 *Hope* and *Wish* About the Past

Complete the conversation by using the correct forms of the words in parentheses
to express hopes or wishes about the past. Use contractions with negatives.

Host: Tell me about the 1988 Yellowstone fire. I wish I __had been__ there to see it.
1 (be)

Scientist: The 1988 fires were the worst I have ever seen. I hope they _____ the last
2 (be)

fires ever of that magnitude in the park.

Host: Were all the fires caused by lightning?

Scientist: I wish that lightning _____ all the fires, but one was caused by
3 (start)

a cigarette.

Host: The fires were originally allowed to burn, right?

Scientist: Yes, that's right. We wish we _____ that nature was going to
4 (know)

work against us. We wish we _____ so long to step in.
5 (not / wait)

Host: What happened?

Scientist: We wish it _____ sooner after the fires started. In previous
6 (rain)

years, rains had put out the fires, so we were expecting the same thing in 1988.

Host: Is there anything else that worked against you?

Scientist: I wish that we _____ fight so many fires at once.
7 (not / have to)

Host: Was there anything good that came out of the fires?

Scientist: Oh, sure. We hope we _____ something that we can share
8 (learn)

with others. We wish we _____ learn these things through
9 (be able to)

other means, but sometimes experience is the best teacher.

11 Writing

On a separate sheet of paper, write two sentences about your hopes for the present or future, two wishes about the present or future, two hopes about the past, and two wishes about the past.

Example: I hope that I see a tornado someday because I've always been fascinated by them. I wish I could go to the moon.

12 Editing

Correct the 7 errors with present and past unreal conditionals, *hope* and *wish*. The first one is corrected for you.

                                                      talk

    If we talk about natural disasters, we often ~~talked~~ about economics. If that hadn't been true in the 1940s, the Weather Bureau, which often predicts weather-related disasters, didn't move from the Department of Agriculture to the Department of Commerce.

    Most Americans don't know that two people died in the Great Plains blizzard of 1886. If they know anything about that blizzard, they usually remember that 90 percent of the cattle on the ranges of the Great Plains died. Ranchers wouldn't have lost so many cattle if the weather wouldn't have been so severe.

    In the 1988 Yellowstone Park fires, one principle concern was for the businesses around the park. If fires threaten private property or Old Faithful, the Park Service would try to put them out, but that year there was another concern. Businesspeople were concerned that if too much of the Park burned, tourists didn't come to the area. In fact, people came to Yellowstone after the fires just to see the damage. They wished that these fires didn't happen, but they were curious to see what had changed. If there hadn't been fires in 1988, they probably wouldn't come that year.

Unit Wrap-up
Writing

Imagine that you live in a house in a forest. A forest fire is approaching. You can rescue only four possessions. On a separate sheet of paper, write a paragraph about what you would choose to save. Use real and unreal conditionals, *wish* and *hope*.

Example: If I had to escape quickly, I would save my photograph albums. I wouldn't be able to replace them if they burned. . . .

TOEFL TIME

Allow yourself 12 minutes to complete the 20 questions in this exercise.
Questions 1 through 10: Circle the letter of the one word or phrase that best completes the sentence.

1. If adults don't have their eyes checked annually, conditions such as glaucoma and cataracts _____ undiagnosed.
   (A) went
   (B) would have gone
   (C) had gone
   (D) might go

2. If current trends _____, four million Americans will receive blood transfusions next year.
   (A) continue
   (B) will continue
   (C) continued
   (D) had continued

3. If the Empire State Building _____, the Chrysler Building would have been the world's tallest building for longer than nine months.
   (A) hadn't built
   (B) hadn't been built
   (C) wasn't built
   (D) weren't built

4. If Earth Day _____ celebrated through the year 2070, it will have existed for over 100 years.
   (A) will be   (C) be
   (B) is   (D) would be

5. If the paperback book hadn't been widely produced and circulated, fewer books _____ in the hands of the reading public at that time.
   (A) had been   (C) were
   (B) would have been (D) would be

6. Travel agents hope the Internet _____ the place of actual travel as it becomes more widely available to people worldwide.
   (A) won't take
   (B) wouldn't take
   (C) didn't take
   (D) weren't taking

7. Solar power would probably have been more popular when it was first introduced if its cost in the early part of the twentieth century _____ so high.
   (A) wouldn't be   (C) hadn't been
   (B) wasn't   (D) weren't

8. Scientists wish that they _____ an earthquake before it strikes.
   (A) could predict
   (B) had predicted
   (C) can predict
   (D) could have predicted

9. If a motorist _____ the island of Hawaii, he or she encounters 11 different climates.
   (A) circles   (C) circled
   (B) has circled   (D) had circled

10. If medieval laws hadn't prohibited ordinary people from wearing linen and lace, buttons _____ status symbols in the fourteenth century.
    (A) didn't become
    (B) wouldn't become
    (C) hadn't become
    (D) might not have become

Go on to the next page.

Questions 11 through 20: Circle the letter of the underlined part of the sentence that is incorrect.

11. Throughout the years, many more people <u>would have</u> <u>died</u>, if Alexander Fleming <u>had</u>
                                    A   B   C

    not <u>discovered</u> penicillin in 1928.
              D

12. <u>If</u> volunteers hadn't <u>helped</u>, the 2159-mile Appalachian Trail probably <u>wasn't</u>
    A   B   C

    <u>constructed</u>.
        D

13. Baseball fans <u>heard</u> the first radio broadcast of a game if their radios <u>would be</u> <u>tuned</u>
               A   B   C

    to Pittsburgh station KDKA, which <u>transmitted</u> the game in 1921.
                                            D

14. If newspaper readers <u>will</u> <u>enjoy</u> doing a crossword puzzle, <u>then</u> they <u>have</u> journalist
                          A   B   C   D

    Arthur Wynne to thank for creating them.

15. If <u>does the moon completely block</u> the <u>sun</u>, <u>does</u> a total eclipse <u>occur</u>?
                       A   B   C   D

16. <u>If</u> the passive-resistance tactics of Mahatma Gandhi <u>hadn't been effective</u>, they
    A   B

    <u>might not have</u> so greatly <u>influence</u> the struggle for civil rights in the United States.
            C   D

17. <u>If</u> settlers on the Great Plains <u>didn't move</u> to river valleys where Rocky Mountain
    A   B

    grasshoppers used to lay their eggs, the grasshoppers <u>might</u> not have <u>become</u> extinct.
                                                  C   D

18. <u>If a writer</u> <u>is</u> unpopular at <u>home he or she</u> may <u>find</u> success abroad.
          A   B   C   D

19. The U.S. policy on dams <u>will</u> <u>be accepted</u> by a large majority of <u>citizens if</u> opposing
                            A   B   C

    views <u>will be</u> reconciled.
          C

20. Clothing <u>would</u> certainly <u>look</u> different <u>today</u> if we <u>don't have</u> the zipper.
          A   B   C   D

Noun Clauses

Chapter 20

Noun Clauses

Overview of Noun Clauses

1 **Identifying Noun Clauses**

In each pair of sentences, one sentence contains a noun clause and the other does not. Write *NC* in front of the sentences that have noun clauses. Then underline the noun clauses.

1. _____ a. Please bring me the book that is on the table.

   __NC__ b. I am sure <u>that I'll read it quickly</u>.

2. _____ a. She thinks that his stories are funny.

   _____ b. The funniest story that I ever read was in one of his books.

3. _____ a. I'm sure about when the book was published.

   _____ b. When he gets here, ask him to come in.

4. _____ a. If you see her, please say hello for me.

   _____ b. We don't know if she'll come.

5. _____ a. What did she say?

   _____ b. I didn't hear what she said.

6. _____ a. That reason isn't good enough for me.

   _____ b. That he loves her is certainly true.

7. _____ a. We don't know who came here.

   _____ b. We don't know the people who came here.

2 Noun Clauses—Form and Function

A. Underline each noun clause and circle the word that introduces it (*that, wh-word, if/whether*). Some sentences have more than one noun clause. (Remember: Do not confuse noun clauses with adjective clauses or time clauses.)

1. Publishers of paperback romance fiction understand (that) book covers are important in selling the books.

2. They think that the book cover should be attractive to a reader.

3. When a cover can invite readers to try a book is when the cover is successful.

4. Readers wonder if a poor cover may hurt an otherwise successful book.

5. Many readers are certain that a cover should indicate what the book is about.

6. One thing that a long-time reader of romance looks for is that the cover has someone or something from the story on it.

7. She thinks about whether some covers are poor because they feature the characters (a handsome man and a beautiful woman, of course) too prominently.

8. She is worried that male models are sometimes used even when they don't match the author's description of the character.

9. Finally, whether the cover embarrasses the readers in public is also important.

B. Look at the noun clauses that you underlined in Part A. Label the function of each noun clause: *S* (= subject); *O* (= object); *O Prep* (= object of a preposition); *SC* (= subject complement); *adj + NC* (= noun clause following adjective).

Example: 1. Publishers of paperback romance fiction understand (that) book covers are important in selling the books .

GRAMMAR PRACTICE 2

Noun Clauses with *That*

3 Forming Sentences with *That* Clauses

Combine the two sentences to form a sentence with a *that* clause. Include *that*.
Omit *this* or preposition + *this*. (Remember: A *that* clause cannot be the object of a
preposition.)

1. Readers know this. Certain elements will occur in romance fiction.

   <u>Readers know that certain elements will occur in romance fiction.</u>

2. Emotional risk and conflict are basic to the romance genre. This is understood.

   _____

3. Readers are certain about this. The conflict will be resolved by the end
   of the book.

   _____

4. They are glad about this. The ending is always happy.

   _____

5. Romance writers insist on this. Their readers are intelligent.

   _____

6. Romance writers realize this. Their books aren't fine literature.

   _____

7. They believe in this. They write well-crafted, entertaining fiction.

   _____

8. Publishers agree with this. Romance fiction is popular.

   _____

9. They notice this. Many romance writers sell over a million copies of each book
   they write.

   _____

4 Writing

On a separate sheet of paper, write a paragraph that gives your opinions about
genre fiction. Answer the following questions: *Who should read genre fiction?*
*When should readers read it? Where should it be read? How often should people
read it? Is it literature? Which genre do you prefer?* Use noun clauses with verbs
such as *agree, believe, suppose,* and *think,* and adjectives such as *certain,
convinced, positive,* and *sure* to express your opinions.

Example: I believe that genre fiction is good for everyone. I am certain that it
            is very popular. I believe that people should read it for fun, but not all
            the time. . . .

Noun Clauses with *Wh*- Words

5 **Noun Clauses with *Wh*- Words**

A detective is asking a suspect some questions. Use each of the questions as a noun clause to complete his indirect requests for information.

1. Where did you find the knife?

   Can you tell me <u>where you found the knife?</u>

2. Why aren't your fingerprints on it?

   Can you explain _____ ?

3. Why did you wipe it off?

   I don't understand _____ .

4. What time was it when you found it?

   Do you remember _____ ?

5. We believe your wife was murdered at about 9:00 last night. Where were you at the

   time of the murder?

   Do you know _____ ?

6. You say you were sleeping then. When do you usually go to bed?

   I'd like to know _____ .

7. Why did you go to bed early that night?

   Can you tell me _____ ?

8. The maid told me that she saw you go out about an hour before the murder took

   place. You couldn't have gone to bed when you say. Why have you lied to me?

   Would you please tell me _____ ?

6 **Noun Clauses with *Wh-* Words—Expressing Uncertainty**

A group of frightened teens are talking to the police about a horrible creature they just encountered in the woods near their neighborhood. Use the questions to complete their statements with noun clauses.

1. You say you saw a monster in the woods. What did the creature look like?

   We're not sure <u>what the creature looked like,</u>

   but it was horrible!

2. How tall was it?

   We're not certain _____,

   but it was taller than we are.

3. Who else has seen the creature?

   We don't know _____

   _____. We just know that it

   is there.

4. Where did you first spot it?

   We didn't notice _____. We were too busy

   looking at it.

5. When did you see it?

   We can't be sure _____ because nobody was

   wearing a watch.

6. What did the creature do when it saw you?

   We don't know _____ when it saw us because

   we didn't wait around to find out.

7. How did you escape?

   We don't know _____, either, but we know we

   were lucky.

8. I'll need to check your story out. Who will go to show me the place where you saw the

   monster?

   We can't decide _____ to show you the place

   where we saw the monster because we're all too afraid!

GRAMMAR PRACTICE 4

Noun Clauses with *If/Whether*

7 | **Noun Clauses with *If/Whether***

Use the questions to complete the sentences with *if/whether* noun clauses. If both *if* and *whether* are possible, use both.

She says:

1. Can he forgive me for leaving?

   I wonder <u>if/whether he can forgive me for leaving.</u>

2. Is he looking for me?

   _____ is something I will never know.

3. Did he see me following him to her house yesterday?

   I can't be sure _____.

4. Have I done the right thing?

   I wonder _____.

5. Does he love me?

   I have thought so much about _____.

6. Will I ever find another love like him?

   The question is _____.

He asks:

7. Has she left for good?

   Do you know _____?

8. Should I go after her?

   Do you know _____?

9. Was that her following me to my house?

   Can you tell me _____?

10. Did I make a mistake to let her go?

    I wonder _____?

11. Could she still love me?

    Will I ever know _____?

12. Will she forgive me and come back?

    How can I be sure _____?

8 Writing

What do you wonder about? What questions would you like to have answered?
On a separate sheet of paper, write sentences and questions with noun clauses.
Use the words given with question words or *if* or *whether* to introduce each
noun clause.

1. I wonder . . .
2. I'm not sure . . .
3. I don't understand . . .

4. I have often wondered . . .
5. I would like to know . . .
6. Can you tell me . . .

Example: I wonder if there is life on other planets in other solar systems.
I'm not sure what I will be doing 10 years from now.

9 Noun Clauses with Past Tense Verbs

Use the verb in parentheses in an appropriate tense to complete each noun clause.
Remember: If the main clause verb is in the past tense, use a past tense verb in the
noun clause if the action occurs at the same time; use *would* or *was/were going to*
if the action occurs later.

1. In the beginning, the heroine was sure that the man of her dreams _didn't love_ _____
   (not / love)

   her. [same time]

2. She wondered why he _____ at her strangely when she told him of
   (look)

   her plan to leave. [same time]

3. The detective believed that the murderer _____ himself
   (reveal)

   eventually. [later]

4. The murderer realized that the clever detective _____ the evidence
   (have)

   he needed to prove his guilt. [same time]

5. The young people were horrified when the door of the mansion _____
   (lock)

   behind them. [same time]

6. They wondered if the monster _____ as people said it would on a
   (appear)

   night with a full moon. [later]

7. The reader wanted to know why the cowboy always _____ into the
   (ride off)

   sunset in Westerns. [same time]

8. It wasn't surprising when the good guy _____ the lady in danger. [same time]
   (save)

10 Editing

Correct the 9 errors with noun clauses. Some errors can be corrected in more than one way. The first error is corrected for you.

No one would disagree ~~if~~ *that* reading is important for teenagers. Diana Tixier Herald, author of *Teen Genreflecting*, believes that good readers were avid readers and often these avid readers are readers of genre fiction. She knows that genre fiction doesn't always get much respect. Nevertheless, Herald is convinced that escapist reading of genre fiction is an ideal outlet for teens. She believes they have different needs from people of other age groups. That the teen years are a time of self-discovery is clear. She feels whether genre fiction fits the needs of teen readers. She wonders that teens can divide the world into more manageable parts by selecting and reading a type of genre fiction that appeals to them.

For her book, Herald wanted to know how did teens select genre fiction. As a librarian, she had noticed that teens pay attention to the labels on the books they read. She believes that they are the only readers who ask for books not by author and title but by the imprint (specific publisher). She thinks that a library should offer genre collections, clearly identified as such, to make books more accessible to teens.

Herald also thought about if the books should be displayed differently. She felt that it is important for teens to see the covers, too. She wondered if would teens read more if a library organized the books in a different way. Herald believes that making the books more accessible to teens will encourage them to become avid, and thus good, readers.

Chapter 21

Quoted Speech; Noun Clauses with Reported Speech

Quoted Speech and Reported Speech

1 **Punctuating Quoted Speech; Identifying Reported Speech**

A. A parent of the future discusses a problem regarding her teen-aged son with an online psychologist. Add the missing punctuation to the conversation.

1. "Hello, Doctor," a woman's voice said. "My name is Margo."

2. Hello, Margo I replied. I can't see you. The video must not be on

3. Oh, I know. I'd like to use only audio for a while if that's okay Margo said

4. Fine. So what's the problem I asked

5. It's my son she said. He says that he's in love with a hologram*

6. I thought to myself Oh, great. Another one. The third this week

7. He told me he's found his life partner, but I want him to spend more time with biological beings she continued

8. Do you know why he doesn't have more biological friends I asked

9. Well, we're a little isolated she said He doesn't have much exposure to biological beings, and he says he doesn't like them. My husband and I try to spend time with him, but we're very busy

*hologram = a picture produced with lasers that appears to be three-dimensional.

B. Underline the sentences in Part A that include reported speech.

2   Quoted Speech; Verbs Introducing Speech

Rewrite the conversation as quoted speech. Fill in the blanks with the words that introduce each quote. Use the past tense, and use *to* before the object pronoun if it is needed. Punctuate carefully.

1. I/ask/her

   <u>I asked her,</u> "Have you met any of his hologram friends**?**"

2. Margo/replied

   Hugo, that's my son, used to introduce me to his holograms _____

   He told me that he understood them better than biological beings. His father and I are, well, intellectuals, so it's no surprise that he is, too.

3. I/suggest

   Well, I think you and your husband should encourage Hugo to develop his physical side, not just his intellect. Swim. Go for a walk. Do things together _____

4. Margo/answer/me

   Doctor, I think I'd better turn on the video now _____. There's something you should know.

5. I/tell/myself

   Oh, great _____ I wonder what this means.

6. Margo/explain

   You see, Doctor, we are computers _____ We took some of my programming and some of my husband's and put them together to form Hugo. We had to have technicians put together the physical components, but Hugo is our son.

7. I/exclaim

   Well, this is a surprise _____ So why did you contact me?

8. she/reply

   _____ I picked your name out of a database of psychologists. I thought that if I could get a human's perspective, I could figure out what to do about Hugo.

9. I/ask/her

   Then you know nothing about me? _____ Because I'm not human, either. I'm an experimental program in an artificial intelligence institute at a major research university.

3 Writing

Choose one of the following topics and, on a separate sheet of paper, write a conversation. Each participant in the conversation should speak at least three times. Use quoted speech and punctuate carefully.

1. Continue the conversation in Exercise 2.
2. Write a conversation between one of the computers and another being.
3. Write a conversation between two characters you create.

Example: "Dave! Dave!" cried Margo. "You'll never believe what just happened!" "You're probably right," said Dave. "But tell me anyway."

GRAMMAR PRACTICE 2

Changes in Reported Speech; Verb Tense in Reported Speech

4 Changes in Reported Speech—Overview

Compare the sheriff's words with the granddaughter's report of what he said. Underline the words that change in the reported speech. (You don't have to underline *Grandpa said that*.) Label the words that you underlined: *V* (= verb); *M* (= modal); *Pro* (= Pronoun); *Pl* (= place); *T* (= time).

1. Sheriff: I like this dry dusty town in western Kansas.

 Pro V Pro

 Granddaughter: Grandpa said that he liked that dry dusty town in western Kansas.

2. Sheriff: I will always remember what happened to the Donovans.

 Granddaughter: Grandpa said that he would always remember what had happened

 to the Donovans.

3. Sheriff: This was long before you were born.

 Granddaughter: Grandpa said that that was long before I was born.

4. Sheriff: You may remember the Donovans, who live north of town.

 Granddaughter: Grandpa said that I might remember the Donovans, who lived north of town.

5. Sheriff: The trouble started when I was out of town.

 Granddaughter: Grandpa said that the trouble started when he was out of town.

6. Sheriff: My deputy had to talk to Mrs. Donovan because I wasn't here.

 Granddaughter: Grandpa said that his deputy had to talk to Mrs. Donovan because he

 wasn't there.

7. Sheriff: I'll tell you the whole story later today.

 Granddaughter: Grandpa said that he would tell me the whole story later that day.

5 **Changes in Verb Tense in Reported Speech**

Mrs. Donovan talked earlier with the deputy. The deputy is now telling the sheriff about their conversation. Finish changing the conversation to reported speech by filling in the appropriate forms of the verbs. Make all changes, including those that are optional. Where a change is not possible, fill in the verb form given in the original speech.

1. Mrs. Donovan: I want to talk to the sheriff. My husband is missing.

   Deputy to Sheriff: She said that she ___wanted_____ to talk to you and that her

   husband ___was missing_____.

2. Mrs. Donovan: He has been gone for about a week, but he had planned to be gone for

   only a couple of days.

   Deputy to Sheriff: She said that he _____ for about a week, but that

   he _____ to be gone for only a couple days.

3. Mrs. Donovan: My husband planned to meet someone here in town.

   Deputy to Sheriff: She said that her husband _____ to meet with

   someone here in town.

4. Mrs. Donovan: Someone was interested in our land and wanted to talk to us.

   Deputy to Sheriff: She said that someone _____ interested in their

   land and _____ to talk to them.

5. Mrs. Donovan: I hoped you had seen my husband.

   Deputy to Sheriff: She said that she hoped I _____ her husband.

6. Deputy to Mrs. Donovan: I'm sorry, but I haven't seen him. If I had seen him, I would
   have told you.

   Deputy to Sheriff: I told her that I _____ sorry, but I _____ her
   husband. I told her that if I _____ him, I
   _____ her.

7. Mrs. Donovan: I'm going to the stable to take care of my horses.

   Deputy to Sheriff: She said she _____ to the stable to take care
   of her horses.

8. Just then, a man ran by the sheriff's office yelling, "Fire! There's a fire at the horse stable!"

   Deputy to Sheriff: That man just said that there _____ a fire at the stable!

GRAMMAR PRACTICE 3

Modals in Reported Speech

6 Changes in Modals in Reported Speech

The sheriff and the deputy ran to the stable. The sheriff pulled the stable owner, John McVee, out of the flames while the deputy helped to put out the fire. Mrs. Donovan wasn't there, but McVee had seen Mr. Donovan earlier in the week. Now he is telling the sheriff about their conversation. Finish changing the speech to reported speech by filling in each modal + verb. Make all possible changes, including those that are optional. Where a change is not possible, fill in as in the original speech.

1. Mr. Donovan: I know that it's raining, but I have to go to Sharon Springs.

   McVee to Sheriff: He said he knew that it was raining but that he _had to go_____ to
   Sharon Springs.

2. Mr. Donovan: I must leave now. I can't wait.

   McVee to Sheriff: He said he _____ then and that he
   _____.

3. Mr. Donovan: I'm going to be back in a few hours. I shouldn't be gone long.

   McVee to Sheriff: He said he _____ back in a few hours and that he
   _____ gone long.

4. Mr. Donovan: I think that the rain might stop. If it doesn't, I may not be able to cross the
   creek.

   McVee to Sheriff: He said that he thought that the rain _____ and that
   if it didn't, he _____ the creek.

5. Mr. Donovan: I should have written a letter to my wife. I could have had you deliver it if something goes wrong.

    McVee to Sheriff: He said he _____ a letter to his wife.

    He _____ me deliver it if something went wrong.

6. Mr. McVee: I'll tell your wife if anything happens.

    McVee to Sheriff: I told him that I _____ his wife if anything happened.

    McVee started coughing even though the fire was almost out. Suddenly a woman screamed. It sounded as if it had come from the hotel. They searched the town, but Mrs. Donovan was nowhere to be found.

GRAMMAR PRACTICE 4

Pronouns and Time and Place Expressions in Reported Speech

7 **Changes in Pronouns and Time and Place Expressions in Reported Speech**

Two days later, Rob Honeywell rode into town. He had seen Mrs. Donovan the day before and went to tell the sheriff about their conversation. Complete the reported speech by filling in pronouns and time and place expressions. Make appropriate changes (some words could be changed in several ways). Where no change is needed, fill in the words from the original speech.

1. Mrs. Donovan: If you want to help me, you can ride into town and bring a horse back here.

    Honeywell to Sheriff: She said that if __I__ wanted to help __her__, __I__ could ride into town and bring a horse back __there__.

2. Mrs. Donovan: I found my husband this morning. He's okay now, but he can't walk to town.

    Honeywell to Sheriff: She said that _____ had found _____ husband _____. _____ was okay _____, but _____ couldn't walk to town.

3. Mrs. Donovan: When we get there, he will need to see a doctor.

    Honeywell to Sheriff: She said that when _____ got _____, _____ would need to see a doctor.

4. Mrs. Donovan: He hurt his ankle two days ago, and both our horses ran away.

   Honeywell to Sheriff: She said that _____ had hurt his ankle _____,

   and both _____ horses had run away.

5. Mrs. Donovan: We can take care of ourselves until you get back to this place.

   Honeywell to Sheriff: She said that _____ could take care of _____ until _____

   got back to _____ place.

6. Mr. Honeywell: I should be there tomorrow. I'll bring horses for you and your husband.

   Honeywell to Sheriff: I told her that _____ should be _____. I said

   _____ would bring horses for _____ and _____ husband.

8 Changes that Occur in Reported Speech

After the Donovans returned to town, they talked to the doctor. The doctor then
went to the sheriff's office and told him about their conversation. Rewrite the
sentences as reported speech. Make all possible changes.

1. Mrs. Donovan: When I realized my danger at the hotel, I turned and ran.

   Doctor to Sheriff: _Mrs Donovan said (that) when she realized her danger at the hotel, she_
   turned and ran.

2. Mrs. Donovan: I must have screamed after the man grabbed me.

   Doctor to Sheriff: Mrs. Donovan said _____

3. Mrs. Donovan: He made my horse run so that I couldn't jump off.

   Doctor to Sheriff: Mrs. Donovan said _____

   _____

4. Mrs. Donovan: If he hadn't tried to cross the river, his horse might not have thrown him off.

   Doctor to Sheriff: Mrs. Donovan said _____

   _____

5. Mrs. Donovan: He couldn't swim, and I couldn't help him.

   Doctor to Sheriff: Mrs. Donovan said _____

   _____

6. Mrs. Donovan: I'm happy to be here in your office, but I'm very tired.

Doctor to Sheriff: Mrs. Donovan said _____

_____

7. Mrs. Donovan: I have to get some sleep now, but I'll talk to the sheriff later.

Doctor to Sheriff: Mrs. Donovan said _____

_____

9 Writing

Finish the story on a separate sheet of paper. Use reported speech to tell what the Donovans said to the sheriff. What happened to Mr. Donovan? Who was the man in the hotel? Why was Mr. Donovan missing? Where and how did Mrs. Donovan find him?

Example: *The Donovans went to talk to the sheriff about what had happened. Mr. Donovan said that he had gotten a message changing the meeting to Sharon Springs. However, shortly after he started out . . .*

GRAMMAR PRACTICE 5

Reported Questions, Commands, and Requests

10 Reported Questions

It's Mitzi's first day as a librarian. When someone asks her a question, she has to ask her supervisor for information about the library. Rewrite the speech as questions reported by Mitzi. Make all possible changes.

1. A woman: Do you have any books by Ray Bradbury?

   This woman asked if we have/had any books by Ray Bradbury. _____

2. A patron: Where are the Westerns?

   Someone asked _____

3. A teenager: What time does the library close?

   Someone else wondered _____

4. A young man: Has anyone turned in my wallet?

   That man asked _____

5. A child: What should I do to get a library card?

   This girl wants to know _____

6. Mike, a college student: Can I check this reference book out of the library?

   The student asked _____

11 Reported Commands and Requests

Rewrite the speech as commands and requests reported by Mitzi. Rewrite requests in two ways. Make all possible changes.

1. A man: Could you hold some books for me? [ask]

   A man asked me to hold some books for him.

   A man asked me if I could hold some books for him.

2. A young woman: Put my name on the list to reserve the next Tony Hillerman novel. [ask]

   _____

   _____

3. A young woman: Please call me when the book comes in. [tell]

   _____

   _____

4. A boy: Could you tell me where the periodicals are located? [ask]

   _____

   _____

5. Another librarian: Put these books back on the shelf. [say]

   _____

   _____

6. The other librarian: Don't worry. It will get easier. [tell]

   _____

   _____

12   Editing

Correct the 9 errors with reported and quoted speech. Some errors can be corrected in more than one way. The first error is corrected for you.

"We go now to our reporter on the street. Marsha, what do you see there"? asked the news broadcaster. [correction shown above: ?"]

"Howard, the scene here is incredible! A car hit a house, and now the car is on fire. There is smoke everywhere. One man told me that he sees a giant ball of fire about 20 minutes ago. Another woman said I was hit by something that knocked her to the ground," responded the reporter.

"Have you talked to the police?" the news broadcaster inquired.

"Yes, Howard, I have. Sargeant Whitney said me earlier that she believed the car hit a gas line in the house. The police are now telling neighbors that they had to leave their homes until the fire is under control," remarked Marsha.

Howard asked, "do you know how this all started?"

"One witness that I talked to said the car had been weaving back and forth across the street before it hit the house. She wondered the driver had fallen asleep," said Marsha.

"Are members of the fire department there?" asked Howard.

"I'm sorry, Howard. I didn't hear what you said," replied Marsha.

"I asked that the fire department was there," said Howard.

"Yes," said Marsha. "Someone from the fire department just told us move away from here because it's too dangerous."

"Okay, Marsha. Thanks. We'll talk to you later," said Howard.

Unit Wrap-up

Writing

From a fiction novel of your choice, select a passage that contains dialogue. It should have at least five lines of quoted speech. On a separate sheet of paper, rewrite the quoted speech as reported speech. Make all the possible changes.

Example: Brent grabbed his coat and, glancing at his watch, told Tom that he was leaving. He said that he had told his clients that they could reach him the next day. . . .

(*Grammar Link*s 3 Student Book, page 403)

10 10 10 10 10 10 10

TOEFL TIME

Allow yourself 12 minutes to complete the 20 questions in this exercise.
Questions 1 through 10: Circle the letter of the one word or phrase that best completes the sentence.

1. Although they have theories, scientists aren't certain why _____.
   - (A) did dinosaurs disappear
   - (B) dinosaurs disappeared
   - (C) would dinosaurs disappear
   - (D) dinosaurs disappear

2. Meteorologists wonder about _____ increase in intensity in the future.
   - (A) that El Niño conditions will
   - (B) that El Niño conditions would
   - (C) if El Niño conditions will
   - (D) whether El Niño conditions will

3. The mother of pop singer Jewel Kilcher wanted _____ to succeed and not even consider failing.
   - (A) that Jewel plan
   - (B) Jewel to plan
   - (C) that Jewel planned
   - (D) whether Jewel would plan

4. Ancient sea-going cultures were aware _____ the position of the moon and stars could be used to navigate.
   - (A) that
   - (B) of
   - (C) if
   - (D) about

5. In an article published six years ago, population experts agreed that there _____ a sizable increase in the number of people on the planet by the end of last year.
   - (A) was
   - (B) will be
   - (C) was going to be
   - (D) is

6. When a hurricane threatens coastal areas, authorities ask residents _____.
   - (A) that they will evacuate
   - (B) will they evacuate
   - (C) to evacuate
   - (D) if they evacuate

7. Stock-market analysts wonder when _____ a downward trend.
   - (A) that the stock market is going to start
   - (B) is the stock market going to start
   - (C) would the stock market start
   - (D) the stock market is going to start

8. Politicians are often asked _____ if they are elected to office.
   - (A) that they will do
   - (B) what will they do
   - (C) what they will do
   - (D) whether they will do

9. The American artist Philemona Williamson believed _____.
   - (A) art should be magical
   - (B) whether art should be magical
   - (C) that should art be magical
   - (D) should art be magical

10. _____ was a meat-packer from New York is a matter of legend.
    - (A) The original "Uncle Sam"
    - (B) That the original "Uncle Sam"
    - (C) Originally, "Uncle Sam"
    - (D) If the original "Uncle Sam"

Go on to the next page.

198

Questions 11 through 20: Circle the letter of the underlined part of the sentence that is incorrect.

11. <u>Its</u> thought <u>that</u> humans probably first <u>domesticated</u> horses <u>to use</u> them for food.
    A   B   C   D

12. Scientists <u>don't agree</u> about <u>if</u> there <u>was</u> ever life <u>on Mars</u>.
               A   B   C   D

13. It's easy to understand <u>why</u> many people believed <u>that</u> strange things <u>will happen</u> to
                           A   B   C

    ships <u>that</u> entered the area of the Atlantic Ocean called the Bermuda Triangle.
          D

14. John F. Kennedy <u>told</u> people <u>not ask</u> what their country could do for them, but rather
                   A   B

    <u>what</u> they <u>could do</u> for their country.
     C   D

15. People <u>are surprised</u> <u>about</u> that Pablo Casals <u>worked</u> until the <u>end of his life</u>.
        A   B   C   D

16. Former Surgeon General C. Everrett Koop <u>believed</u> <u>in</u> every American <u>should take</u>
                                    A B   C

    charge of his or her own health and <u>not be</u> afraid to ask questions about a medical
                                      D

    condition.

17. <u>The possibility</u> <u>that</u> the sleep-deprived mind <u>be</u> prone to "microsleeps," lapses of
      A   B   C

    consciousness so brief <u>that</u> the subject may not be aware of them, has been suggested
                         D

    in recent studies.

18. Albert Einstein is reported to have said <u>that</u> the single most important decision any of
                                  A

    us will ever make is <u>if</u> to believe <u>that</u> the universe <u>is</u> friendly.
                   B   C   D

Go on to the next page.

19. Scientists think <u>if</u> cheetahs evolved in the area <u>that</u> <u>is</u> now the western United States,
                         A   B C

and then they later <u>spread</u> into Europe, Asia, and Africa.
                    D

20. The Mattel toy company <u>says</u> <u>that</u> an average American girl <u>have</u> 10 Barbie dolls and
                           A   B   C

that every second, two <u>are</u> sold somewhere in the world.
                         D

Adverb Clauses;
Connecting Ideas

Chapter 22

Adverb Clauses

Adverb Clauses

1 **Identifying Adverb Clauses**

The passage contains five adverb clauses, including the example. Underline each adverb clause and circle its subordinating conjunction. In each adverb clause, write *S* above the subject and *V* above the verb. (Remember: A clause has a subject and a verb.)

                          S   *V*

     (Because) they want to meet the needs of their clients or customers, successful

business owners need to know the reasons behind people's purchases. Owners need

to budget time and money for market research when they are thinking about starting

a new business. Although they might not have all the information, they need to know

the likelihood of the success of their product. They should try to find out as much as

possible about their potential customers before they invest a lot of time and money.

In the end, if they have the right information to make good decisions, they are more

likely to succeed.

Types of Adverb Clauses I

2 Adverb Clauses of Time, Condition, and Reason

Underline the adverb clause in each sentence. Then write **T** for time, **C** for condition, or **R** for reason to indicate what kind of adverb clause each sentence contains.

1. <u>Because I was interested in this TV program,</u> I started to watch it. __R__

2. We've seen seven commercials since we started watching this program. _____

3. When the program was getting more exciting, they broke for a commercial. _____

4. I lose interest in sitting here as soon as the commercials start. _____

5. If this happens, I start to think about food. _____

6. Since the program isn't on, I might as well get a sandwich. _____

7. Television can be dangerous as it can make you fat. _____

3 Adverb Clauses of Time and Reason

Use the subordinating conjunction in parentheses to combine each pair of sentences into one sentence containing an adverb clause of time or reason. Use the sentences in the order in which they are given. Use commas where needed.

1. The message was confusing. I didn't understand the commercial.
   Because the message was confusing, I didn't understand the commercial.
   (because)

2. I forget a commercial. It is over.
   I forget a commercial as soon as it is over.
   (as soon as)

3. I didn't notice the name of the product. I was paying attention to the beautiful model.
   _____
   (since)

4. A commercial starts. I stop paying attention.
   _____
   (once)

5. I've seen a lot of commercials recently. I can't remember which products they advertise.
   _____
   (as)

6. I haven't seen those commercials. I have few opportunities to watch television.
   _____
   (because)

7. A commercial is really funny. I hardly notice the product.
   _____
   (whenever)

8. There will be commercials. People watch television.
   _____
   (as long as)

4 **More Practice with Adverb Clauses of Time and Reason**

Complete the sentences with the subordinating conjunctions in the boxes. Use each conjunction only once. Use commas where needed.

> ✓as   since   until   whenever

1. __As_____ she drinks her AWAKE coffee,

   Margie comes to life.

2. _____ she started drinking AWAKE

   Margie used to be sleepy all day.

3. She has had much more energy _____ she started drinking AWAKE.

4. Try AWAKE. _____ you drink it you'll have more energy, too!

> because   as long as   as soon as   before

5. End your day with a smooth cup of Assured Herbal Tea. _____ you take a sip

   you'll feel calm and relaxed.

6. Even _____ you finish the cup you'll feel warm and secure.

7. You'll enjoy Assured _____ we use only the freshest herbs.

8. _____ she can remember Evelyn has ended her day with Assured.

   You can, too.

Types of Adverb Clauses II

5 **Adverb Clauses of Contrast and Opposition**

In the sentences contrasting men and women shoppers, use the subordinating conjunction in parentheses to combine each pair of sentences into one sentence containing an adverb clause. Use the sentences in the order in which they are given. Use commas where needed. Write each sentence in two ways.

1. Men shop, too. Women are still the target market for retailers. (although)

   Although men shop, too, women are still the target market for retailers. OR Men shop, too,

   although women are still the target market for retailers.

2. Men stay an average of nine minutes in a store. Women stay over 12 minutes. (while)

_____

_____

3. Both men and women need to be enticed to buy accessories. They buy them at different times and places. (even though)

_____

_____

4. Men will pick up accessories when they pick up pants to try on. Women will look for accessories after they've tried on the pants. (although)

_____

_____

5. Men are able to make choices in style and size. They prefer help in matching colors. (though)

_____

_____

6 Using *While* to Show Contrast

Use the words given to write sentences with *while*. Write each sentence in two ways.

1. most teens/follow/fads   some teens/be/influencers

   While most teens follow fads, some teens are influencers. OR Most teens follow fads, while some teens are influencers. OR While some teens are influencers, most teens follow fads. OR Some teens are influencers, while most teens follow fads.

2. teens in the past/not be/the main shoppers in the family
   teens today/make/many of the shopping decisions

   _____

   _____

   _____

3. adults/often buy/a product/for practical reasons
   teens/usually choose/a product/because it's cool

   _____

   _____

   _____

4. teens in the past/not have/much money to spend
   teens today/spend/at least $264.00 each month

   _____

   _____

   _____

7 **Reason Versus Contrast and Opposition**

Use the subordinating conjunctions in the boxes to complete the sentences.
Use each conjunction only once. There is more than one possible answer in
some sentences.

although	✓because	even though	since

Because they are surveyed so often and studied so much, teens are claiming
1

that they no longer set fads. _____ small groups of hip teens used to think up
2

something new and different and watch it spread to the mainstream, teens today may be under

the influence of marketing firms that control what the trends will be. _____ the
3

marketers are in control, teens wonder if they are being coerced into wearing, watching, and

eating what the adult marketers want them to. _____ teens today may be just
4

followers, they continue to buy what is currently cool.

as	because	though	while

_____ businesses want to sell more and more products to teens, they keep
5

coming up with new fads. _____ they are not setting the trends, teens today are
6

still savvy shoppers who know what they want. _____ they may be influencing
7

teens, marketers know they must work to keep teens interested in their products.

_____ Levi Strauss did not stay in tune with what teens want, the company lost
8

customers to smaller brands of jeans considered "way cooler" by teens.

8   **Adverb Clauses of Purpose**

Use *so that* to combine the sentences to form one sentence with an adverb clause of purpose. Use *can* for ability. Otherwise, use *will*.

1. Marketing research firms look for teens who are trendsetters. They want to identify teens that they call "influencers."

    Marketing research firms look for teens who are trendsetters so that they can identify

    teens that they call "influencers."

2. The firms seek out influencer teens. They want to get their opinions on the latest trends in fashion and other areas.

    _____

    _____

3. They survey influencer teens. They want to find out what's hip in the mind of a teen.

    _____

    _____

4. Teen responses are analyzed. The firm wants to make recommendations to companies like Nike and Pepsi.

    _____

    _____

5. Companies pay for market research. They want their products to be successful with teens.

    _____

    _____

9   **Writing**

On a separate sheet of paper, write a paragraph about yourself as a consumer. What do you buy? How much do you spend? Do you follow trends? What is your purpose for the things you buy? How do you spend money? Use the following subordinating conjunctions in your paragraph: 1) time—*when/as soon as/as long as*; 2) reason—*because/since/as*; 3) contrast and opposition—*while/although/even though*; and 4) purpose—*so that*.

Example: Although I know I should save some money, I often spend all the money I have. Because I like to wear the latest fashions, as soon as I have any money, I spend it on clothes. When I shop, I look for clothing that is unique. Even though I like to look stylish, I don't always follow the latest trends. Sometimes I buy an outfit so that I'll look different from others.

10 Editing

Correct the 8 errors with adverb clauses. Some errors may be corrected in more than one way. The first error is corrected for you.

Paco Underhill, managing director of Envirosell, has been called a retail

because/since/as

anthropologist ~~when~~ he has been recording and analyzing what customers do in

stores for the last 20 years. As he has spent hours studying videotapes of shoppers he

is an expert on shopper behavior. He knows that until the merchandise in a store is

important, the layout of the physical space of a store is just as important to the

success of that store. When he enters a store, he quickly evaluates where and how the

merchandise is displayed. Paco Underhill observes the movement of shoppers since

he is able to advise his clients on how to set up their stores for success.

As they enter a store, shoppers are walking at a fast pace. Although they are

walking fast, they need time to slow down. A shopper will miss anything in the first

15 to 20 feet of the store, since she is moving too fast. As a shopper is going too fast

to really see the merchandise, retailers shouldn't put anything of value in the first

15 feet of the store. Because he has studied thousands of hours of videotape of

customers entering stores, Paco Underhill also believes in the invariant right.

This means that because they enter the store, shoppers invariably turn to the right.

While a store knows this, the display department will put anything of value to the

right of the door so that customers can see it.

Chapter 23

Connecting Ideas

Coordinating Conjunctions

1 Coordinating Conjunctions with Clauses, Phrases, and Words

Underline the coordinating conjunction in the sentences. Then identify the content the coordinating conjunction is connecting by writing **C** for clauses, **P** for phrases, or **W** for words above the coordinating conjunction.

1. Leroy watches TV, <u>but</u> Amy listens to the radio.
    (C above "but")

2. Leroy and Amy both hear commercials.

3. Leroy usually likes the commercials, yet sometimes he thinks they are annoying.

4. If the commercials are annoying, Leroy goes to the kitchen and gets something to eat.

5. Amy doesn't like commercials, so she doesn't listen to them.

6. She would rather listen to music or news.

7. Sometimes she waits for the commercials to end, and sometimes she turns off the radio when the commercials are on.

8. Amy likes the radio, but she can also listen to CDs.

2 Coordinating Conjunctions—Meaning

Complete the sentences with the coordinating conjunctions in the box. Use each conjunction only once.

> and   but   ✓or   or   so   yet

1. Most computer users like using just one kind of computer: a personal computer (PC)
   _or_____ a Macintosh (Mac).

2. Personal-computer companies promoted security, compatibility, _____ service. These companies promoted all three areas.

3. Because Mac users are different from PC users, the Mac company wanted a different approach to advertising. Users are different, _____ the advertising is different.

4. The commercials showed that Macs were fun, _____ they could also be used for serious work. Being both fun and serious may have seemed surprising.

5. The Macs were easy to use, _____ they were also capable of doing interesting things.

6. Some young people may have been attracted by the Macintosh computers' different colors _____ by their modern-looking exterior design.

3 Parallel Structures; Subject—Verb Agreement

Each of the sentences contains one error in using parallel structures or subject/verb agreement. Correct the errors.

1. Several companies are working on ways to blend the Internet and ~~to advertise on television.~~ _television advertising_

2. The technology allows the viewer to see the product on TV, to split the TV screen, and clicks on a website for more information.

3. One piece of technology allows consumers to block advertising and controlling what advertising they watch.

4. Interactive advertising will give both advertisers and consumers more choice, convenience, and they can control it better.

5. However, privacy issues and the use of information is important to address.

6. Advertisers must control who gets access to information and to use it.

7. The advertising industry has to regulate itself to protect consumer privacy or losing the trust

of the consumer.

8. New laws or government control are possible if there is poor internal regulation.

4 Punctuating Sentences with Coordinating Conjunctions

Some of these sentences contain one or more errors in punctuation. Other
sentences contain no errors. Correct the errors. If a sentence contains no errors,
write **NC**.

1. Every product has to find a way to stand out, it has to look different from its competitors.
   ,and (above "out, it")

2. Personal computer (PC) manufacturers found that many of their products were similar to

their competitors' products, so they needed to differentiate their products.

3. The products needed to be different enough but, not too different.

4. The PC companies tried to show that they had a good product and good service.

5. The PC companies "sold" their computers their knowledge and their service.

6. Customers could buy a prepackaged system, or put together their own systems.

7. They could ask for help, or they could use their own judgment.

8. The customers were helped while they were buying the computers and after they got home.

9. Many PC customers appreciated the extra support once they got the computer home so selling

after-the-sale service seemed to be effective and successful.

GRAMMAR PRACTICE 2

Connecting Main Clauses That Have the Same Verb Phrase

5 Connecting Main Clauses

Combine the sentences by using *so, too, either,* or *neither*. Each pair of sentences can be combined in two ways.

1. You liked our shoes when you were growing up. Your mother liked our shoes when you were growing up.

    You liked our shoes when your were growing up, and _so did your mother. / your mother did,_

    too. _____

2. You couldn't wait to get a new pair of shoes. Your friends couldn't wait to get a new pair of shoes.

    You couldn't wait to get a new pair of shoes, and _____

    _____

3. You've changed over the years. Our shoes have changed over the years.

    You've changed over the years, and _____

    _____

4. You haven't forgotten what you like. We haven't forgotten what you like.

    You haven't forgotten what you like, and _____

    _____

5. You need to see our new line of shoes. Your friends need to see our new line of shoes.

    You need to see our new line of shoes, and _____

    _____

6. Your eyes are going to like these shoes. Your feet are going to like these shoes.

    Your eyes are going to like these shoes, and _____

7. Your feet aren't going to be tired at the end of the day. Your legs aren't going to be tired at the end of the day.

    Your feet aren't going to be tired at the end of the day, and _____

    _____

8. You're not going to be disappointed in our shoes. Your friends aren't going to be disappointed in our shoes.

You're not going to be disappointed in our shoes, and _____

_____

9. You'll want to wear these shoes every day. Everyone else will want to wear these shoes every day.

You'll want to wear these shoes every day, and _____

_____

Transitions I

6 Punctuating Sentences Connected by Transitions

Use commas, semicolons, and periods to punctuate the sentences. Add capital letters where necessary. There may be more than one way to punctuate the sentences.

In the late 1990s, one of the most popular investments was in companies associated with the Internet; however, (OR . However,) since many of these companies weren't making a profit, their values were hard to assess. Many investors saw the Internet as a new way of doing business they therefore didn't want to be left out of any important future developments in addition buying Internet stocks became trendy, even though there were no dividends. Other investors recognized the potential of an accelerating trade in Internet stocks consequently they were able to buy low and sell high. One company more than tripled its initial opening price on the first day that it was traded for example.

GRAMMAR PRACTICE 4

Transitions II

7 **Addition Transitions**

Connect the second sentence to the first using the connectors in parentheses. Put the connector in the second sentence in the position indicated in the parentheses.

1. (*furthermore* / beginning) HealthyDog dog food tastes great. HealthyDog dog food is good for your dog's health.

   HealthyDog dog food tastes great. Furthermore, (OR ; furthermore,) HealthyDog dog food

   is good for your dog's health.

2. (*besides* / beginning) Your dog will be healthier. You'll spend less time and money at the veterinarian's office.

   _____

   _____

3. (*in addition* / middle) Your dog's coat will be shiny. Your dog will be more active.

   _____

   _____

4. (*also* / middle) HealthyDog will change the way your dog feels. It will make you happy.

   _____

   _____

8 **Time Transitions**

Connect the ideas by inserting the time connectors at the beginning of sentences where they are appropriate.

1. (after that, first) I'm going to address two aspects of consumer behavior in the
   ....**First,**......................................**After that,**
   United States. ᴧI'll speak about planned obsolescence. ᴧI'll address need versus want.

2. (meanwhile, then) The products we buy are designed to wear out. Models and parts change.

   We have to buy something new because we can't repair our "old" stuff.

3. (finally, next) Often, before we buy something, advertisers have tried to convince us that we

   not only want but need their products. We ourselves begin to believe that we need the

   products. We buy what we want, not necessarily what we need.

9 Writing

On a separate sheet of paper, write a paragraph about a time you went shopping. What happened? What did you buy? Use at least two connectors of addition and two connectors of time.

Example: One time when I went Christmas shopping, I was looking for a gift for my nephew. The store was crowded; in addition, I was tired and hungry. . . .

10 Result Transitions

Combine the two sentences using the transitions given. Use the sentences in the order they are given. Punctuate carefully.

1. The logo of this product is well known. Consumers recognize the product.

    The logo of this product is well known; consequently, consumers recognize the product.
    (consequently)

2. The ad was effective. The company sales increased.

    _____
    (as a result)

3. The company used a multimedia campaign. It reached a wider audience.

    _____
    (therefore)

11 Contrast and Opposition Transitions

Combine the two sentences using the transitions given. Use the sentences in the order they are given. Punctuate carefully.

1. People remember the jingle. They don't remember the product.

    People remember the jingle; however, they don't remember the product.
    (however)

2. Famous people are often used in ads. They sometimes have a negative effect on the product.

    _____
    (nevertheless)

3. The slogan is recognizable. The company may stop using it.

    _____
    (nonetheless)

4. This company's logo is good. Its slogan is poor.

    _____
    (however)

12 Writing

On a separate sheet of paper, write sentences that give examples for each of the statements in the box. Use *for example* or *for instance*.

> 1. I buy clothes that are comfortable.
> 2. I buy jeans that are stylish.
> 3. I buy shoes that are practical.
> 4. That company sells cars that are sporty.
> 5. That company sells snacks that are delicious.
> 6. That company sells games that are fun.

Example: I buy clothes that are comfortable. For instance, I only buy loose-fitting
         T-shirts made of soft cotton.

13 Editing

Correct the 7 errors with coordinating conjunctions and transitions. Some errors may be corrected in more than one way. The first error is corrected for you.

                        and

As fiber-optic, digital, ~~or~~ satellite technologies all advance in the next 10 years, they will give advertisers new tools to use television and the Internet interactively. However, advertisers will be able to target very specific markets. For instance, custom-made ads. These ads will target specific markets such as a particular age group or what zip code someone has. While advertisers' messages were delivered to large general audiences before, so they'll soon be delivered to the narrow audiences most interested in the product or service. For example, advertisers can target sports fans but dog lovers. Furthermore, the technology will give consumers the power to order products, in addition, they will be able to get information instantly. Whenever they want a product, consumers will only have to click a button to get it.

Unit Wrap-up

Writing

Choose two ads from a magazine or a newspaper: one that is effective and one that is not. On a separate sheet of paper, write two paragraphs in which you compare and contrast them. Give reasons why one works and the other doesn't. In your paragraph, use subordinating conjunctions, coordinating conjunctions, and transitions of addition, result and reason; and contrast and opposition.

Example: I prefer this ad for jeans that shows an active woman wearing them to
           that one because it doesn't show the jeans. While this one lets me see
           the product, that one tries to appeal to young people who like a
           particular type of music. . . .

TOEFL TIME

Allow yourself 12 minutes to complete the 20 questions in this exercise.
Questions 1 through 10: Circle the letter of the one word or phrase that best
completes the sentence.

1. _____ with a live virus, the Salk polio
   vaccine is safer than the Sabin polio vaccine.
   (A) As a result, it isn't made
   (B) Because
   (C) As it isn't made
   (D) In addition

2. In the fall, gardeners are advised to cover
   their outdoor plants at night so that the
   plants _____ by an early frost.
   (A) not killed
   (B) didn't kill
   (C) can't kill
   (D) won't be killed

3. _____, artist David Hollowell creates
   images of the game.
   (A) So he loves baseball
   (B) While he loves baseball
   (C) Yet he loves baseball
   (D) Since he loves baseball

4. Akitas tend to be fairly big dogs with well-
   defined muscles, _____ they used to hunt
   bears.
   (A) for
   (B) when
   (C) therefore
   (D) however

5. A bacterium may produce chemicals that cut
   viral DNA into pieces _____ it can protect
   itself from the DNA.
   (A) either
   (B) so that
   (C) for
   (D) therefore

6. _____ pronghorn are often called antelope,
   they are not related to African and Asian
   antelopes.
   (A) However
   (B) Because
   (C) Though
   (D) Futhermore

7. The National Transportation Safety Board
   investigates _____.
   (A) while a plane crashes
   (B) after a plane crashes
   (C) consequently, a plane crashes
   (D) yet a plane crashes

8. Looking up genealogy has become a leading
   Internet subject, and _____.
   (A) so has finding lost relatives and friends
   (B) finding lost relatives has so
   (C) too has finding lost relatives
   (D) and finding lost relative hasn't either

9. _____ they are mammals, bears are warm-
   blooded.
   (A) Also
   (B) So
   (C) Consequently
   (D) Since

10. The human body needs salt; _____, most
    Americans consume too much.
    (A) yet
    (B) however
    (C) therefore
    (D) or

Go on to the next page.

Questions 11 through 20: Circle the letter of the underlined part of the sentence that is incorrect.

11. In autumn, chlorophyll is no longer produced in trees; so other pigments in the leaves
    A   B   C

    are exposed.
    D

12. Since high-level chess matches are very strenuous activities, so professionals train for
                         A   B   C

    them like athletes train for sporting events.
         D

13. Excitement and if you are afraid produce rapid heart rates and
             A   B

    increased adrenaline flow; in addition, they produce stress.
            C   D

14. There are benefits of higher education besides increasing knowledge,
                             A   B

    for instance, educated people usually earn more money and have more self-confidence.
            C   D

15. Because only a fraction of our communication being verbal, our bodies often convey a
            A   B

    message; the tone of our voices can carry meaning, also.
                       C   D

16. Although Roger Maris' single-season homerun record was thought to be untouchable,
         A   B

    nevertheless, Mark McGuire and Sammy Sosa broke his record in 1998.
         C   D

17. Because arthroscopic surgery has reduced the recovery time and decreasing
         A   B   C

    the chance of infection, knee-surgery patients can start rehabilitation sooner.
         D

18. As they had waited for the Mars Climate Orbiter to reach Mars, when the craft was
       A   B

    lost, the engineers who built it were disappointed and astronomers who were waiting
                                      C

    to receive data were so.
                 D

19. Though botox contains a highly purified neurotoxin, it is used to control severe muscle
       A

    spasms and smoothing out wrinkles, too; furthermore, it can relieve headaches.
              B   C   D

20. Cormorants, diving birds, don't have external nostrils but any other way to breathe
                                A   B

    when their mouths are closed.
       C   D

218

Answer Key

Unit One
Present and Past: Simple and Progressive

Chapter 1: Simple Present and Present Progressive

Simple Present and Present Progressive I

1 Simple Present—Form and Spelling

A. 2. Do people schedule   3. don't think
4. Does the human body follow   5. run
6. don't use   7. are   8. do they follow
9. Does Phil go; is   10. goes; finishes
11. doesn't stay   12. does she get up
13 hurries; goes   14. doesn't realize; depends
15. do you depend

B. 2. plays /z/   3. mixes /ĭz/   4. starts /s/
5. watches /ĭz/   6. stays /z/   7. goes /z/
8. talks /s/   9. misses /ĭz/   10. tries /z/
11. carries /z/   12. ends /z/   13. reaches /ĭz/
14. finishes /ĭz/   15. studies /z/   16. sleeps /s/
17. pays /z/   18. annoys /z/   19. has /z/
20. drives /z/   21. blows /z/

2 Present Progressive—Form and Spelling

A. 2. aren't paying   3. are trying   4. aren't
always complaining   5. are we doing
6. 'm sleeping; waking up   7. 's eating
8. Is natural time working   9. 're still trying
10. Are you listening   11. is it saying
12. Is it telling

B. 2. leaving   3. fixing   4. shopping   5. seeing
6. beginning   7. crying   8. running
9. waving   10. stopping   11. going
12. tying   13. flying   14. paying   15. tasting
16. showing   17. doing   18. planning
19. coming   20. letting   21. hopping
22. hoping   23. hiking   24. dying

Simple Present and Present Progressive II

3 Simple Present—Uses

2. a   3. a   4. b   5. b   6. a

4 Present Progressive—Uses

2. b   3. b   4. b   5. a   6. a   7. a

5 Adverbs of Frequency and Time Expressions with Simple Present and Present Progressive

2. Do you exercise on the weekends?
3. They aren't watching a lot of TV these days.
4. He goes to bed at 10:00.
5. Are you leaving at this time?
6. She doesn't eat dinner in the evening.

6 Simple Present and Present Progressive; Time Expressions

2. He often gets up at sunrise.
3. This week we're eating big breakfasts.
4. Jon relaxes at home on weekends.
5. Are you studying more these days?
6. Briana doesn't exercise every day.
7. What classes does Sarah have on Tuesdays?
8. Is Lisa getting enough sleep at night?

7 Writing

Answers will vary.

8 Simple Present Versus Present Progressive

2. do they do   3. studies   4. think
5. are trying / try   6. is asking
7. do we remember   8. don't remember
9. does time run / is time running
10. is the universe going

AK-1

Verbs with Stative Meaning

9 **Identifying Verbs with Active Meaning and Verbs with Stative Meaning**

A. My husband <u>has</u> an irregular schedule, so he stays up late to watch TV programs that he <u>doesn't</u> really <u>hear</u>. He rarely exercises and <u>looks</u> tired all the time. He says he(̓s being) lazy, but he <u>is</u>n't lazy. He <u>seems</u> unwell in the morning. He <u>knows</u> his schedule is making him unhappy, and he <u>wants</u> to do something about it.

Nowadays, I'm listening to my body's internal clock and paying attention to natural time and my natural work cycle. I'm going to work early and leaving early, too. I go to bed when my body tells me I'<u>m</u> tired, so I <u>do</u>n't <u>mind</u> getting up early now. I <u>like</u> my new schedule. (I̓m feeling) great.

Are you following your natural cycle, or are you following clock time?

B. See circled text in Part A.

10 **Verbs with a Stative and an Active Meaning**

2. a. are looking; b. looks   3. a. have; b. 're having   4. a. are weighing; b. weigh
5. a. are feeling; b. feels   6. a. are; b. are being

11 **Editing**

move
2. However, the earth doesn't ~~moves~~ around the sun on a consistent basis.

varies
3. It is ~~varying~~ from day to day by as much as 16 minutes.

realize
4. Nowadays, we seldom ~~realizing~~ that clock time and sun time don't match.

usually make
5. We are ~~usually making~~ appointments by our watches, not by the position of the sun in the sky.

is
6. Watches help us agree on what time it ~~is being~~.

Chapter 2: Simple Past and Past Progressive

Simple Past and Past Progressive I

1 **Simple Past—Form**

2. blew   3. brought   4. dug   5. drank   6. ate   7. felt   8. found   9. flew   10. gave   11. left
12. let   13. made   14. rose   15. read   16. ran   17. said   18. slept   19. taught   20. woke

2 **Simple Past—Form and Pronunciation**

A. 2. did he do

3. (wanted)

4. (increased)

5. fell

6. (dropped)

7. What was

8. set up

9. (rolled)

10. was Galileo able to

11. (needed)

12. didn't have

13. knew

14. did he play

15. put

16. hit

17. took

18. got

19. (showed)

20. went

B. See the circled words in Part A.

/t/	/d/	/ɪd/
increased dropped	used rolled showed	wanted needed

3 **Past Progressive—Form**

2. Was the river hurting   3. was bringing   4. were getting   5. weren't making   6. were they failing
7. were any people doing   8. were studying
9. were observing

GRAMMAR PRACTICE 2

Simple Past and Past Progressive II

4 **Simple Past and Past Progressive—Meaning**

A. 2. PP   3. PP   4. PP   5. SP   6. PP   7. PP

B. 2. were arguing   3. started   4. pulled
5. forgot   6. fought   7. were fighting
8. cut   9. wore

5 **Simple Past and Past Progressive**

2. died   3. was studying   4. broke out
5. closed   6. stayed   7. was waiting / waited
8. thought / was thinking   9. was sitting
10. fell   11. helped   12. became
13. was working / worked   14. made   15. was

6 **Writing**

Answers will vary.

GRAMMAR PRACTICE 3

Simple Past and Past Progressive in Time Clauses

7 **Simple Past and Past Progressive in Time Clauses—Meaning**

3. [In the 1880s, (when) the United States was thinking about instituting standardized time, the railroads were very powerful.]

4. Farmers and factory owners needed to get their products to the railway station (before) the train arrived. Knowing the arrival time of the train became very important.

5. (After) the farmers and factory owners started paying attention to clock time, other business owners and professionals began using it, too.

6. [(While) clock time was taking over the business world, natural time remained important in people's personal world.]

8 **Simple Past, Past Progressive, and Time Clauses**

2. After Lauren went to work, Paul got up. OR Paul got up after Lauren went to work.

3. While Lauren was working, Paul got up. OR Paul got up while Lauren was working.

4. Paul got up before Lauren ate lunch. OR Before Lauren ate lunch, Paul got up.

5. When Lauren left /was leaving work, Paul went/was going to work. OR Lauren left/was leaving work when Paul went /was going to work. OR Paul went /was going to work when Lauren left/was leaving work. OR When Paul went /was going to work, Lauren left/ was leaving work.

6. Lauren left work before Paul ate dinner. OR Before Paul ate dinner, Lauren went to work.

7. Lauren went to bed while Paul was working. OR While Paul was working, Lauren went to bed.

8. After Lauren went to bed, Paul met friends. OR Paul met friends after Lauren went to bed.

10 **Writing**

Answers will vary.

11 **Editing**

2. Einstein's theory of relativity predicted that motion and gravity ~~used to affect~~ **affected** time.

3. However, Einstein never ~~doing~~ **did** an experiment to prove his theory.

4. An experiment ~~on~~ **in** 1971 tested his theory.

5. While one airplane was traveling west carrying an atomic clock, another ~~is~~ **was** traveling east with another atomic clock.

6. The atomic clock on the plane traveling east gained time while the one on the plane going west ~~losed~~ **lost** time.

9. Lauren was sleeping when Paul came home. OR When Paul came home, Lauren was sleeping. OR When Lauren was sleeping, Paul came home. OR Paul came home when Lauren was sleeping.

GRAMMAR PRACTICE 4

Used To

9 *Used To*—**Form**

A. 2. didn't use to have
3. Did your teacher play
4. used to use
5. did you use to check
6. used to check
7. used to help
8. used to help

B.
3. Would your teacher play
4. would use
5. would you check
6. would check
7. would help
8. would help

Unit Wrap-up

Writing

Answers will vary.

TOEFL TIME

Questions 1–10

1. C   2. D   3. C   4. A   5. B   6. D   7. A
8. B   9. B   10. B

Questions 11–20

11. D (*omit* being)   12. C (building)
13. D (creates)   14. D (refused OR were refusing)
15. C (used to think OR thought)
16. D (used to)   17. B (died)   18. C (when)
19. C (cost)   20. C (opened)

Unit Two
Present and Past: Perfect and Perfect Progressive

Chapter 3: Present Perfect and Present Perfect Progressive

GRAMMAR PRACTICE 1

Present Perfect and Present Perfect Progressive I

1   Past and Past Participle Forms

2. caught; caught   3. drew; drawn   4. fell; fallen
5. heard; heard   6. kept; kept   7. led; led
8. lay; lain   9. mistook; mistaken   10. quit; quit
11. rode; ridden   12. saw; seen   13. sold; sold
14. sank; sunk   15. struck; struck
16. swam; swum   17. told; told
18. thought; thought   19. won; won
20. wrote; written

2   Present Perfect—Form

2. hasn't given   3. 've invented   4. haven't done
5. has happened   6. hasn't technology saved
7. has our time gone   8. have needed
9. have spent   10. haven't changed

3   Present Perfect Progressive—Form

2. haven't been enjoying   3. have been feeling
4. have they been feeling   5. 've been trying
6. have we been doing   7. 've been speeding up
8. 've been doing   9. 've been trying
10. have we been getting   11. we haven't

4   Contractions with Present Progressive, Present Perfect, and Present Perfect Progressive

2. is   3. is   4. has   5. has   6. is   7. has

GRAMMAR PRACTICE 2

Present Perfect and Present Perfect Progressive II

5   Present Perfect with *Already, Yet, Still,* and *So Far*

2. has already gotten a job; hasn't had a baby yet
3. have already bought; still haven't started
4. have already reached; haven't achieved all our goals yet
5. have they already retired; still haven't retired
6. have you done so far; haven't you done yet

6   Time Expressions of Duration

2. since   3. since   4. for   5. all   6. since
7. for   8. since   9. for   10. for

7   Using Present Perfect Progressive

A. 2. Q: How long have we been communicating by e-mail?
   A: We've been communicating by e-mail since 1972.
3. Q: How long have people been surfing the Internet?
   A: People have been surfing the Internet since 1973.
4. Q: How long have we been using the World Wide Web?
   A: We've been using the World Wide Web since 1989.
5. Q: How have most people been communicating lately?
   A: They've been communicating by cell phone.

B. *Answers will vary.*

GRAMMAR PRACTICE 3

Present Perfect Versus Present Perfect Progressive

8   Present Perfect and Present Perfect Progressive

2. e   3. b   4. d   5. c

9 Present Perfect Versus Present Perfect Progressive

2. I have written / (have been writing) a movie script for two years.

3. I (have gone) / have been going to six writers' conventions in the last two years.

4. I (haven't watched) / (haven't been watching) TV since I started writing the script.

5. My children and husband (haven't seen) / (haven't been seeing) much of me recently, either.

6. I (have traveled) / have been traveling overseas, and I'd like to do that again.

7. I (have made) / have been making a decision to relax more when I finish this script.

8. (Have you had) / Have you been having time for all the things you want to do recently?

9. Is there anything that you (haven't done) / (haven't been doing) lately because you (have had) / have been having no time?

10 Writing

A and B: *Answers will vary.*

GRAMMAR PRACTICE 4

Present Perfect Versus Simple Past

11 Present Perfect Versus Simple Past

2. became; c   3. has lived; b   4. have had; a
5. have been; a   6. saw; d   7. has painted; b
8. saw; d

12 Present Perfect Versus Simple Past

2. read   3. 've been   4. Have you ever driven
5. drove   6. still haven't driven   7. 've always
wanted   8. 've never had   9. started
10. Have you saved   11. 've saved

13 Writing

Answers will vary.

14 Present Perfect, Present Perfect Progressive, and Simple Past

2. 've lived / 've been living   3. moved
4. did you leave   5. were   6. didn't have
7. Have your lives been   8. 've lived / 've been
living   9. has been building   10. hasn't finished
11. 've taught / 've been teaching   12. 've had
13. has spent / has been spending   14. 's written
15. Have you been   16. 've been   17. were

15 Editing

    Recently I have been reading a book about people who use their time well. I have been

                              1. found

trying to be more like them since I ~~have found~~ this book.

    Herb Kelleher, CEO of Southwest Airlines, is a person who uses his time well. During an

interview, someone asked him, "What does a typical day look like for you

                              2. looked

now?" He said that he didn't know. He said, "I have never ~~look~~ back. I have always tried to

                            3. set/been setting

remain directed forward." He has decided what is important and has ~~setting~~ his priorities based

on those decisions.

                      4. delegated

    Several years ago, he ~~has delegated~~ control of his schedule to his executive vice president,

Colleen Barrett. Herb Kelleher said that before Colleen began handling his appointments,

scheduling his day took up too much time of his time. When he spent time on scheduling, he

5. didn't focus   **6. has concentrated**

~~hasn't focused~~ on other important matters. Since then, Herb ~~concentrated~~ on running the

company, while she has managed his daily activities.

                      7. has been

    So far, Herb Kelleher ~~was~~ a good role model for me while I have been trying to use my time

                               8. finished

well. I have managed my time better since I ~~have been finishing~~ the book. There is just one

problem. I don't have an executive vice president to schedule my day!

Chapter 4: Past Perfect and Past Perfect Progressive

GRAMMAR PRACTICE 1

Past Perfect and Past Perfect Progressive

1 Past Perfect—Form

A. 2. Before he came to the United States, he had (driven) a car.

     3. Before he came to the United States, he had (caught) a fish.

     4. Before he came to the United States, he had (made) a lot of friends.

     5. Before he came to the United States, he had (ridden) a horse.

     7. Before he came to the United States, he hadn't (slept) in a tent.

     8. Before he came to the United States, he hadn't (gone) skiing.

     9. Before he came to the United States, he hadn't (heard) a coyote howl.

   10. Before he came to the United States, he hadn't (written) e-mail to his parents.

   11. Before he came to the United States, he hadn't (read) a novel in English.

   12. Before he came to the United States, he hadn't (had) so much fun.

B. Miami, Florida

2 Past Perfect Progressive—Form

2. had been playing; hadn't been gathering
3. Had the ants been doing 4. had been working; had been searching 5. had the ants been looking for 6. had been been looking

GRAMMAR PRACTICE 2

Past Perfect

3 Past Perfect and Simple Past

2. asked; had stored 3. had sung; (had) danced; had worked 4. didn't have; had played 5. had been; wasn't able to 6. thought about; had done; had gathered 7. made; had requested 8. picked up; threw 9. realized; hadn't used 10. begged; didn't change

4 Past Perfect and Simple Past in Sentences with Time Clauses

2. In 1885, Karl Benz invented the automobile.
3. When Karl Benz invented the automobile, Etienne Lenoir had already built the first internal combustion engine. OR Etienne Lenoir had already built the first internal combustion engine when Karl Benz invented the automobile.
4. Henry Ford didn't mass produce the Model T until 1908. OR Henry Ford hadn't mass produced the Model T until 1908. OR Until 1908, Henry Ford didn't mass produce the Model T. OR Until 1908, Henry Ford hadn't mass produced the Model T.
5. Humans had used the wheel for thousands of years before Nicholas-Joseph Cugnot invented

the steam-powered tricycle. OR For thousands of years before Nicholas-Joseph Cugnot invented the steam-powered tricycle, humans had used the wheel. OR Before Nicholas-Joseph Cugnot invented the steam-powered tricycle, humans had used the wheel for thousands of years.

6. By 1904, the Wright brothers had achieved powered flight. OR The Wright brothers had achieved powered flight by 1904.

7. Charles Lindbergh flew the first transatlantic solo flight after Paul Cornu had designed the first helicopter. OR After Paul Cornu had designed the first helicopter, Charles Lindbergh flew the first transatlantic solo flight.

8. The first supersonic jet passenger service hadn't begun until 1976. OR Until 1976, the first supersonic jet passenger service hadn't begun.

9. Frank Whittle had performed a test flight on the first jet engine before the first supersonic jet service began. OR Before the first supersonic jet service began, Frank Whittle had performed a test flight on the first jet engine.

10. The Wright brothers had already achieved powered flight when Paul Cornu designed the first helicopter. OR When Paul Cornu designed the first helicopter, the Wright brothers had already achieved powered flight.

GRAMMAR PRACTICE 3

Past Perfect Progressive; Past Perfect Progressive Versus Past Perfect

5 Past Perfect Versus Past Perfect Progressive

1. A: had been looking for

2. Q: Had the clock struck
   A: had gotten; had been climbing

3. Q: had struck
   A: had struck; had never heard

4. Q: Had it been feeling
   A: hadn't been thinking

6 Past Perfect, Past Perfect Progressive, and Simple Past

2. bragged; teased   3. had been telling
4. challenged   5. hadn't run; had won
6. accepted   7. were   8. had danced/had been dancing   9. had gone   10. took   11. got
12. realized   13. crossed/had crossed   14. didn't stop/hadn't stopped

7 Editing

                                    1. have
For a number of years now, career coaches ~~had~~ been giving advice on managing time on the
                                              2. required/been requiring
job. One company asked a career coach about one of its policies. The company had ~~requiring~~ its

employees to work 60 or 70 hours per week, but most of the people weren't working very

efficiently. The company found out that most workers are not very productive after
                                                              3. started
50 hours per week. After the company cut back on each person's work time, it ~~had started~~ to see

better time management.

    "We hadn't been taking vacations," said one employee, "but the career coach asked each of
                      4. was
us to take just a couple of days off. I ~~had been~~ surprised at how much better I felt at work after

a short break away from the office."

Another problem that the career coach noticed was that little things, such as making phone
                5. began
calls, had been distracting the workers. When the workers ~~had began~~ scheduling time to do the
little things, they could focus better on the bigger projects. "Answering e-mail was my big time
               6. came
waster," said another employee. "Before the career coach ~~had come~~, I had been looking at my
e-mail constantly. I hadn't been able to concentrate on my work very well. Now I use the time
between meetings to read e-mail, and I concentrate better on my projects."

Unit Wrap-up
Writing

Answers will vary.

TOEFL TIME
Questions 1–10

1. A 2. C 3. D 4. B 5. A 6. D 7. C
8. B 9. B 10. D

Questions 11–20

11. A (have been) 12. A (*omit* had) 13. C (for)
14. C (confirmed) 15. B (had) 16. B (had)
17. B (already OR *omit* ever) 18. B (when OR after) 19. D (won) 20. B (has)

Unit Three
Future; Phrasal Verbs; Tag Questions
Chapter 5: Future Time

GRAMMAR PRACTICE 1
Will and *Be Going To* I

1 *Will*—Form

2. will we ride 3. will be 4. won't be able to
5. will we go on 6. will be 7. 'll be 8. 'll take
care of 9. 'll ride 10. won't ride 11. will you
wave

2 *Be Going To*—Form

2. is going to carry 3. is going to dive
4. 're going to reach 5. 're going to experience
6. 're not/aren't going to return 7. is going to
take 8. are you going to ride

GRAMMAR PRACTICE 2
Will and *Be Going To* II; Future Time Clauses

3 *Will*—Function

2. 2 prediction or expectation; 11 request
3. 7 prediction or expectation; 8 offer or promise
4. 4 prediction or expectation; 10 refusal

4 *Be Going To*—Function

A. First, the train is going to carry you up a
156-foot-tall hill.

Within seconds, the train is going to dive 146
feet into a vertical loop.

You're going to reach a top speed of 65 mph.

You're going to experience inversions where
you're riding upside down.

You're not/You aren't going to return to the
platform until you experience a gravity-defying
upward spiral.

B. Which one are you going to ride next?

5 *Will* and *Be Going To*—Function

2. prediction 3. expectation 4. offer
5. prediction about the immediate future
6. request 7. expectation 8. refusal

**6 Expressing the Future in Sentences with
Time Clauses**

A. 2. is going to dive; reaches 3. travel; 're going
to experience 4. go; are going to proceed
5. is; are going to travel 6. arrives; are going
to be

B. 2. After you experience the first drop of 188 feet, you will go into the first vertical loop. OR You will go into the first vertical loop after you experience the first drop of 188 feet.

3. Before the train enters a high-speed 180-degree turn, it will go through two more vertical loops. OR The train will go through two more vertical loops before it enters a high-speed 180-degree turn.

4. As soon as the train goes through the loops, it will fly up a hill. OR The train will fly up a hill as soon as it goes through the loops.

5. When you go through the last inversion, you will finish the ride. OR You will finish the ride when you go through the last inversion.

7 Writing

Answers will vary.

GRAMMAR PRACTICE 3

Expressing the Future with Present Progressive, Simple Present, and *Be About To*

8 Expressing the Future with Present Progressive, Simple Present, and *Be About To*

2. c   3. b   4. a

9 Future Time with Present Progressive and Simple Present

A. 2. scheduled action   3. planned event
4. plan   5. planned event   6. prediction
7. planned event   8. plan   9. prediction

B. 2. opens   3. 'm packing   4. is going OR goes
5. will probably be   6. are we visiting OR do we visit   7. 'm bringing   8. isn't going OR doesn't go   9. will be

10 Expressing the Future with Present Progressive, Simple Present, and *Be About To*

2. 'm about to call   3. are you going   4. 'll know
5. closes   6. 'll be   7. 'm telling   8. 're going
9. 're making   10. 'm about to pick up
11. 'm going

11 Writing

Answers will vary.

12 Editing

USA Weekend, a newspaper magazine, recently chose the 10 most beautiful places in

1. 'm going to visit

America. My friends and I are making plans to visit the spot of our choice. I ~~going to visit~~ the

2. I'll see OR I'm going to see

number one spot, Sedona, California. With its dramatic red sandstone rock towers, ~~I'm seeing~~

3. to travel

one of the most beautiful places in the U.S. My friend is going ~~travel~~ to the number four spot

4. arrives   5. hike

this summer. When she ~~will arrive~~, she'll ~~hikes~~ the Kalalau Trail on Kauai, Hawaii's oldest

island. She'll see volcanic peaks and waterfalls surrounded by tropical flowers. Another

6. is

friend ~~are~~ going to drive the Great River Road along the upper Mississippi River as it goes

through many nineteenth-century towns. We won't go to the number two spot, the city of

Pittsburgh, or the number five spot, The Golden Gate Bridge in San Francisco. Which one

7. will you

~~you will~~ visit?

Chapter 6: Future Progressive, Future Perfect, and Future Perfect Progressive

GRAMMAR PRACTICE 1

Future Progressive I

1 Future Progressive with *Will*—Form

2. won't be carrying   3. will they be doing
4. will be carrying out   5. 'll be going
6. 'll be traveling   7. 'll be passing
8. will be helping

2 Future Progressive with *Be Going To*—Form

2. 's also going to be researching   3. is going to be taking on   4. are going to be carrying out   5. are going to be saving   6. are these scientists going to be doing   7. 're going to be devoting

GRAMMAR PRACTICE 2

Future Progressive II; Future Progressive Versus Future with *Will* or *Be Going To*

3 Future Progressive Versus Future with *Will* or *Be Going To*

A. 2. will be   3. will fly/will be flying   4. will be waiting   5. will cheer/will be cheering   6. Are you going to ride/Will you be riding   7. will depart/is going to be departing   8. Will you be

B. 5

4 Future Progressive in Sentences with Time Clauses

2. drive; will be using   3. drive; will be controlling
4. use; won't be causing   5. will be riding; install
6. have; will be living   7. build; won't be commuting

GRAMMAR PRACTICE 3

Future Perfect and Future Perfect Progressive I

5 Future Perfect with *Will* and *Be Going To*—Form

A. 2. will we have solved   3. 'll have found
4. 'll have put   5. will have discovered
6. won't have changed   7. Will anything have changed   8. 'll have gotten   9. will have learned

B. 2. 're going to have launched   3. 're going to have developed   4. is going to have provided
5. 's going to have mapped   6. Are they going to have sent   7. aren't going to have done
8. 're going to have continued   9. Are they going to have found

6 Future Perfect Progressive with *Will* and *Be Going To*—Form

A. 2. will have been blowing   3. will have been running   4. won't have been blowing   5. will have been writing

B. 2. 's going to have been reading   3. is Ron going to have been looking at   4. 's going to have been observing

GRAMMAR PRACTICE 4

Future Perfect and Future Perfect Progressive II

7 Future Perfect and Future Perfect Progressive with *Will* and *Be Going To*

2. a   3. a   4. a, b   5. a, b   6. a

8 Time Clauses, Future Perfect, and Future Perfect Progressive

A. 2. Before he begins plans for a moon base, he will have worked on the Mars missions for three years. OR He will have worked on the Mars missions for three years before he begins plans for a moon base.

3. When he goes into space, he will have trained as an astronaut for two years. OR He will have trained as an astronaut for two years when he goes into space.

4. By the time he goes into space, he won't have worked for NASA for 10 years. OR He won't have worked for NASA for 10 years by the time he goes into space.

B. 2. Before he starts working on the moon base, he will have been working on the Mars mission for three years. OR He will have been working on the Mars mission for three years before he starts working on the moon base.

3. When he starts working on the moon base, he will have been working for NASA for five years. OR He will have been working for NASA for five years when he starts working on the moon base.

4. By the time he goes into space, he will have been working for NASA for six years. OR He will have been working for NASA for six years by the time he goes into space.

Answers will vary.

10 Editing

1. will be landing

In the future, robots and other devices that ~~will be land~~ on Mars will probably have gone to Antarctica before they ever leave Earth. Scientists will be using this cold continent more and more as they design devices for Mars exploration. They want to try out the machines there because of the similarities in climate between Mars and Antarctica. Both of these places have frozen soil, and Antarctic lakes resemble the Martian lakes of long ago. Before anyone

2. sets   3. been exploring OR explored

~~will be setting~~ foot on Mars, scientists are going to have ~~exploring~~ Lake Hoare in Antarctica for many years. They will have been looking at the algae that lives at the bottom of the ice-covered lake. They want to know about it because it is a very simple form of life. In the future, they

4. will search OR will be searching

~~searching~~ for similar algae under the surface of Mars in what they think are old lake beds. The water dried up long ago, but the remains of the algae, if there are any, might still be there.

5. returned

By 2010, a spacecraft is going to have ~~been returning~~ to Earth with soil samples. When the spacecraft comes back, scientists may find algae fossils in the soil. Regardless of what they find, scientists aren't going to give up their search for life too easily. They will keep looking in other

6. have

places until they ~~will have~~ reached their goal.

Chapter 7: Phrasal Verbs; Tag Questions

GRAMMAR PRACTICE 1

Phrasal Verbs I

1 **Phrasal Verbs Without Objects**

A.

B. 2. started out
   3. came back OR have come back
   4. will go on OR am going to go on
   5. broke down
   6. set in
   7. turned out OR had turned out
   8. showed up

2 **Phrasal Verbs; Placement of Pronoun Objects**

2. Q: <u>pull along</u> (his sled?)

   A: pulled it along

3. Q: <u>carry out</u> (his plan)

   A: carried it out

4. Q: <u>did keep up</u> (the pace)

   A: kept it up

5. Q: <u>did try out</u> (the parasail)

   A: didn't try it out

6. Q: <u>held up</u> (Borge Ousland)

   A: held him up

7. Q: <u>make up</u> (the time)

   A: make it up

8. Q: <u>took off</u> (his skis)

   A: took them off

GRAMMAR PRACTICE 2

Phrasal Verbs II

3 Phrasal Verbs—Meaning

2. on   3. off   4. out; off   5. up   6. up; off
7. down

4 Particle Versus Preposition

3. She turned it up.   4. We turned up it.
5. Turn down it.   6. She turned it down.
7. The police ran him/her down.   8. I ran down it.

GRAMMAR PRACTICE 3

Verb–Preposition Combinations; Phrasal Verbs with Prepositions

5 Verb–Preposition Combinations

2. depend on   3. plan for   4. learned from
5. protected; from   6. happened to   7. worry
about / think about   8. think about / worry about
9. suffered from   10. recovered from   11. come
from   12. care about   13. write about
14. will / 'll talk about   15. will / 'll pay for
16. will / 'll read about

6 Phrasal Verbs with Prepositions

A. 2. e   3. a   4. f   5. b   6. g   7. d

B. 2. get back from   3. put up with   4. get down
to   5. come up with   6. put up with / watch
out for / get along with   7. meet up with

7 Writing

Answers will vary.

GRAMMAR PRACTICE 4

Tag Questions I

8 Tag Questions—Form

2. Q: didn't they?
   A: they did.

3. Q: did it?
   A: it didn't.

4. Q: wasn't he?
   A: he was.

5. Q: had they?
   A: they hadn't.

6. Q: don't they?
   A: they do.

7. Q: haven't they?
   A: they have.

8. Q: aren't they?
   A: they are.

9. Q: won't we?
   A: we will.

10. Q: are there?
    A: there aren't.

11. Q: doesn't it?
    A: it does.

12. Q: aren't I?
    A: you are

GRAMMAR PRACTICE 5

Tag Questions II

9 Writing

Answers will vary.

10 Editing

   NASA, the National Aeronautic and Space Administration, is preparing a report on the

future of space travel. It may be considering sending astronauts back to the moon. This is a
          1. isn't it
good idea, ~~is it~~? Buzz Aldrin, a former astronaut, says it may not be the best idea. He hopes
                          2. over
that they will think the idea ~~up~~ carefully and he has suggested setting up a new space port in
                    3. it up
an area of space called L 1. If NASA sets ~~up it~~ there, it will offer a place to launch spaceships

to the moon, Mars, and anywhere else humans decide to travel in the future. Unlike the moon

or the International Space Station, L 1 has low gravitational pull, so a spaceship will require

4. off   _5. it_

little energy to leave it. It can take ~~up~~ easily. This space port will cost a lot, won't ~~this~~? How will

6. it off

we pay ~~off it~~? In fact, it will be relatively cheap. NASA can bring it off for less money than the

current International Space Station costs.

Unit Wrap-up

Writing

Answers will vary.

TOEFL TIME

Questions 1–10

1. A   2. D   3. A   4. A   5. C   6. B   7. D
8. C   9. A   10. B

Questions 11–20

11. B (have figured out)   12. D (completes)
13. A (will have)   14. C (_omit_ will)   15. C (get it
out)   16. C (are)   17. B (get along with)
18. B (succeed in)   19. B (is about to start)
20. C (run out of them)

Unit Four
Noun Phrases

Chapter 8: Nouns, Articles, and Quantifiers

GRAMMAR PRACTICE 1

Nouns; Proper Nouns and Common Nouns

1 **Identifying Proper and Common Nouns**

Conquest, travel, and trade have helped spread different kinds of food and methods of

R

cooking throughout the world. For example, romans redesigned the gardens of the countries

M   E

they conquered, and Christian soldiers returned from religious wars in the middle east and

N   A

north africa with new ingredients and recipes. The travels of marco polo of venice, italy,
M   P   V   I

C   I   E

helped establish trade with china and india, which gave europeans tea, spices, and the practice

C   E

of heating the cooking pot with coal. When columbus and other explorers returned to europe

A   I

from america, they brought new food and recipes with them. Then, italians traded these

T   E

things with turks, who in turn traded with other Eastern europeans, thereby helping to spread

E

new food throughout most of europe.

2 Article Use with Proper Nouns

3. the   4. the   5. NA   6. NA   7. the   8. the
9. NA   10. the   11. the   12. NA   13. the
14. NA   15. the   16. the   17. the   18. NA
19. NA   20. the   21. NA   22. the   23. NA
24. the

3 Articles and Numbers with Proper Nouns

2. the   3. NA   4. NA   5. a   6. two   7. NA
8. NA

5 Count and Noncount Nouns

                                                   C   N

The Internet has also been instrumental in spreading **ideas** about **cooking**. Many

                C   C   C   C

online **bookstores** have a **section** for **cookbooks** that includes **reviews** about the

     C   C   C

books. Television and radio **programs** often have corresponding **websites** that give

    C   N   N   C   N

recipes and further **information** and **advice** about **kinds** of **food**. Some

     C   C   N   C

companies use the Internet to give **consumers help** with their **products**. For

                C   C   C

example, one **company** that sells frozen **turkeys** has a very popular **website** about the

            C

Thanksgiving **holiday**.

6 Count Nouns Versus Noncount Nouns; Plural Count Nouns

A. 2. bosses   3. work   4. advice   5. parties
6. Fun   7. husbands   8. wives   9. children
10. vegetables   11. lives   12. Flies
13. enemy OR enemies   14. Mice   15. teeth
16. bacteria   17. health   18. customers
19. money   20. men   21. tomatoes
22. crates   23. garlic   24. boxes   25. heads

B. The boxes will break, and the heads of garlic will fall out and roll on the floor.

7 Subject–Verb Agreement

2. have   3. enters   4. have   5. plays   6. rests
7. aren't   8. is

8 Nouns Used as Count and Noncount Nouns

2. a business   3. A pressure   4. pressure
5. a chance   6. chance   7. a fire

Count Nouns and Noncount Nouns

4 Identifying Count and Noncount Nouns

3. N   4. SC data   5. N   6. N   7. N
8. SC sheep/PC   9. N   10. PC   11. SC people
12. N   13. N   14. SC potatoes   15. N   16. N
17. N   18. SC children   19. N   20. SC theses
21. N   22. SC wives   23. PC   24. N

Articles

9 The Definite Article

2. e   3. b   4. g   5. a   6. c   7. f

10 The Indefinite Article (*A/An*) and [0] Article

2. a   3. d   4. f   5. c   6. e

11 Definite and Indefinite Articles

2. a   3. [0]   4. the   5. an   6. the   7. the
8. the   9. a   10. [0]   11. [0] OR a   12. [0]
13. [0]   14. a   15. the   16. the   17. a
18. The   19. [0]   20. the   21. a   22. [0]
23. the

12 *The, A, Some*, [0]

2. [0], some   3. a   4. the   5. the   6. the
7. the   8. [0], some   9. [0]   10. the   11. the
12. a   13. the   14. the   15. some, the   16. the

GRAMMAR PRACTICE 4
General Quantifiers

13 General Quantifiers

3. recipes   4. recipes   5. food   6. recipe
7. food, recipes   8. food, recipe, recipes
9. recipes   10. recipes   11. food   12. food,
recipes   13. recipes   14. food   15. food
16. food, recipes   17. food, recipes
18. food, recipes

14 *Much* and *Many*

2. How many   3. How much   4. How much
5. How much   6. How many

15 General Quantifiers

2. a great many   3. no   4. quite a few
5. one of   6. years   7. several   8. a great
deal of   9. none   10. all of   11. several/some
12. each/every   13. Plenty of/Lots of   14. not all
15. none/not any   16. some   17. many/most

16 Writing

Answers will vary.

17 Editing

                                        1. an
    The Food Guide Pyramid is ~~a~~ outline of what to eat each day. It's a general guide that lets

people choose a diet that's right for them. The Pyramid calls for eating a variety of foods to stay

                                              2. [0]
healthy. The Pyramid also focuses on ~~the~~ fat because most Americans' diets are too high in fat.
3. The top   4. few
~~Top~~ of the pyramid shows fats, oils, and sweets. These foods provide ~~little~~ nutrients and are
                    5. don't provide any/provide no
high in calories. They ~~don't provide no~~ vitamins either, so people should eat less of them. The

next level has two groups of foods that come from animals: milk, cheese, meat, fish, eggs, and
                                              6. servings   7. [0]
nuts. The guidelines recommend two to three ~~serving~~ a day. The next level is ~~the~~ foods from

plants—fruit and vegetables. Many people don't eat enough of these foods. People should eat
8. plenty of   9. a good source/good sources
~~plenty~~ vegetables and fruit because they are ~~good source~~ of vitamins. At the base of the pyramid
                                              10. many
are grains—breads, cereal, rice, and pasta. How ~~much~~ grains should you eat? Get at least four or

five servings a day.

Chapter 9: Modifiers, Pronouns, and Possessives

GRAMMAR PRACTICE 1
Modifiers

1 Identifying Modifiers

A. Every <u>good</u> (cook) knows that even a <u>great</u> (recipe) isn't going to result in a <u>delicious</u> (dish)

without <u>quality</u> (ingredients). Professional (chefs) use only <u>fine, fresh</u> (produce). They usually

prefer to buy <u>healthy organic</u> (fruit) and (vegetables) at <u>small farmer-owned</u> (stands) at <u>local</u>

(markets) instead of in <u>large grocery</u> (stores). For example, they select <u>dark green leafy</u> (lettuce)

and <u>smooth, round</u> (tomatoes) at the peak of freshness for their <u>summer</u> (salads). They pick <u>ripe</u>

<u>red</u> (strawberries), <u>sweet Persian</u> (melons), and <u>exotic tropical</u> (fruit) for <u>luscious, light</u> (desserts).

B. *Opinion*: good OR great OR delicious OR quality OR fine OR fresh OR luscious
Appearance: small OR large OR leafy OR smooth
Shape: round
Color: green OR red OR dark
Origin: Persian
Find a noun used as a modifier: grocery OR summer
Find a compound modifier: farmer-owned

2 -*ing* and -*ed* Adjectives

2. Interested; tempting   3. stimulated   4. healing
5. exciting   6. refreshed; refreshing   7. confusing

3 Noun Modifiers; Compound Modifiers

A. 2. Bread Machine   3 Clay Pot   4. Chili Sauce

B. 2. Four-Course Meals   3. Award-Winning Recipes
4. 20-Minute Meals   5. 300-Calorie-Meal

4 Order of Modifiers

2. really quick, easy meals   3. great American food   4. famous art   5. modern nonstick
6. French herb   7. very interesting regional
8. delicious international coffee

5 Writing

Answers will vary.

GRAMMAR PRACTICE 2
Reflexive Pronouns; Reciprocal Pronouns; *Other*

6 Reflexive and Reciprocal Pronouns

2. by myself   3. himself   4. by yourself
5. yourself   6. each other   7. by ourselves
8. each other   9. him   10. one another
11. itself   12. us   13. each other

B.

Form	Function
2. singular possessive noun *Mexico's* OR *pepper's*	1. ownership *traders'* OR *her* OR *his* OR *your* OR *mine* OR *their*
3. plural possessive noun *traders'*	2. amount *of a century*
4. possessive pronoun *his* OR *mine*	3. something that is part of another thing *pepper's*
5. possessive phrase *of Mexico* OR *of a century*	4. origin *of Mexico* OR *Mexico's*

7 Forms of *Other*

2. another   3. another   4. Another
5. The other   6. others   7. the others   8. others

GRAMMAR PRACTICE 3
Indefinite Pronouns

8 Indefinite Pronouns

2. anything OR something   3. anything
4. Someone OR Somebody was   5. No one OR Nobody has   6. Everyone OR Everybody wants
7. anything   8. nothing   9. anyone OR anybody
10. anything   11. something

GRAMMAR PRACTICE 4
Possessives

9 Possessives—Form and Uses

A. 2. In the 1500s, European <u>traders'</u> <u>ships</u> carried the chilies to other places.

3. The <u>length</u> <u>of a century</u> was the time needed for chilies to spread throughout the world.

4. A Hungarian cook has <u>her</u> <u>recipes</u> for chili peppers, and a Chinese cook has <u>his</u>, too.

5. <u>Mexico's</u> chili <u>peppers</u> are especially famous for <u>their</u> <u>flavor</u> and <u>heat</u>.

6. The chili <u>pepper's</u> <u>seeds</u> and <u>ribs</u> make it hot.

7. If <u>your</u> <u>skin</u> is as sensitive as <u>mine</u> is, wear gloves when handling hot chilies.

10 **Forming Possessive Determiners, Possessive Pronouns, and Possessive Nouns**

2. China's   3. their   4. theirs   5. South Carolina's
6. the world's   7. people's   8. its   9. Asians'
10. my   11. Her   12. my   13. family's
14. Our   15. hers

11 **Possessive Nouns Versus Possessive Phrases**

2. center of the house's activities   3. stove's warmth OR warmth of the stove   4. gossip of the neighborhood and wider community   5. my parents' house   6. smells of cooking holiday food
7. my uncles' funny stories

12 **Editing**

1. much-loved

Cacao seeds are valued for producing a ~~much-loving~~ product: chocolate. Researchers

2. another   3. exact origins

disagree with one ~~other~~ about the ~~origins exact~~ of chocolate, but they tend to agree that the first

domestication of cacao trees was at least 3000 years ago in the low-lying forests of what is now

4. is 5. surprised

Mexico. Almost everyone ~~are surprising~~ to find out that the Mayans, who lived in that part of

6. chili

Mexico, had several ways of preparing chocolate, including flavoring it with ~~chilies~~ peppers, and

almost always drank it. The Mayans probably spread their chocolate-drinking habits to others in

Central America, eventually reaching the Aztecs in the highlands of Mexico.

The Aztecs valued the caffeine-rich seeds so much that they used them as currency. Because

of this, only royalty and the upper class consumed the rich chocolate drinks. Montezuma

7. himself   8. Aztecs' last OR last Aztec

~~by himself~~, one of the ~~Aztec last~~ rulers, probably gave chocolate to Hernán Cortés, a Spanish

explorer. The Spanish introduced chocolate into Europe, where the bitter drink was first

9. appreciated

mixed with sugar. Nowadays, people from all over the world enjoy this highly ~~appreciating~~ treat

from the Americas.

Unit Wrap-up

Writing

Answers will vary.

TOEFL TIME

Questions 1–10

1. C   2. D   3. A   4. A   5. B   6. C   7. D   8. A   9. B   10. A

Questions 11–20

11. A (Some archaeologists)   12. D (a shorter stay)   13. C (furniture)   14. B (interesting)
15. D (the Western world)   16. D (sunflowers)   17. C (the person)   18. A (her)   19. C (*omit* the)
20. B (other)

Unit Five
Adjective Clauses
Chapter 10: Adjective Clauses

GRAMMAR PRACTICE 1

Adjective Clauses

1 Identifying Adjective Clauses

2. One Harvard (professor) who has studied intelligence and creativity for over 30 years is Howard Gardner.

3. Gardner developed his theories on intelligence by doing research on artistic (talents) that children have.

4. He proposed that intelligence is (something) which is made up of different aspects.

5. Gardner called the (aspects) that make up intelligence "multiple intelligences."

6. Gardner reported on the (relationship) that he found between types of intelligence and creativity.

7. Gardner first studied two (men) who demonstrated different kinds of intelligence, Sigmund Freud and Pablo Picasso.

8. Both men were considered creative because of the (innovations) which they made in their fields.

9. The traits of the (people) he studied helped Gardner develop ideas about creativity.

2 Position of Adjective Clauses

2. A psychologist is a person who helps us learn about our personalities.   3. A personality test is something which helps people understand their unique traits.   4. Almost everyone who takes a personality test can know herself or himself better.   5. People that know their positive traits can make better career decisions.   6. Something that you should think about carefully is your career.

GRAMMAR PRACTICE 2

Adjective Clauses with Subject Relative Pronouns

3 Subject Relative Pronouns

2. who/that is adventurous   3. who/that are talkative   4. which/that is dangerous
5. which/that are stressful

4 Adjective Clauses with Subject Relative Pronouns; Combining Sentences

2. They are personality tests which/that indicate a person's traits.   3. People who/that have the right personality traits for a certain job will probably succeed.   4. These are traits which/that are important for a particular job.   5. Someone who/that doesn't have these traits probably won't be happy at a job.

GRAMMAR PRACTICE 3

Adjective Clauses with Object Relative Pronouns

5 Adjective Clauses with Object Relative Pronouns

2. who/whom/that/[0] we consider enterprising
3. who/whom/that/[0] we consider conscientious
4. which/that/[0] we consider exciting
5. which/that/[0] we consider important

6 Adjective Clauses with Object Relative Pronouns; Combining Sentences

2. His job is a difficult job which/that/[0] not many people would want.   3. The hours which/that/[0] he spends at work are long.   4. People who/whom/that/[0] he meets want something from him.   5. That man who/whom/that/[0] we saw on television is the president.

7 Subject and Object Relative Pronouns

2. who/that   3. which/that   4. which/that
5. who/whom/that/[0]   6. which/that   7. who/that   8. who/that   9. who/that   10. who/that
11. which/that/[0]   12. which/that

8 Writing

Answers will vary.

9 **Editing**

1. that/which

The Greek philosopher Plato wrote about four kinds of characters ~~who~~ humans have.

Because Plato was interested in the societal role that these types of characters played, he focused

2. displayed

on the actions that each type ~~displayed them~~. He wrote about artisans, guardians, idealists, and

rationals.

Aristotle, Plato's student, also defined four types of people, but he defined them on the

3. who

basis of happiness. Someone ~~who he or she~~ found happiness in sensual pleasure was different

4. who

from someone ~~whom~~ wanted to acquire assets. Others found happiness in acting in a moral

fashion, while Aristotle's fourth type of person enjoyed logic.

While Plato was alive, Hippocrates, a Greek physician, proposed that people have distinct

5. were

temperaments from birth. He identified four personality types that ~~was~~ based on bodily fluids:

eagerly optimistic, doleful, passionate, and calm. A Roman physician in the second century

A.D., Galen, furthered Hippocrates' ideas.

6. which/that

The four personality temperaments ~~who~~ Hippocrates and Galen described complemented

Plato's four descriptions of social actions. Hundreds of years later, others interested in

personality types also found four types. Perhaps our personalities haven't changed much in the

last 2000 years.

Chapter 11: More About Adjective Clauses

GRAMMAR PRACTICE 1

Adjective Clauses with Relative Pronouns That Are Objects of Prepositions

1 **Adjective Clauses with Relative Pronouns That Are Objects of Prepositions**

2. For a short time, you can probably do a job <u>that your personality isn't well suited for</u> / which your

personality isn't well suited for / [0] your personality isn't well suited for / for which your personality isn't

well suited

3. In the long run, however, you will be better off if you do a job <u>that you are happy at</u> / which you are

happy at / [0] you are happy at / at which you are happy

4. A person <u>that you can talk with honestly</u> may help you decide on a good career / who you can talk

with honestly / whom you can talk with honestly / [0] you can talk with honestly / with whom you can

talk honestly

2 **Adjective Clauses with Relative Clauses That Are Objects of Prepositions; Combining Sentences**

2. She is an employment counselor at the company at which I have a job/that I have a job at/which I have a job at/I have a job at.   3. I'm not particularly suited for the job that I'm working in/which I'm working in/I'm working in/in which I am working.   4. Nora encourages me to look for a position that I can get excited about/which I can get excited about/I can get excited about/about which I can get excited.   5. I may find a new job that I can move into/which I can move into/I can move into/into which I can move.

GRAMMAR PRACTICE 2

Adjective Clauses with Possessive Relative Pronouns

3 **Combining Sentences; Clauses with *Whose***

2. An immediate response on these tests is preferred to a later response whose accuracy may decrease with too much thought.   3. People whose responses are slow may answer as they wish they were, not as they really are.   4. Answers based on wishes will not help a person whose personality is actually quite different.   5. A person whose answers tend toward a specific trait has a strong preference in one aspect of work.   6. For example, a person whose responses indicate an outgoing personality probably prefers to work with other people.

4 **Relative Pronouns as Objects of Prepositions; Possessive Relative Pronouns**

2. which/that/[0]   3. whose   4. whom
5. which   6. whose   7. which/that/[0]
8. who/whom/that/[0]

5 **More Practice with Relative Pronouns**

2. which/that/[0]   3. which/that/[0]
4. who/that   5. whom   6. whose   7. which
8. which/that   9. who/that   10. which/that/[0]

GRAMMAR PRACTICE 3

Adjective Clauses with *Where* and *When*

6 **Adjective Clauses with *Where***

A. 2. The place where John eats is at a small table alone.
The place which George eats at is a large round table with friends. OR The place at which George eats is a large round table with friends.

3. The place where John relaxes is home with a good book.
The place to which George goes is a lively night spot. OR The place which George goes to is a lively night spot.

4. The place where John feels comfortable is in a small group of close friends.
The place in which George feels comfortable is in a large noisy crowd. OR The place which George feels comfortable in is in a large noisy crowd.

B. introvert: John   extrovert: George

7 **Adjective Clauses with *When***

A. 2. when we feel confused or frustrated
3. when an employee feels nervous   4. when students feel many emotions   5. when an artist feels creative   6. when you felt bored

B. 2. in which we feel confused or frustrated/which we feel confused or frustrated in/that we feel confused or frustrated in/we feel confused or frustrated in   3. in OR at which an employee feels nervous/which an employee feels nervous in OR at/that an employee feels nervous in OR at/an employee feels nervous in OR at   4. in which students feel many emotions/which students feel many emotions in/that many students feel many emotions in/many students feel many emotions in   5. in OR at which an artist feels creative/which an artist feels creative in OR at/that an artist feel creative in OR at/an artist feels creative in OR at   6. in OR at which you feel bored/which you feel bored in OR at/that you feel bored in OR at/you feel bored in OR at

8 **Writing**

Answers will vary.

9 Editing

Traditionally, a creative person is someone ~~whose~~ **1. who is** able to find a new solution to a problem.

Many "creativity tests" were created during a time ~~when this position was taken in~~. However,
2. when this position was taken/which this position was taken in/ in which this position was taken/that this position was taken in

this definition has been expanded by psychologists ~~who their~~ work enlarges older views of
3. whose

creativity. A place where there is some disagreement is in the idea of general creativity. The

definition that Howard Gardner came up with says that people are creative in a specific domain.

A gifted musician may show innovation in music but not in another area ~~in that she has less~~
4. in which she has less talent/that she has less talent in/which she has less talent in

~~talent~~. An expansion of the traditional theory says that there are many periods of time when

people are creative. There can also be many different ways ~~in which creativity is demonstrated in~~.
5. in which creativity is demonstrated/which creativity is demonstrated in

Two areas ~~where~~ are not part of traditional creativity tests, fashioning new products and
6. which/that

asking new questions, are part of Gardner's definition of creativity. Gardner's definition also differs

in that a judgment about creativity must be made by a group of people, not by a single individual.

Unit Wrap-up
Writing

Answers will vary.

TOEFL TIME
Questions 1–10

1. C   2. B   3. A   4. B   5. B   6. C   7. B
8. D   9. C   10. D

Questions 11–20

11. A (that/which OR *omit* who)   12. D (*omit* them)   13. D (which hang down)
14. C (that/which covered)   15. A (that/which)
16. B (*omit* their)   17. D (*omit* in)
18. B (whose)   19. C (that people knew)
20. B (the Little Big Horn River)

Unit Six
Gerunds and Infinitives
Chapter 12: Gerunds and Infinitives

GRAMMAR PRACTICE 1

Gerunds

1 Gerunds as Subjects, Objects of Verbs, and Objects of Prepositions

A. ~~Appear~~ on television helped the career of musician Ricky Martin. At the 1999 Grammy
1. Appearing

Awards, ~~sing~~ "The Cup of Life" earned Martin a standing ovation. He certainly must have
2. singing

been happy about ~~receive~~ this recognition of his music, and he also must have enjoyed ~~accept~~
3. receiving   **4. accepting**

the award for Best Latin Pop Performance. After his appearance on the Grammys, Martin's

5. increasing

fame kept ~~increase~~. His song "Livin' La Vida Loca" soared to the top of the pop charts, and

           6. buying   **7. growing up**   **8. living**

people looked forward to ~~buy~~ his album. From ~~grow up~~ in San Juan, Puerto Rico, to ~~live~~ the

                        9. singing

crazy life, Martin has always been fond of ~~sing~~.

B. *Subject of a sentence*: singing
Object of a verb: accepting, increasing
Object of a preposition: buying, growing up, living
Be + adjective + preposition: receiving, singing

2 Gerunds; *By* + Gerund; *Go* + Gerund

A.   **1. becoming**
     By ~~become~~ famous, Ricky Martin increased both his problems and his pleasures. If he
     2. dancing   **3. blending**   **4. approaching**
goes ~~dance~~ or on a date, he has a problem ~~blend~~ into the crowd. Fans can't help ~~approach~~
                 5. Maintaining
him for an autograph. ~~Maintain~~ his private life is hard. On the other hand, he has a good
     6. performing   **7. exposing**
time ~~perform~~. When he goes out on stage, he stands there ~~expose~~ his thoughts and feelings
                     8. shopping   **9. drawing**   **10. reminding**
to his fans. Perhaps he can't go ~~shop~~ by himself without ~~draw~~ attention, but by ~~remind~~

himself of the line between his personal life and his private life, he may be able to live quite

well with his fame.

B. *By + gerund*: reminding
Go + gerund: dancing, shopping
Subject: Maintaining
Object of a preposition: drawing
Gerunds used with other expressions: blending,
approaching, performing, exposing

3 Writing

Answers will vary.

GRAMMAR PRACTICE 2
Infinitives I

4 *It* + Infinitive; Infinitive as Subject

A. 2. It takes time to learn about all the programs.
3. It is difficult to decide what to watch.
4. It is a good idea not to waste time on
programs that don't interest you.

B. 2. To have a remote control is necessary.
3. To see how quickly you can become
interested in each program is interesting.

4. Not to channel surf when someone else is
watching a program is a good idea. OR To
channel surf when someone else is watching a
program isn't/is not a good idea.

5 Verb + Infinitive Patterns

2. to rescue   3. to take   4. to take care of
5. him to let   6. to know   7. them to put
8. them not to work   9. them to do   10. to do
11. to keep up   12. to wrap   13. to give up
14. (her) to keep   15. to fire

GRAMMAR PRACTICE 3
Infinitives II

6 Adjectives Followed by Infinitives

2. were/are ashamed to admit   3. were stunned to
learn   4. were delighted to hear   5. will you be
surprised to hear

7 Infinitive of Purpose

2. (In order) To figure out if they are lying   3. (in order) to conceal his or her guilt   4. (In order) To fool us   5. (in order) to arrest the murderer
6. (in order) to find out who committed the crime

8 Infinitives with *Too* and *Enough*

A. 2. Jon is too young to watch an R-rated movie at a theater alone.
Matt is old enough to watch an R-rated movie at a theater alone.

3. Jon is young enough to buy a child's ticket to a movie.

Matt is too old to buy a child's ticket to a movie.

B. 2. Matt has enough money to go to a concert.
3. Matt doesn't have enough time to play video games all day.
4. Jon doesn't have enough money to buy a lot of CDs.

9 Infinitives as Noun Modifiers

Answers will vary.

10 Writing

Answers will vary.

11 Editing

1. launching

One result of ~~launch~~ Music Television (MTV) in 1981 was that both the television and the

2. to see

music industries took off in new directions. Before this time, it was unusual ~~seeing~~ music

videos, but televising them 24 hours a day became a winning formula for attracting young

viewers. News and documentaries about music and performers were included on the broadcasts

to supplement the videos. Young "VJ's," or Video Jockeys, hosted the programs and

3. listening

recommended ~~to listen~~ to artists that they liked to hear. By promoting rock concerts and by

holding interviews with artists, MTV attracted and exposed viewers to a wide variety of

4. popular enough   5. ~~to launch~~

performers. Since the early 1980s, MTV has become ~~enough popular~~ for launching another

6. to keep

channel, MTV2, and it is always looking for ways ~~keeping~~ bringing in new viewers.

Chapter 13: More About Gerunds and Infinitives

GRAMMAR PRACTICE 1

Verbs + Gerunds and Infinitives

1 Verbs That Take Only Gerunds or Only Infinitives

2. to go   3. them to go   4. going   5. going
6. to go   7. to go   8. them to go   9. going
10. going   11. going   12. them to go   13. going
14. to go   15. to go   16. them to go

2 More Practice with Verbs That Take Only Gerunds or Only Infinitives

2. to earn   3. getting   4. feeling   5. hearing
6. to say   7. to thank   8. speaking

3 Gerunds and Infinitives

2. to turn   3. to vanish   4. experiencing
5. standing/to stand   6. to create   7. seeing/to see   8. getting/to get

4 Verbs That Take Gerunds and Noun Phrases + Infinitives

2. searching   3. to explore   4. to see   5. to examine   6. to be   7. believing

5 Verbs That Take Gerunds and Infinitives but with a Difference in Meaning

2. going   3. to go   4. seeing   5. holding
6. to repair   7. opposing   8. to enjoy

6 Writing

Answers will vary.

GRAMMAR PRACTICE 2

Performers of the Actions of Gerunds and Infinitives

7 Performers of Gerunds and Infinitives

3. for the audience to recognize   4. watching
5. the humans' looking   6. us to believe
7. Buzz's becoming   8. Woody's feeling   9. (for)
popular actor Tom Hanks to do   10. for him to
make   11. for Tim Allen to do   12. these two
actors to bring

GRAMMAR PRACTICE 3

Verbs Followed by Base Forms

8 Forms Following Causative Verbs, Verbs of Perception, and Other Verbs

1. b. disappear   2. a. grow, growing; b. appear
3. a. battle, battling; b. create; c. create   4. a. fire,
firing; b. add; c. believe, to believe

9 Writing

Answers will vary.

10 Editing

                                        1. playing
Eric Clapton earned his fame through ~~play~~ his guitar, but he may have kept his solo career

alive because of his singing. As a teenager, Clapton took up playing the guitar, and he later

started performing in public. Practicing the guitar improved his music but left little time for
                            2. going
schoolwork, so he stopped ~~to go~~ to school to pursue a career in music. After he joined the

Yardbirds, he became known for being one of the best blues guitarists playing at that time. As

his reputation grew, Clapton seemed to be moving from one band to another. Within 10 years
  3. his
of ~~he~~ having dropped out of school, Clapton was considered to be a leading rock guitarist.

However, he didn't appreciate having become so well-known, and at one time he seemed to be

trying to hide in an unknown band. Clapton's popularity faded for a while, but he continued to
                                                            4. Clapton's
record albums. The soundtrack of the 1992 film *Rush* included ~~for Clapton~~ singing "Tears in

Heaven," a tribute to his son, who had recently died. Clapton's performance of "Tears in
                                                            5. him
Heaven" and other songs on a special television program made it possible for ~~his~~ to reach a new
                        6. release
audience. This success let him ~~to release~~ another album, and he kept on writing and performing

songs for other movies.

Unit Wrap-up

Writing

Answers will vary.

TOEFL TIME

Questions 1–10

1. B   2. C   3. A   4. D   5. A   6. C   7. C
8. D   9. C   10. A

Questions 11–20

11. A (stampede)   12. D (waking up)
13. D (to master)   14. C (was)   15. B (seeing)
16. A (To prepare)   17. D (diversifying)
18. C (to work)   19. B (people to eat OR eating)
20. D (not loud enough)

Unit Seven
Modals
Chapter 14: Modals

`GRAMMAR PRACTICE 1`
Overview of Modals

1 Overview of Modals

Tony's Tips for Meeting People

(Can) you walk into a room full of people and start talking immediately? You ought to try it ✓
sometime. All of us <u>are supposed to</u> <u>be able to</u> meet new people, but some of us find that a
little hard. Try my tips and start making new friends today!

- You (must) show confidence! If you think you are worth knowing, other people (will)
  agree! You (could) try saying to yourself, "I am an interesting person!" Believe it.

- You (should) look people in the eye! People <u>aren't going to</u> speak to you if you look at
  their shoes!

- Of course, you ought to ✓ smile! You (may) <u>be able to</u> get someone else to speak with just a
  nice smile. Try it and see!

- You <u>have got to</u> say something! "Hi!" is a good start! You <u>are allowed to</u> keep your
  remarks simple. You <u>don't have to</u> be funny; just be sincere!

- You (must) not talk only about yourself! In fact, you had better ✓ let the other person talk
  more than you do. You (might) learn interesting things if you just listen.

So, what do you think? <u>Are you going to</u> <u>be able to</u> do these simple things? Of course you
are! Start today! You (should) see results soon!

`GRAMMAR PRACTICE 2`
Modals of Ability

2 Present, Past, and Future Ability

2. weren't able to/couldn't   3. were able to/could   4. was able to/could
5. were able to   6. was able to   7. were able to/could   8. isn't able to/can't
9. are able to/can   10. is able to/can   11. will be able to   12. won't be able to
13. are able to/can/will be able to   14. won't be able to/aren't able to/can't

`GRAMMAR PRACTICE 3`
Belief Modals Used to Talk About the Present

3 Belief Modals and Other Ways of Expressing Degrees of Certainty

A. 2. They may be engaged.   3. He must be single.   4. They might not be happy together.

B. 2. It's not/It isn't likely that he's at work today.   3. It's possible that she's at home.
   4. It's impossible that they're on their honeymoon.

4 **Belief Modals About the Present**

2. may/might/could   3. may/might/could
4. may/might/could   5. may/might
6. should/ought to   7. must/could
8. must/have to/have got to   9. should/ought to
10. shouldn't

5 **Writing**

Answers will vary.

GRAMMAR PRACTICE 4

**Belief Modals Used to Talk About
the Future**

6 **Belief Modals About the Future**

2. should/ought to   3. may   4. will we
5. might/could   6. may/might   7. should
8. may/could   9. might   10. may   11. will

GRAMMAR PRACTICE 5

**Social Modals I: Modals for Permission,
Requests, and Offers**

7 **Permission, Requests, and Offers**

1. b. will OR could; c. Shall; d. Could OR Will
2. a. May OR Can; b. Can OR May; c. Would

8 **Writing**

Answers will vary.

GRAMMAR PRACTICE 6

**Social Modals II: Modals for Suggestions,
Advice, Expectations, Warnings, and
Necessity**

9 **Social Modals**

A. 2. d   3. a   4. g   5. b   6. f   7. e

B. 2. should   3. are supposed to   4. had better
not   5. don't have to   6. have got to

10 **Suggestions, Expectations, Advice,
and Necessity**

2. must OR have to OR have got to   3. is
supposed to OR is to   4. mustn't OR must not OR
cannot OR can't OR are not allowed to   5. doesn't
have to OR does not have to   6. could OR might
7. don't have to OR do not have to   8. should OR
ought to   9. should OR ought to   10. must OR
has to OR has got to   11. should OR ought to
12. had better

11 **Writing**

Answers will vary.

12 **Editing**

                                    1. find
    Anthropologists have seldom been able to ~~finding~~ a society in which men and women don't

marry, even though when and how they marry might vary. In some cultures, couples are

                                                                    2. may
supposed to marry as soon as they reach adulthood. In others, couples ~~may be~~ delay marriage

                                                                    3. marry
until they want children. But most cultures believe that couples should ~~to marry~~.

    Types of marriage also vary. The most prevalent practice is monogamy, a marriage between

one husband and one wife. There are also polygamous societies. In these, a man may have more

                    4. may/might   **5. may not**
than one wife, but he ~~must~~ not. A wife, however, ~~mayn't~~ have more than one husband

Polyandry, in which a wife can have more than one husband, is extremely rare, occurring in

only 1 percent of the world population.

                    6. Will you/Can you
    Will you marry? ~~Will you can~~ choose your own mate? Many societies are changing, and

                    7. change
attitudes about marriage should ~~changing~~ along with them. It is unlikely, however, that

marriage, in some form, is going to disappear anytime soon.

Chapter 15: More About Modals

GRAMMAR PRACTICE 1
Perfect Modals

1 Perfect Modals—Form

2. may not have made   3. could have been
4. might have married   5. shouldn't have told
6. must have gotten   7. couldn't have been
8. could have had   9. must have said
10. ought to have told   11. shouldn't have raised
12. might not have chosen

GRAMMAR PRACTICE 2
Belief Modals Used to Talk About the Past

2 Belief Modals About the Past

1. b. couldn't have / mustn't have; c. should have / ought to have; d. must have / has to have / has got to have

2. a. may have / might have / could have; b. couldn't have / mustn't have/ can't have; c. must have / has to have / has got to have; d. may have / might have / could have

3. a. may have / might have / could have; b. mustn't have / couldn't have / can't have

3 Writing

Answers will vary.

GRAMMAR PRACTICE 3
Social Modals Used to Talk About the Past

4 Social Modals About the Past

2. should have OR ought to have   3. shouldn't have   4. 'd better not have   5. couldn't   6. could have OR might have   7. was to have OR was supposed to have   8. might have OR could have   9. didn't have to   10. should have OR ought to have

5 Belief and Social Modals About the Past

2. must, has to   3. might, could   4. couldn't
5. mustn't have had   6. had to   7. couldn't talk
8. might, could   9. shouldn't   10. didn't have to accept   11. must, has to   12. was supposed to call

6 Writing

Answers will vary.

7 Editing

1. couldn't
My boyfriend has disappeared. I ~~can't~~ find him all day, and he hasn't answered his phone.

2. couldn't stay
Last night he was really tired. While we were eating dinner, he tried, but he ~~couldn't have stayed~~

awake. He kept falling asleep, so he went home early. He told me that he had some work he

3. had to
~~must have to~~ do this weekend. It was really important to him to finish it today. It's possible that

4. may not /might not
he went to his office to work. He could have or he ~~couldn't~~ have; I really don't know. He ought to

5. may not
have called me, but his phone ~~mayn't~~ have been turned on. Sometimes he turns it off when he

6. had to
wants to concentrate. He had better not have gone fishing with his friends. He knew he ~~must to~~

go shopping with me earlier, but I went by myself since I didn't know where he was. Maybe I

7. called
should have ~~call~~ the police earlier. Now I'm really beginning to worry.

Unit Wrap-up
Writing

Answers will vary.

TOEFL TIME
Questions 1–10

1. A   2. C   3. B   4. C   5. A   6. D   7. A
8. C   9. C   10. B

Questions 11–20

11. D (have happened)   12. D (be able to)
13. A (might OR may)   14. C (was able)
15. A (*omit* will)   16. D (try)   17. B (come)
18. B (*omit* must)   19. D (responded)
20. B (cost)

Unit Eight
Passives

Chapter 16: Introduction to the Passive

GRAMMAR PRACTICE 1

The Passive I

1 Passive Sentences in the Simple Present

2. are used   3. is dribbled; (is) thrown
4. are pitched; (are) hit   5. is kicked
6. are knocked down   7. is thrown; (is) caught
8. is driven; (is) putted

2 Passive Sentences in the Simple Past

2. weren't published   3. was formed
4. was played   5. was later called   6. were added
7. was won   8. wasn't won

GRAMMAR PRACTICE 2

The Passive II

5 Meaning of Passive Sentences

    Most football teams in the United States have their team logos on both sides of their team helmets, but the logo of the Pittsburgh Steelers is painted on only one side. In 1962, the logo was created for the Steelers by the United States Steel Corporation (US Steel). At that time, the public's reaction to the logo wasn't known, so it was put on only one side of the helmets in case the Steelers decided to change it. The team is often asked about their helmets. To keep people talking about the logo and the team, the logo is still painted on only one side of Steeler helmets.

3 Forming Passive Sentences

2. Q: When was the number of players reduced to six from seven?
   A: The number of players was reduced to six from seven in 1912.

3. Q: Who is appointed for each game?
   A: A team captain is appointed for each game.

4. Q: What is permitted only to the team captain?
   A: Discussions with the referee are permitted only to the team captain.

5. Q: How many goalkeepers are allowed for each team?
   A: Only one goalkeeper is allowed for each team.

6. Q: When were goalkeepers permitted to fall to the ice to make "saves"?
   A: Goalkeepers were permitted to fall to the ice to make "saves" in 1911.

7. Q: What happens when a player is injured?
   A: Another player is substituted when a player is injured./When a player is injured, another player is substituted.

4 Transitive and Intransitive Verbs

3. The event was covered by both news reporters and sports announcers from a major U.S. television network.   4. The Nike logo was worn on their jackets during their broadcasts.   5. Why was the Nike logo worn?   6. Was Nike endorsed by these news reporters and sports announcers?   7. No change.   8. No change.   9. Now, corporate logos aren't worn by news reporters.   10. But sports announcers are allowed to wear corporate logos by the network.   11. No change.   12. No change.

2. US Steel designed the logo.   3. The team didn't know if the public liked the logo.
4. People ask the players questions about the helmets.   5. Players still wear the logo.

6 Receivers in Active and Passive Sentences

The most remarkable growth of a sport in the twentieth century **wasn't achieved** by basketball or baseball. Soccer **achieved** this increase. This fast-growing sport **was** originally **played** by amateurs in British-influenced countries, but now it **is dominated** by professionals worldwide. Much of the growth occurred in the second half of the century, and three reasons **are** usually **given** for the spread of soccer.

First, the World Cup **is televised** throughout the world. During the Cup, work schedules **are rearranged** and millions of people **watch** the games.

Second, the growth of the game **was influenced** by the high-level play of the club teams. The best players from all over the world **are recruited** to keep the clubs competitive with one another, and the careers of these players **are followed** by the fans in their home countries.

Third, the fans also **play** soccer. Youth clubs **are organized** throughout the world, and children **start** their practice sessions at ages four, five, and six. In the last 50 years, soccer has truly become the world's game.

7 Omitting the *By* Phrase

3. He was named Secretariat by his owner, and he was voted Horse of the Year ~~by people~~ in both of his competitive years.

4. The Triple Crown is awarded ~~by racing officials~~ to any horse winning the Kentucky Derby, the Preakness, and the Belmont Stakes all in the same year.

5. The 1973 Triple Crown was won by Secretariat in grand style.

6. Horse racing's Triple Crown wasn't won ~~by a horse~~ in any of the previous 25 years.

7. The Kentucky Derby was run by Secretariat in world-record time.

8. Secretariat won the Belmont Stakes by 31 lengths, a distance so great that the images of Secretariat and the next-closest horse weren't captured at the same time by TV cameras.

8 The *By* Phrase

3. This sport was used by the ancient Greeks and Romans to train warriors.
4. Table tennis was first played by the English on dining room tables.
5. Table tennis was also called Ping-Pong in the early 1900s.
6. Tournaments in the U.S. are governed today by the U.S. Table Tennis Association.
7. The sport of mountain climbing was started in eighteenth-century Europe.
8. Mt. Everest was conquered in 1953 by Edmund Hillary and Tenzing Norgay.
9. Many of the highest mountains in South America still aren't climbed today.
10. Ice skates were first used as transportation.
11. Speed races were held in the Netherlands in the fifteenth century.
12. "Clap skates" were developed by the Dutch in 1997 so that skaters could go faster.

9 **Writing**

Answers will vary.

10 **Editing**

1. dominate

Every year, four tournaments ~~are dominated~~ the men's professional golf season. They are

called the Majors and define the best players in the sport. The tournaments—the Masters, the

U.S. Open, the British Open, and the PGA—are considered to be challenging and pressure-

2. is called

filled. No player ~~called~~ great unless he has won a Major.

In 1953, three of the four tournaments were won by the same man, Ben Hogan. That year,

3. became

Hogan ~~was become~~ the only golfer to have won these three tournaments in the same year.

Hogan didn't enter the PGA, partly because it was held too soon after the British Open and

partly because Hogan hadn't fully recovered from a near-fatal accident in 1949. Perhaps, too,

4. given

Hogan didn't enter the PGA because it was never ~~giving~~ the same respect as the other

tournaments.

5. won by

A record 18 Major tournaments were ~~won~~ a single individual: Jack Nicklaus. Nicklaus made

it clear that these four tournaments were the ones he was training to win. Because Nicklaus was

6. was copied

the best golfer of his era, he ~~copied~~ by other professional golfers, and the Majors truly became

the tournaments to win.

After the PGA tournament finishes in August, other tournaments on the professional tour

7. played

are still ~~play.~~ Competition isn't stopped after the last of the Majors is over, but some golfers may

already be looking ahead to the next year.

Chapter 17: More About Passives

GRAMMAR PRACTICE 1

Passives in Progressive and Perfect Tenses

1 **Passive Sentences in Present Progressive**

2. The opening pitch isn't / is not being thrown out by the governor. It's / It is being thrown out by the mayor.   3. The first inning isn't / is not being pitched by Jay White. It's / It is being pitched by Mark Erikson.   4. The ball isn't / is not being hit into right field by Bill Watson. It's / It is being hit into left field by Bill Watson.   5. It isn't / is not being caught by the outfielder, Sam Jacobs. It's / It is being caught by a fan in the stands.   6. The bases aren't / are not being run by the fans. They're / They are being run by Bill Watson.

2 **Active and Passive Sentences in Past Progressive**

A. 2. was being watched   3. were attending
4. were being thrown   5. were being hit
6. was flying   7. was moving   8. was being given   9. were being honored   10. was being treated

B. *Answers will vary,* but a suggested version is:

It's Mother's Day, May 14, 1939. The baseball game is being played in Chicago. It's being watched by the parents of pitcher Bob Feller, who plays for Cleveland, Ohio. They are attending the game to watch their son throw baseballs to the batters. Today, the balls that are being thrown are hard, and the balls that are being hit are like rocks. Feller is throwing a ball, and Marv Owen is hitting it. As the ball is flying through the air, it is moving with force and speed. By chance, that baseball hits Feller's mother, breaks her glasses, and cuts her above her eye. While his mother is being given medical attention, Feller is going to see if she is all right. Feller returns to the game and strikes out Owen. On a day when mothers across the country are being honored, Feller's mother is being treated for her injuries.

3 Passive Sentences in Perfect Tenses

2. had been painted   3. had been practiced
4. had been tested   5. had been hired   6. had been sold   7. had been prepared   9. have been entertained   10. has been eaten   11. have been spilled   12. have been sung   13. have been told
14. has been made

Passives with Modals

4 Passives with Modals

2. must not/mustn't be given   3. can be picked
4. ought to be appointed   5. will be considered
6. have to be considered   7. are going to be given
8. may be offered   9. must be prepared

5 Passive Sentences with Verbs in Different Tenses

2. were held   3. weren't begun   4. have been held   5. weren't held   6. were scheduled
7. were included   8. have been realized

9 Editing

1. selected

Athletes and teams that get ~~select~~ to be on the *Sports Illustrated* magazine cover may be

both happy and sad. They may feel that they are being honored by the magazine. However, they

may believe in the jinx, or bad luck, that comes with being on the cover.

Sports Illustrated (*SI*) got started in 1954. At the end of 1955, the editors decided to name a

"Sportsman of the Year" and put his picture on the cover of the magazine. Unfortunately, the
                2. had been/was   3. shot
man who ~~has been~~ chosen, William Woodward, Jr., accidentally got ~~shoot~~ by his wife and
4. died/had died
~~had been died~~ before he had his picture taken for the cover. One story says that Mr. Woodward's
                    5. been following/followed
ghost is responsible for the bad luck that has ~~been followed~~ the people on the cover.

9. have been broken   10. have been won
11. is usually chosen   12. had been chosen
13. were canceled   14. shouldn't be held
15. can be kept   16. are (being) attended
17. will be chosen   18. are led   19. is played
20. is raised   21. was lighted/lit   22. has been carried   23. is being lighted/lit

Get Passives

6 *Get* Passives

2. have gotten burned   3. have gotten tossed
4. got pitched   5. are getting put   6. are getting added OR will get added   7. will get burned OR are going to get burned   8. will get traded OR are going to get traded   9. will get fired OR are going to get fired   10. may get sold

7 Writing

Answers will vary.

Passive Causatives

8 Passive Causatives

2. The players have/get their bags carried.
3. The players have/get their practice gear bought for them.   4. The players have/get their rooms booked in nice hotels.   5. The players had/got a postcard of the team sent to a late-night TV program for publicity.   6. The players have/get their many contracts handled for them by agents.

Over the years since *SI* first got published, about 37 percent of the athletes and teams that

have been featured on the cover have had bad luck. Some have lost games that they were

6. suffered

expected to win. Others have ~~been suffered~~ family tragedies or personal injuries that have ended

their careers in sports. These people may have been affected by the *SI* jinx just by believing it

They may have thought that they would have bad luck after they were on the *SI* cover. But if

7. did they get

that was true, why ~~they got~~ their photos taken?

The belief in the *SI* jinx may continue, but it won't stop athletes from posing for the cover.

Just ask professional basketball player Michael Jordan, who was successful despite being on the

cover more than 50 times.

Unit Wrap-up
Writing

Answers will vary.

TOEFL TIME

Questions 1–10

1. C   2. A   3. C   4. B   5. D   6. B   7. C   8. B   9. C   10. A

Questions 11–20

11. A (disappeared)   12. D (by their instructors)   13. A (*omit* was)   14. B (introduced)
15. D (will be)   16. C (being)   17. D (improved)   18. A (*omit* was)   19. B (*omit* been)
20. D (appear)

Unit Nine
Conditionals
Chapter 18: Factual Conditionals; Future Conditionals

GRAMMAR PRACTICE 1
Overview of Conditionals

1 **Conditional Statements and Questions**

        R   C
A. 2. Snow reflects less heat back into space if it melts fast.

        C   R
   3. If less heat is reflected back into space, more heat is kept around Earth.

          R   C
   4. The temperature of the planet rises if more heat is kept around Earth.

        C   R
   5. If the temperature of the planet rises, many different climate changes occur.

B. 2. Does snow reflect less heat back into space if it melts fast? OR If snow melts fast, does it reflect less heat back into space?

3. If less heat is reflected back into space, is more heat kept around Earth? OR Is more heat kept around Earth if less heat is reflected back into space?

4. Does the temperature of the planet rise if more heat is kept around Earth? OR If more heat is kept around Earth, does the temperature of the planet rise?

5. If the temperature of the planet rises, do many different climate changes occur? OR Do many different climate changes occur if the temperature of the planet rises?

GRAMMAR PRACTICE 2
Factual Conditionals

2 Factual Conditionals with Present Tense Verbs and Modals

3. If trade winds relax, then   4. Cooler, nutrient-rich water is pushed deeper if   5. If El Niño conditions exist, then   6. For example, there is flooding in Peru if   7. Scientists can get a wide range of accurate information on the Pacific if 8. If scientists understand El Niño better, then

3 Factual Conditionals with Past Tense Verbs

2. If they built new cities, then   3. If they built on the coast, then   4. The Incas suffered if   5. Therefore, the Incas made sacrifices to their gods if

4 Using Factual Conditionals with Modals and Imperatives

Answers will vary.

GRAMMAR PRACTICE 3
Future Conditionals

5 Future Conditionals—Form and Function

2. If it is an El Niño year, Peru and parts of the United States and Europe will suffer from damaging floods.   3. Many countries will have flash floods if El Niño brings too much rain.   4. Indonesia, Australia, and India will experience drought if El Niño happens.   5. If El Niño occurs, the next year will be a La Niña year.   6. If countries have drought during El Niño, they will have too much rain during La Niña.

6 Writing

Answers will vary.

7 Editing

If people live in a snow ~~region~~ **1. region,** they will probably see snow every year. Snow is often fun and beautiful, but it can be dangerous if it is heavy and accompanied by strong winds. This combination of snow and wind is called a blizzard. If the blizzard ~~be~~ **2. is** so bad that no one can see very far, "white-out" conditions may exist. In white-out conditions, everything looks white and it's easy to get confused. People may know an area well, but ~~they go out in white outs, if they~~ **3. if they go out in white outs, they** can still get lost.

There are many stories about people in blizzards. These people had a better chance of surviving if they had shelter. If they were ~~outside. They~~ **4. outside, they** probably got very cold very quickly. If they got too cold, they ~~freeze~~ **5. froze**. They could even have been close to shelter but not known it.

If you ~~will be~~ **6. are** in a blizzard, stay home. You should survive a blizzard if you are warm and have food and water. We can't control snow or wind, but if we ~~will prepare~~ **7. prepare** for snowstorms, we can lessen their damage.

Chapter 19: Present and Past Unreal Conditionals; *Hope* and *Wish*

GRAMMAR PRACTICE 1

Present Unreal Conditionals

1 **Present Unreal Conditionals—Form**

2. weren't; wouldn't get   3. would answer; asked
4. were; would be   5. wanted; wouldn't forget

2 **Present Unreal Conditionals—Meaning**

2. a. F   3. a. T   4. a. F
   b. T   b. T   b. F

3 **Factual Versus Unreal Conditionals**

2. didn't hurt; would still have   3. lived; would
respect   4. wouldn't hit; were   5. go; are

4 **Writing**

Answers will vary.

GRAMMAR PRACTICE 2

Past Unreal Conditionals

5 **Past Unreal Conditionals**

2. would have caused; had erupted
3. might/could have taken; hadn't been
4. had seen; could have told   5. had happened;
would have died

6 **Past Unreal Conditionals—Meaning**

2. a. T   3. a. T   4. a. F   5. a. F
   b. F   b. T   b. T   b. F

7 **Past Unreal Conditionals**

2. If the chamber had been above sea level, ocean
water wouldn't have rushed into it.

3. The volcano would have remained standing if it
hadn't collapsed in the explosion.

4. If the explosion hadn't been so loud, people in
Australia couldn't have heard it.

5. The wind from the explosion would have circled
the earth more times if the force of the explosion
hadn't decreased.

8 **Writing**

Answers will vary.

GRAMMAR PRACTICE 3

Sentences with *Hope* or *Wish*

9 ***Hope* and *Wish* About the Present
and Future**

2. started/would start   3. doesn't start/won't start
4. were   5. will cooperate/cooperates
6. will burn/burns   7. could
8. can also save/will also save/also save   9. could
10. will work/can work/work

10 ***Hope* and *Wish* About the Past**

2. were   3. had started   4. had known
5. hadn't waited   6. had rained   7. hadn't had to
8. learned   9. had been able to

11 **Writing**

Answers will vary.

12 **Editing**

                                              1. talk
If we talk about natural disasters, we often ~~talked~~ about economics. If that hadn't been true
                                                                    2. wouldn't have moved
in the 1940s, the Weather Bureau, which often predicts weather-related disasters, ~~didn't move~~

from the Department of Agriculture to the Department of Commerce.

Most Americans don't know that two people died in the Great Plains blizzard of 1886. If

they know anything about that blizzard, they usually remember that 90 percent of the cattle on

the ranges of the Great Plains died. Ranchers wouldn't have lost so many cattle if the weather
     3. hadn't
~~wouldn't have~~ been so severe.

In the 1988 Yellowstone Park fires, one principle concern was for the businesses around the

4. threatened

park. If fires ~~threaten~~ private property or Old Faithful, the Park Service would try to put them

out, but that year there was another concern. Businesspeople were concerned that if too much

5. wouldn't

of the Park burned, tourists ~~didn't~~ come to the area. In fact, people came to Yellowstone after

6. hadn't happened

the fires just to see the damage. They wished that these fires ~~didn't happen~~, but they were

7. wouldn't have

curious to see what had changed. If there hadn't been fires in 1988, they probably ~~wouldn't~~

come that year.

Unit Wrap-up
Writing

Answers will vary.

TOEFL TIME
Questions 1–10

1. D   2. A   3. B   4. B   5. B   6. A   7. C   8. A   9. A   10. D

Questions 11–20

11. B (*omit comma*)   12. C (wouldn't have been)   13. B (were)   14. A (*omit* will)   15. A (the moon
completely blocks)   16. D (influenced)   17. B (hadn't moved)   18. C (*add a comma after* home)
19. D (are)   20. D (didn't have)

Unit Ten
Noun Clauses

Chapter 20: Noun Clauses

GRAMMAR PRACTICE 1
Overview of Noun Clauses

1 Identifying Noun Clauses

2. a. She thinks <u>that his stories are funny</u>.

3. a. I'm sure about <u>when the book was published</u>.

4. b. We don't know <u>if she'll come</u>.

5. b. I didn't hear <u>what she said</u>.

6. b. <u>That he loves her</u> is certainly true.

7. a. We don't know <u>who came here</u>.

2 Noun Clauses—Form and Function

2. They think (that) the book cover should be attractive to a reader. [O]

3. (When) a cover can invite readers to try a book is (when) the cover is successful. [S] [SC]

4. Readers wonder (if) a poor cover may hurt an otherwise successful book. [O]

5. Many readers are certain (that) a cover should indicate (what) the book is about. [adj + NC] [O]

6. One thing that a long-time reader of romance looks for is (that) the cover has someone or something from the story on it. [SC]

7. She thinks about (whether) some covers are poor because they feature the characters (a handsome man and a beautiful woman, of course) too prominently. [O Prep]

8. She is worried (that) male models are sometimes used even when they don't match the author's description of the character. [adj + NC]

9. Finally, (whether) the cover embarrasses the readers in public is also important. [S]

GRAMMAR PRACTICE 2

Noun Clauses with *That*

3 Forming Sentences with *That* Clauses

2. That emotional risk and conflict are basic to the romance genre is understood. OR It is understood that emotional risk and conflict are basic to the romance genre.

3. Readers are certain that the conflict will be resolved by the end of the book.

4. They are glad that the ending is always happy.

5. Romance writers insist that their readers are intelligent.

6. Romance writers realize that their books aren't fine literature.

7. They believe that they write well-crafted, entertaining fiction.

8. Publishers agree that romance fiction is popular.

9. They notice that many romance writers sell over a million copies of each book they write.

4 Writing

Answers will vary.

GRAMMAR PRACTICE 3

Noun Clauses with *Wh-* Words

5 Noun Clauses with *Wh-* Words

2. why your fingerprints aren't on it   3. why you wiped it off   4. what time it was when you found it   5. where you were at the time of the murder   6. when you usually go to bed   7. why you went to bed early that night   8. why you have lied to me

6 Noun Clauses with *Wh-* Words—Expressing Uncertainty

2. how tall it was   3. who else has seen the creature   4. where we first spotted it   5. when we saw it   6. what the creature did   7. how we escaped   8. who will go

---

GRAMMAR PRACTICE 4

Noun Clauses with *If/Whether*

7 Noun Clauses with *If/Whether*

2. Whether he is looking for me
3. if/whether he saw me following him to her house yesterday
4. if/whether I have done the right thing
5. whether he loves me
6. whether I will ever find another love like him

7. if/whether she has left for good
8. if/whether I should go after her
9. if/whether that was her following me to my house
10. if/whether I made a mistake to let her go
11. if/whether she could still love me
12. if/whether she will forgive me and come back

8 Writing

Answers will vary.

9 Noun Clauses with Past Tense Verbs

2. was looking   3. was going to/would reveal
4. had   5. locked   6. was going to/would appear
7. rode off   8. saved

10 Editing

1. that
No one would disagree ~~if~~ reading is important for teenagers. Diana Tixier Herald, author of

2. are
Teen Genreflecting, believes that good readers ~~were~~ avid readers and often these avid readers are

readers of genre fiction. She knows that genre fiction doesn't always get much respect.

Nevertheless, Herald is convinced that escapist reading of genre fiction is an ideal outlet for

teens. She believes they have different needs from people of other age groups. That the teen

3. that
years are a time of self-discovery is clear. She feels ~~whether~~ genre fiction fits the needs of teen

4. if/whether
readers. She wonders ~~that~~ teens can divide the world into more manageable parts by selecting

and reading a type of genre fiction that appeals to them.

5. teens selected
For her book, Herald wanted to know how ~~did teens select~~ genre fiction. As a librarian, she

6. paid
had noticed that teens ~~pay~~ attention to the labels on the books they read. She believes that they

are the only readers who ask for books not by author and title but by the imprint (specific

publisher). She thinks that a library should offer genre collections, clearly identified as such, to

make books more accessible to teens.

7. whether   **8. was**
Herald also thought about ~~if~~ the books should be displayed differently. She felt that it ~~is~~

9. teens would
important for teens to see the covers, too. She wondered if ~~would teens~~ read more if a library

organized the books in a different way. Herald believes that making the books more accessible

to teens will encourage them to become avid, and thus good, readers.

Chapter 21: Quoted Speech; Noun Clauses with Reported Speech

GRAMMAR PRACTICE 1

Quoted Speech and Reported Speech

1 **Punctuating Quoted Speech; Identifying Reported Speech**

A. & B. "Hello, Doctor," a woman's voice said. "My name is Margo."

"Hello, Margo," I replied. "I can't see you. The video must not be on."

"Oh, I know. I'd like to use only audio for a while if that's okay," Margo said.

"Fine. So what's the problem?" I asked.

"It's my son," she said. "He says that he's in love with a hologram."

I thought to myself, "Oh, great. Another one. The third this week."

"He told me he's found his life partner, but I want him to spend more time with

biological beings," she continued.

"Do you know why he doesn't have more biological friends?" I asked.

"Well, we're a little isolated," she said. "He doesn't have much exposure to biological

beings, and he says he doesn't like them. My husband and I try to spend time with

him, but we're very busy."

2 **Quoted Speech; Verbs Introducing Speech**

2. "Hugo, that's my son, used to introduce me to his holograms," Margo replied. "He told me that he understood them better than biological beings. His father and I are, well, intellectuals, so it's no surprise that he is, too."

3. "Well, I think you and your husband should encourage Hugo to develop his physical side, not just his intellect. Swim. Go for a walk. Do things together," I suggested.

4. "Doctor, I think I'd better turn on the video now," Margo answered me. "There's something you should know."

5. "Oh, great," I told myself. "I wonder what this means."

6. "You see, Doctor, we are computers," Margo explained. "We took some of my programming and some of my husband's and put them together to form Hugo. We had to have technicians put together the physical components, but Hugo is our son."

7. "Well, this is a surprise!" I exclaimed. "So why did you contact me?"

8. She replied, "I picked your name out of a database of psychologists. I thought that if I could get a human's perspective, I could figure out what to do about Hugo."

9. "Then you know nothing about me?" I asked her. "Because I'm not human, either. I'm an experimental program in an artificial intelligence institute at a major research university."

3 **Writing**

Answers will vary.

GRAMMAR PRACTICE 2

Changes in Reported Speech; Verb Tense in Reported Speech

4 Changes in Reported Speech—Overview

                         Pro M   V

2. Granddaughter: Grandpa said that <u>he would</u> always remember what <u>had happened</u> to

the Donovans.

                            Pro   Pro V

3. Granddaughter: Grandpa said that <u>that</u> was long before <u>I was</u> born.

                         Pro M   V

4. Granddaughter: Grandpa said that <u>I</u> <u>might</u> remember the Donovans who <u>lived</u> north

of town.

                                                  Pro

5. Granddaughter: Grandpa said that the trouble started when <u>he</u> was out of town.

                            Pro   Pro

6. Granddaughter: Grandpa said that <u>his</u> deputy had to talk to Mrs. Donovan because <u>he</u>

         Pl

wasn't <u>there</u>.

                          Pro M   Pro   T

7. Granddaughter: Grandpa said that <u>he</u> <u>would</u> tell <u>me</u> the whole story later <u>that day</u>.

5 Changes in Verb Tense in Reported Speech

2. had been gone; had planned   3. had planned
4. had been; had wanted 5. had seen 6. was;
hadn't seen; had seen; would have told 7. was
going 8. was

GRAMMAR PRACTICE 3

Modals in Reported Speech

6 Changes in Modals in Reported Speech

2. had to leave; couldn't wait   3. was going to be;
shouldn't be 4. might stop; might not be able to
cross 5. should have written; could have had
6. would tell

GRAMMAR PRACTICE 4

Pronouns and Time and Place Expressions in Reported Speech

7 Changes in Pronouns and Time and Place Expressions in Reported Speech

2. she; her; that morning; He; then; he 3. they;
here; he 4. he; two days before/three days ago;
their 5. they; themselves; I; that 6. I; here
today; I; her; her

8 Changes That Occur in Reported Speech

2. Mrs. Donovan said (that) she must have
screamed after the man had grabbed her.
3. Mrs. Donovan said (that) he had made her horse
run so that she couldn't jump off.
4. Mrs. Donovan said (that) if he hadn't tried to
cross the river, his horse might not have thrown
him off.
5. Mrs. Donovan said (that) he couldn't swim and
(that) she couldn't help him.
6. Mrs. Donovan said (that) she was happy to be
there in my office, but (that) she was very tired.
7. Mrs. Donovan said (that) she had to get some
sleep then, but (that) she would talk to you later.

9 Writing

Answers will vary.

GRAMMAR PRACTICE 5

Reported Questions, Commands, and Requests

10 Reported Questions

2. where the Westerns were/are 3. what time the
library closed/closes 4. if anyone had/has turned
in his wallet 5. what she should do to get a
library card 6. if he could/can check that
reference book out of the library

11 **Reported Commands and Requests**

2. A young woman asked me to put her name on the list to reserve the next Tony Hillerman novel. OR A young woman asked me if I would/could put her name on the list to reserve the next Tony Hillerman novel.   3. A young woman told me to call her when the book came in.
4. A boy asked me if I could tell him where the periodicals were located. OR A boy asked me to tell him where the periodicals were located.   5. Another librarian said that I should put these/those books back on the shelf. OR Another librarian said to put these/those books back on the shelf.   6. The other librarian told me not to worry.

12 **Editing**

1. ?"

"We go now to our reporter on the street. Marsha, what do you see there"? asked the news

broadcaster.

"Howard, the scene here is incredible! A car hit a house, and now the car is on fire. There is

2. saw

smoke everywhere. One man told me that he sees a giant ball of fire about 20 minutes ago.

3. she

Another woman said I was hit by something that knocked her to the ground," responded the

reporter.

"Have you talked to the police?" the news broadcaster inquired.

4. said to me/told me

"Yes, Howard, I have. Sargeant Whitney said me earlier that she believed the car hit a gas

5. have

line into the house. The police are now telling neighbors that they had to leave their homes

until the fire is under control," remarked Marsha.

6. Do

Howard asked, "do you know how this all started?"

"One witness that I talked to said the car had been weaving back and forth across the street

7. wondered if

before it hit the house. She wondered the driver had fallen asleep," said Marsha.

"Are members of the fire department there?" asked Howard.

"I'm sorry, Howard. I didn't hear what you said," replied Marsha.

8. if

"I asked that the fire department was there," said Howard.

9. to move

"Yes," said Marsha. "Someone from the fire department just told us move away from here

because it's too dangerous."

"Okay, Marsha. Thanks. We'll talk to you later," said Howard.

Unit Wrap-up

Writing

Answers will vary.

TOEFL TIME

Questions 1–10

1. B   2. D   3. B   4. A   5. A   6. C   7. D
8. C   9. A   10. B

Questions 11–20

11. A (It's)   12. B (whether)   13. C (would happen)   14. B (not to ask)   15. B (*omit* about)
16. B (that OR *omit* in)   17. C (is)
18. B (whether)   19. A (that)   20. C (has)

Unit Eleven
Adverb Clauses; Connecting Ideas
Chapter 22: Adverb Clauses

GRAMMAR PRACTICE 1

Adverb Clauses

1 Identifying Adverb Clauses

(Because) they want to meet the needs of their clients or customers, successful business

owners need to know the reasons behind people's purchases. Owners need to budget time and

money for market research (when) they are thinking about starting a new business. (Although)

they might not have all the information, they need to know the likelihood of the success of their

product. They should try to find out as much as possible about their potential customers (before)

they invest a lot of time and money. In the end, (if) they have the right information to make good

decisions, they are more likely to succeed.

GRAMMAR PRACTICE 2

Types of Adverb Clauses I

2 Adverb Clauses of Time, Condition, and Reason

2. We've seen seven commercials since we started watching this program. T   3. When the program was getting more exciting, they broke for a commercial. T   4. I lose interest in sitting here as soon as the commercials start. T   5. If this happens, I start to think about food. C   6. Since the program isn't on, I might as well get a sandwich. R   7. Television can be dangerous as it can make you fat. R

3 Adverb Clauses of Time and Reason

3. I didn't notice the name of the product since I was paying attention to the beautiful model.
4. Once the commercial starts, I stop paying attention.   5. As I've seen a lot of commercials recently, I can't remember which products they advertise.   6. I haven't seen those commercials because I have few opportunities to watch television.   7. Whenever a commercial is really funny, I hardly notice the product.   8. There will be commercials as long as people watch television.

4 More Practice with Adverb Clauses of Time and Reason

2. Until   3. since   4. Whenever   5. As soon as
6. before   7. because   8. As long as

GRAMMAR PRACTICE 3

Types of Adverb Clauses II

5 Adverb Clauses of Contrast and Opposition

2. While men stay an average of nine minutes in a store, women stay over 12 minutes.

   Men stay an average of nine minutes in a store, while women stay over twelve minutes.

3. Even though both men and women need to be enticed to buy accessories, they buy them at different times and places.

   Both men and women need to be enticed to buy accessories even though they buy them at different times and places.

4. Although men will pick up accessories when they pick up pants to try on, women will look for accessories after they've tried on the pants.

   Men will pick up accessories when they pick up pants to try on although women will look for accessories after they've tried on the pants.

5. Though men are able to make choices in style and size, they prefer help in matching colors.

   Men are able to make choices in style and size though they prefer help in matching colors

6 Using *While* to Show Contrast

2. While teens in the past were not the main shoppers in the family, teens today make many of the shopping decisions. OR While teens today make many of the shopping decisions, teens in the past were not the main shoppers in the family. OR Teens in the past were not the main shoppers in the family, while teens today make many of the shopping decisions. OR Teens today make many of the shopping decisions, while teens in the past were not the main shoppers in the family.

9 Writing

Answers will vary.

10 Editing

    Paco Underhill, managing director of Envirosell, has been called a retail anthropologist
1. because/since/as
~~when~~ he has been recording and analyzing what customers do in stores for the last 20 years. As
                    2. shoppers
he has spent hours studying videotapes of ~~shoppers~~ he is an expert on shopper behavior. He

3. While adults often buy a product for practical reasons, teens usually choose a product because it's cool. OR While teens usually choose a product because it's cool, adults often buy a product for practical reasons. OR Adults often buy a product for practical reasons, while teens usually choose a product because it's cool. OR Teens usually choose a product because it's cool, while adults often buy a product for practical reasons.

4. While teens in the past didn't have much money to spend, teens today spend at least $264.00 each month. OR While teens today spend at least $264.00 each month, teens in the past didn't have much money to spend. OR Teens in the past didn't have much money to spend, while teens today spend at least $264.00 each month. OR Teens today spend at least $264.00 each month, while teens in the past didn't have much money to spend.

7 Reason Versus Contrast and Opposition

2. Even though/Although 3. Since
4. Even though/Although 5. As/Because
6. While/Though 7. While/Though
8. As/Because

8 Adverb Clauses of Purpose

2. The firms seek out influencer teens so that they can get their opinions on the latest trends in fashion and other areas.

3. They survey influencer teens so that they can find out what's hip in the mind of a teen.

4. Teen responses are analyzed so that the firm can make recommendations to companies like Nike and Pepsi.

5. Companies pay for market research so that their products will be successful with teens.

3. even though/although/though/while
knows that ~~until~~ the merchandise in a store is important, the layout of the physical space of a

store is just as important to the success of that store. When he enters a store, he quickly
4. Since Paco Underhill observes the movement of shoppers, he OR Paco Underhill observes the movement of shoppers so that he
evaluates where and how the merchandise is displayed. ~~Paco Underhill observes the movement~~

~~of shoppers since he~~ is able to advise his clients on how to set up their stores for success.
                                                            5. Because/As/Since
    As they enter a store, shoppers are walking at a fast pace. ~~Although~~ they are walking fast,

they need time to slow down. A shopper will miss anything in the first 15 to 20 feet of
    6. store since
the ~~store, since~~ she is moving too fast. As a shopper is going too fast to really see the

merchandise, retailers shouldn't put anything of value in the first 15 feet of the store.

Because he has studied thousands of hours of videotape of customers entering stores, Paco
                                                7. as soon as/when
Underhill also believes in the invariant right. This means that ~~because~~ they enter the store,
                                8. When
shoppers invariably turn to the right. ~~While~~ a store knows this, the display department will put

anything of value to the right of the door so that customers can see it.

Chapter 23: Connecting Ideas

GRAMMAR PRACTICE 1
Coordinating Conjunctions

1 **Coordinating Conjunctions with Clauses, Phrases, and Words**
                    W
2. Leroy <u>and</u> Amy both hear commercials.
                                            C
3. Leroy usually likes the commercials, <u>yet</u> sometimes he thinks they are annoying.
                                                        P
4. If the commercials are annoying, Leroy goes to the kitchen <u>and</u> gets something to eat.
                                    C
5. Amy doesn't like commercials, <u>so</u> she doesn't listen to them.
                                W
6. She would rather listen to music <u>or</u> news.
                                                    C
7. Sometimes she waits for the commercials to end, <u>and</u> sometimes she turns off the radio when the

commercials are on.
                            C
8. Amy likes the radio, <u>but</u> she can also listen to CDs.

2 **Coordinating Conjunctions—Meaning**

2. and   3. so   4. but/yet   5. but/yet   6. or

3 Parallel Structures; Subject-Verb Agreement

2. The technology allows the viewer to see the product on TV, to split the TV screen, and ~~clicks~~ *to click*

on a website for more information.

3. One piece of technology allows consumers to block advertising and ~~controlling~~ *to control* what

advertising they watch.

4. Interactive advertising will give both advertisers and consumers more choice, convenience,

and ~~they can control it better.~~ *control*

5. However, privacy issues and the use of information ~~is~~ *are* important to address.

6. Advertisers must control who gets access to information and ~~to use it.~~ *how they use it*

7. The advertising industry has to regulate itself to protect consumer ~~privacy or losing~~ *privacy, or it will lose* the trust

of the consumer.

8. New laws or government ~~control are~~ *controls are/control is* possible if there is poor internal regulation.

4 Punctuating Sentences with Coordinating Conjunctions

2. NC   3. The products needed to be different enough but not too different.   4. NC   5. The PC companies "sold" their computers, their knowledge, and their service.   6. Customers could buy a prepackaged system or put together their own systems.   7. NC   8. NC   9. Many PC customers appreciated the extra help once they got the computer home, so selling after-the-sale service seemed to be effective and successful.

GRAMMAR PRACTICE 2

Connecting Main Clauses That Have the Same Verb Phrase

5 Connecting Main Clauses

2. your friends couldn't, either./neither could your friends.   3. so have our shoes./our shoes have, too.   4. we haven't, either./neither have we.   5. so do your friends./your friends do, too.   6. so are your feet./your feet are, too.   7. your legs aren't, either./neither are your legs.   8. your friends aren't, either./neither are your friends.   9. so will everyone else./everyone else will, too.

GRAMMAR PRACTICE 3

Transitions I

6 Punctuating Sentences Connected by Transitions

In the late 1990s, one of the most popular investments was in companies associated with the Internet; however, (OR . However,) since many of these companies weren't making a profit, their values were hard to assess. Many investors saw the Internet as a new way of doing business; (OR . They) they, therefore, didn't want to be left out of any important future developments. In addition, buying Internet stocks became trendy, even though there were no dividends. Other investors recognized the potential of an accelerating trade in Internet stocks; (OR Consequently) consequently, they were able to buy low and sell high. One company more than tripled its initial opening price on the first day that it was traded, for example.

GRAMMAR PRACTICE 4

Transitions II

7 Addition Transitions

2. Your dog will be healthier; besides, you'll spend less time and money at the veterinarian's office. OR Your dog will be healthier. Besides, you'll spend less time and money at the veterinarian's office.

3. Your dog's coat will be shiny. Your dog, in addition, will be more active. OR Your dog's coat will be shiny; your dog, in addition, will be more active.

4. HealthyDog will change the way your dog feels. It will also make you happy. OR HealthyDog will change the way your dog feels; it will also make you happy.

8 Time Transitions

2. The products we buy are designed to wear out. Meanwhile, models and parts change. Then, we have to buy something new because we can't repair our "old" stuff.

12 Writing

Answers will vary.

13 Editing

3. Often, before we buy something, advertisers have tried to convince us that we not only want but need their products. Next, we ourselves begin to believe that we need the products. Finally, we buy what we want, not necessarily what we need.

9 Writing

Answers will vary.

10 Result Transitions

2. The ad was effective; as a result, the company sales increased. 3. The company used a multimedia campaign; therefore, it reached a wider audience.

11 Contrast and Opposition Transitions

2. Famous people are often used in ads; nevertheless, they sometimes have a negative effect on the product. 3. The slogan is recognizable; nonetheless, the company may stop using it. 4. This company's logo is good; however, its slogan is poor.

                                  1. and
As fiber-optic, digital, ~~or~~ satellite technologies all advance in the next 10 years, they will give
                        2. Therefore
                (or any subject-verb that makes sense)
advertisers new tools to use television and the Internet interactively. ~~However~~, advertisers will be
                  3. instance, they may use
           (or any subject-verb that makes sense)
able to target very specific markets. For ~~instance,~~ custom-made ads. These ads will target
                        4. zip code
specific markets such as a particular age group or ~~what zip code someone has~~. While
                    5. before, they'll
advertisers' messages were delivered to large general audiences ~~before, so they'll~~ soon be
delivered to the narrow audiences most interested in the product or service. For example,
             6. or
advertisers can target sports fans ~~but~~ dog lovers. Furthermore, the technology will give
        7. products; in OR products. In
consumers the power to order ~~products, in~~ addition they will be able to get information
instantly. Whenever they want a product, consumers will only have to click a button to get it.

Unit Wrap-up
Writing

Answers will vary.

TOEFL TIME
Questions 1–10

1. C 2. D 3. D 4. A 5. B 6. C 7. B
8. A 9. D 10. B

Questions 11–20

11. C (trees, so) 12. C (*omit* so) 13. B (fear)
14. B (knowledge;) 15. B (is) 16. C (*omit*
nevertheless) 17. C (decreased) 18. D (, too)
19. B (smooth OR to smooth) 20. B (or)